AMERICA'S NEW COMPETITORS

Economic Policy Council of the UNA-USA

AMERICA'S NEW COMPETITORS
The Challenge of the
Newly Industrializing Countries

edited by
THORNTON F. BRADSHAW
DANIEL F. BURTON, JR.
RICHARD N. COOPER
ROBERT D. HORMATS

BALLINGER PUBLISHING COMPANY
Cambridge, Massachusetts
A Subsidiary of Harper & Row, Publishers, Inc.

International Standard Book Number: 0-88730-135-5

Library of Congress Catalog Card Number: 87-19295

Printed in the United States of America

Library of Congress Cataloging-in-Publication Data

America's new competitors.

Includes index.
1. United States—Foreign economic relations—Developing countries. 2. Developing countries—Foreign economic relations—United States. 3. Competition, International.
I. Bradshaw, Thornton F.
HF1456.5.D44T65 1987   337.730172'4   87-19295
ISBN 0-88730-135-5

The United Nations Association of the USA (UNA-USA) is a private, nonprofit organization which conducts programs of research, study and information to broaden public understanding of the activities of the United Nations and other multilateral institutions. Through its nationwide membership and network of affiliated national organizations, UNA-USA informs and involves the public in foreign affairs issues, and encourages constructive U.S. policies on global issues.

The UNA-USA Economic Policy Council is comprised of a cross-section of U.S. business, labor and academic leaders who are brought together in study panels to analyze important international issues affecting long-run U.S. relationships with both developed and developing countries. The EPC both identifies critical policy questions and makes recommendations which are then published and presented to officials within the executive and legislative branches of the U.S. and officials of the U.N. and other international organizations. As part of this process, a number of papers are commissioned from leading specialists.

This UNA-USA Economic Policy Council Book is based on rewritten and edited versions of some of these papers. UNA-USA is responsible for the choice of the subject areas and the decision to publish the volumes, but the responsibility for the content of the papers and for opinions expressed in them rests with the individual authors and editors.

This book was made possible by generous grants from the Alfred P. Sloan Foundation, The Ford Foundation, and The Rockefeller Foundation.

CONTENTS

LIST OF TABLES

PREFACE

The Economic Policy Council (EPC) of the United Nations Association of the United States of America chose to undertake this study in an effort to analyze the new international role of the newly industrializing countries (NICs) and to come to grips with the impact these nations are having on the United States and the international economy. The NICs are often still viewed as marginally prosperous developing countries that export a narrow range of labor-intensive, light-manufactured goods. Whereas this description may have been accurate fifteen years ago, it is seriously inaccurate today. The NICs are increasingly encroaching on the economic territory that has been the traditional preserve of industrialized nations, and in the process they are causing serious adjustment problems. Many NICs are capable of producing and exporting a broad range of sophisticated manufactured goods in large volumes, and some have extensive international debts. The United States is inextricably linked to these countries through trade, financial flows, and investments, and our economic policies do not adequately take into account the NICs' expanded international economic roles. The purpose of this study was to examine the economic emergence of the NICs and to assess the consequences for U.S. policy.

Participants in this project included corporate executives, commercial bankers, investment bankers, labor leaders, and economists.

Some panel members contributed papers and all actively participated in our panel discussions; thus the final product reflects a diversity of perspectives. The chapters that constitute this volume therefore serve a twofold purpose. They offer a detailed analysis of how the NICs are changing the face of the international economy, as well as insights into how different sectors of the U.S. economy and foreign observers view these problems.

This project is part of an ongoing effort by the EPC to orchestrate a systematic and constructive involvement of the American private sector in international economic problems. The EPC is committed to representing the views of both management and labor, who work in close cooperation with economists and other professionals to analyze international economic problems facing the United States and develop policy recommendations. Because these policy recommendations are grounded in extensive research and discussion, and because they are backed by a broad domestic consensus, they have a special legitimacy for U.S. policymakers. The EPC is one of the most experienced labor and management groups working in the area of international economic policy, and it is our hope that, by contributing to a more thorough awareness of the critical policy implications of our new economic setting, this study will help foster the increased cooperation and understanding that are so important to sound U.S. policy.

We would like to express our appreciation to the Alfred P. Sloan Foundation, The Ford Foundation, and The Rockefeller Foundation for providing grants that helped make this study possible. We would also like to thank Rose Carcaterra for directing the coordination of all aspects of this manuscript.

The views expressed in these chapters are solely those of the individual authors. The consensus findings and recommendations of the panel members who participated in this study were published in a separate report of the Economic Policy Council of the UNA-USA.

Thornton F. Bradshaw
Daniel F. Burton, Jr.
Richard N. Cooper
Robert D. Hormats

INTRODUCTION

1 COPING WITH THE NICs

Thornton F. Bradshaw

As the cochairman of the EPC panel on the newly emerging industrial countries, my problem is that I am not sure there is a problem. We have settled on the two questions we should like to address: (1) How will the newly industrializing countries affect the international economy over the next five to ten years? and (2) how should the United States respond to these changes? We have spent time trying to define the NICs, which I do not think is a viable exercise. At any one time in history some countries are on their way up, some are on their way down, and maybe for one brief shining moment a country stands still. That's only for one brief moment, and I'm not sure that defining a class of countries as newly emerging can be useful.

I think that much can be learned at any one time in history by observing countries that are on their way down, observing those that on their way up, and then trying to define or work out some exchange of positions—and if you cannot do that, trying to work out balanced relationships so that the world does not fall apart because some countries are getting richer and some are getting poorer. I think that's our basic problem.

The countries that are getting richer rather rapidly today have some common characteristics. They are countries with a large labor supply. They are countries that have low wage rates, not because they lack labor unions but because they are in a different sociological phase of their history.

In Taiwan, for instance, the prevailing wage in mass production industries such as my own is about $1.80 an hour; this includes about sixty to seventy cents cash and the rest in benefits. The comparable wage in the state of Indiana, where comparable workers can accomplish similar tasks, is now $15.00 an hour. This wage differential represents countries at two different phases of history and cannot easily be overcome. The wage rates in Taiwan are determined by its very large labor supply. Young girls on the farms and in the barrios are willing, and indeed anxious, to come to the factories; to live at at the factories in dormitories; to spend four, five, six years there at the cash wage of sixty to seventy cents an hour; to get their food at the factory cafeterias; to get their entertainment and their education there, such as it is; to go home very seldom because of the lack of transportation facilities; to save their money; and then at the end of six years, to go back to their villages with their dowries. There is no comparable system in the state of Indiana. The problem is that these nations, which have the large labor supply and are at a different phase of their economic history, will get richer while we will continue to get relatively poorer.

Also involved in this rapid shifting of position is the easy transfer of technology. We used to think that the nation that had the technology had all the advantages, but technology is extremely easy to transfer. Trained management is easily transferred, too. About two years ago the prime minister of Taiwan said to me, "We know that we got you here because of our low labor rates" (RCA went to Taiwan some fifteen years ago because of low labor rates), "but we know that we can't keep you here because of low labor rates, since there are other nations in the world that have lower labor rates. Instead, we're going to keep you here because we're going to supply you with the very best technically trained management that you can get throughout the world." And indeed their managers are trained. They are trained in their universities, and the proof is that of RCA's almost 10,000 employees in Taiwan, there are only seventeen Americans, and they are liaison. All the rest are Taiwanese. A great entrepreneurial spirit in some of these nations is another important factor in their success.

All these things add up to rapid change, with the emphasis on *rapid*. Change has always been evident, such as during the Roman Empire, but it occurred very slowly. Today it happens very fast, and that's why we notice. This kind of change must take place, but we have difficulty adjusting to it in the rich, slowly growing U.S. economy. We have to adjust to this situation, just as the NICs have to adjust because their growth is not going to last forever. There are new NICs on the horizon, and as the old NICs phase out, the new NICs will come in. This bouncing ball of industrialization is moving around the world very fast. That is the principle problem that we have to address: How do we live in a world where rapid adjustment must be undertaken—today in the United States, tomorrow in some other country?

The adjustment is especially critical for people. This kind of change is going to be very disruptive of social institutions and people—particularly people—and I think that social disruption is the heart of our problem. Because of progress in economics, communications, and technology, we cannot remain static. We must learn to live with these changes, and I think that is what this study is all about. It is not about the NICs. It spotlights the NICs to help gain insights into new aspects of this overall problem.

2 NEW PLAYERS IN THE INTERNATIONAL ECONOMY

Robert D. Hormats

Just as the growth of the United States' economic power posed a competitive threat to—and provided a large market for—the nations of Western Europe in the last century, the newly industrialized countries both pose competitive threats and provide market opportunities for the United States and other mature industrialized economies in the latter years of this one. Their rise is part of the cycle of constant change—of the ebb and flow of economies—that has characterized the world as far back as the great city-states of Rome, Carthage, and Troy. Those who cannot compete fall behind, both economically and politically; those who can, usually thrive on both fronts.

The fundamental policy question for the United States is whether we will respond to these successful economies defensively (by erecting barriers around our country) or competitively (by strengthening our productivity and our export performance). A second challenge is to structure a series or rules and understandings that industrialized and developing nations find mutually acceptable. A willingness to compete with the NICs does not imply that such competition should take place without any rules to promote fairness and reciprocity. The United States has for years been expected to play by a broadly agreed set of international rules. So have Australia, Canada, Europe, and Japan. And so must the newly industrializing nations.

Three goals must be kept in mind as we consider the question of the United States' capacity to compete with the NICs and its role in seeking mutually acceptable rules that govern the conduct of trade with them. First, the ability of the United States to respond constructively to competitive pressures from the NICs will depend heavily on the quality of its domestic economic policy and performance. To the extent that U.S. domestic policies produce a high rate of growth and the vigorous creation of new jobs, the ability of Americans to adapt to intense competition from the developing nations will be sharply enhanced. And the U.S. private sector must respond by concentrating greater effort on selling to these expanding economies the products in which the United States has a strong competitive advantage. Moreover, national policy will need to pay greater attention to the basic underpinnings of U.S. competitiveness: capital formation, research and development, and education. The debate over the recent tax bill and the effort to cut government expenditures have tended to neglect these three vital areas; yet unless the United States moves soon to strengthen its performance in all three, our competitive position will inevitably slip.

Second, there will need to be a broad consensus on the international ground rules for promoting adjustment. Internally, the NICs will need to accept the principle that if they are to be convincing in their arguments for greater access to markets of industrialized nations for products in which they have competitive strength, they must allow access to their markets for the goods and services in which the industrialized countries are highly competitive. And there will need to be a consensus among the industrialized nations that they must more broadly share the burden of adjustment to the competitiveness of the developing nations—with Europe and Japan (which import a considerably smaller portion of LDC manufactured goods than does the United States) accepting a greater share of the manufactured exports of these countries.

Third, the international trading system needs to be updated to promote conditions under which increases in trade can occur smoothly, thereby providing appropriate returns for new investment and highly competitive producers. At the same time, there must be mutually acceptable rules that govern the circumstances under which governments may temporarily slow imports to cushion the human effects of adjustment and enable firms and workers time to improve their competitiveness or move into areas in which they are more competitive. And the rules governing protection of intellectual property (such as protecting patents, discouraging counterfeiting, and stiffening penalties for trademark violations) should be tightened.

But laying out a framework for improving the prospects for greater U.S. competitiveness and better managing U.S. relations with the NICs is only a start. Two philosophical issues lie at the heart of the challenge for both industrialized and developing nations. The first concerns the inevitable conflict that arises when one group of countries sees its position slipping while others become stronger. The former frequently attempts to devise artificial means to maintain a comparative advantage (through tariffs, subsidies, and voluntary restraint arrangements), while the latter often presses its advantage with little sensitivity to the adverse effect that sharp surges in exports have on workers and industries in the former. Too often in history, such conflicts have led to intense bitterness and confrontation—as the countries and industries that see themselves being passed fail to recognize that drastic improvements in their own practices are the only real way to maintain or improve their competitive positions and instead blame the more competitive countries or industries for their problems. Unless the United States draws appropriate conclusions—that its economic fate lies primarily in its own hands—it will find itself increasingly vulnerable to imports from the more competitive nations of the globe, will seek to artificially maintain its position, and will blame its problems on others rather than improve its own policies and practices.

The second concerns the role of the state. In many NICs the state plays a far greater role in economic decisions than it does in the United States. When the NICs did little trade with this country, the difference hardly mattered. But as trade increases, this difference can lead to major distortions and bitter conflict over whether government policies are unduly distorting market forces. In some NICs, the government encourages efficiency and avoids prolonged subsidies; in others it provides only temporary support and seed money for research; in others it encourages close cooperation among companies, works closely with private industry in order to provide focus, and targets specific sectors for enhanced exports; and in still others it provides large subsidies and prolonged protection. Without some type of understanding on which types of government intervention are acceptable and which are not, distortions are inevitable.

Finally, two policy dilemmas pose problems for the United States and the NICs. The United States has underscored the need for other nations to rely heavily on market forces. Yet the more trade competitive the LDCs become, the greater the domestic pressures grow in this country to limit their imports. A particularly troublesome conflict arises because the high-debt LDCs are urged by governments in industrialized nations to improve their competitiveness and boost exports in order to earn the funds required to service their debt while at the same time domestic pressures in the United States and other industrialized countries resist the increases in imports from the LDC that would result from such efforts. Somehow the two considerations must be reconciled, or the incentives for the LDCs to move toward more efficient policies will be blunted. If we do not want to accept goods in certain sectors, it is better to say so early on rather than wait until the capacity is put in place and then render it useless by restricting market access of its product.

Among the NICs there is a growing disparity. The Asian NICs have grown far more rapidly than their counterparts in Latin America. In the area of manufactured goods the East Asian NICs are in a dominant market position, while Latin America tends to rely more heavily on the export of raw materials. If the Latin American NICs fail to create a better environment for private investment and for export efficiency—as those of East Asia have—they will find their world market share slipping away. Yet there is a certain reluctance on the part of the Latin American nations to undertake major policy changes necessary to strengthen their competitive positions. A long history of a heavy state hand in their economies and high levels of employment (often the result of political favors) in state-owned enterprises have made leaders reluctant to reduce the role of the state—and the inefficiency that comes from such reluctance continues to exert a drag on growth. The East Asian model may not be one that Latin Americans can totally embrace; but it has some very attractive features that the Latin Americans would do well to emulate.

The following chapters describe these issues in greater detail and offer useful insights into many aspects of the role of the NICs and the U.S. policy response. In the 1960s the United States responded to Sputnik not by digging a hole and hiding but with a dramatic surge in rocket and space technology that involved great cooperation between the public and private sectors. In a sense, Japanese and Korean cars, Taiwanese televisions, Hong Kong VCRs, and Brazilian small airplanes are collectively the Sputniks of the 1980s; we must respond today in much the same way as we did then.

3 THE CHALLENGE OF THE NICs

Richard N. Cooper

We are drawn to the newly industrialized countries (NICs) because they are seen as a new challenge to the United States, and so they are in some respects. But that challenge needs to be put in the broader perspective of the evolution of the U.S. and world economies over the last thirty to forty years. In that perspective we should be celebrating the economic success of these countries, not lamenting it or accepting it with reluctance and misgiving. Moreover, if the economic success of the NICs is joined by corresponding political progress, as has occurred in Spain and Portugal and seems to be occurring in Argentina and Brazil, they can look forward to joining the community of prosperous, democratic, humane, and peaceful societies with shared values. Economic growth alone does not assure this development, but without economic growth an assured evolution in that direction is surely impossible.

In this chapter I would like to make six points with respect to the newly industrialized countries and the U.S. relationship to them. The first noteworthy point about the NICs is that they represent successful examples of economic development, something that many doubters and cynics thought was impossible twenty-five years ago. We now have half a dozen to a dozen countries that have experienced substantial increases in real per capita income over the last quarter century.

11

Second, their success has been associated with quite a remarkable variety of circumstances and policies. It is not possible to make sweeping generalizations, as former Senator Buckley did on behalf of the Reagan administration in a United Nations conference in Mexico in 1984, that the success stories are all due to free enterprise. It is true that the "four tigers" of Asia all espouse private property, but Hong Kong among them is the only really free enterprise entity. The role of government is very important in most of the successful NICs. In some cases the role is subtle and indirect, while in others it is very direct and even heavy handed.

The United States can take some credit for some of the successes. It was the United States that pressed Taiwan and Korea (following the experience of postwar Japan) into land reform and then persuaded them, and later Brazil, to change their trade policies toward an outward-looking, export-oriented one in the 1960s, rather than relying on import substitution. But in many other cases the United States can claim no credit other than being a source of capital and goods and offering a market for their goods. For example, the United States had no direct role in the policies of Singapore or Hong Kong. So a wide variety of circumstances surrounds the economic emergence of the NICs. We do not know precisely what leads to success in economic development.

Third, instead of celebrating the success, there is considerable ambivalence about it, and we tend to see the NICs rather as problems. A recent issue of *Business Week* proclaimed on its title page, "The Koreans Are Coming," in reference to the famous line about British troops at a time when the British were not considered friendly. What exactly is the problem? It is that these countries produce goods that compete with U.S. products. They sell goods both in the United States and in competition with U.S. goods elsewhere in the world, and that is seen as a threat to U.S. profits and employment.

There is perhaps some factual basis to these concerns and anxieties, which will be taken up below, but in focusing on them we neglect that millions of people are better off than they were twenty-five years ago as a result of this process. Being better off, they want to buy much more from the United States. But in order to buy more from the United States they must be able to sell more overseas, including to the United States.

It generally has been the case that all these countries spend every penny that they earn and then some. A number of them now have substantial external debt, the accumulation of past borrowings. Koreans are fond of pointing out that for seventeen of the last twenty years they ran consequential deficits with the United States. It is true that during 1984 and 1985 they ran a surplus with the United States; but few countries did not run a surplus with the United States during those years. U.S. trade deficits exceeded $100 billion in each of the two years. The problem can hardly be blamed on Korea or other NICs. Singapore ran payments deficits in all but one of the years from the early 1960s up until 1985. Over time, these countries taken as a group spend everything they can earn and borrow for imports from abroad.

Furthermore, the process of their economic transformation also leaves the average American—but not every single American—better off because it provides cheaper goods than Americans can produce and it creates demand for the high-quality goods that Americans are good at producing. That process makes U.S. consumers and producers better off and leads to a higher standard of living for the United States as well as higher standards of living in the NICs.

My fourth point is that the process of this economic transformation raises questions about our capacity to adjust to structural change brought about by the emergence of the newly industrialized countries. Notwithstanding the several advantages that I have mentioned, the pace of change required of the U.S. economy could conceivably be so great as to overwhelm them. It could lead to high unemployment, low profits, and low growth. Although this is theoretically possible for some period of time, we are not operating in an area of ignorance with respect to these problems of transitional adjustment. We have much experience concerning our capacity to adapt to change. It is worth noting that historically, including up to the present time, the major sources of structural change in the U.S. economy, and hence the factors that call for major adaptation of the economy, are not imports but technical change. New innovations are constantly dislocating our inherited ways of doing things. Industries both rise and decline from decade to decade as a result of technological progress and of new patterns of demand. These factors are the most important source of dislocation, but they are also the most important source of higher standards of living for Americans. Quite properly, we do not call for great restraint on technical progress.

The second major source of dislocation in the U.S. economy has been U.S. government spending. Historically, changes in the pattern of federal spending have been a major cause for the need to readjust employment in terms both of occupation and of geographical location. We built a space industry from nothing to a substantial industry in the course of about eight years with the Apollo program. Then we reduced the industry by half in the following three years. Defense spending has waxed and waned by huge amounts over the years, calling for substantial changes in the structure of U.S. output and employment. The output of U.S. defense industries in early 1986 was 80 percent higher than it had been in 1977, compared with an increase of only 26 percent in total U.S. industrial production. After the current round of major procurement, and in the presence of substantial pressure to reduce the U.S. budget deficit, it seems certain that the defense industry will once again go into a period of decline. Government policy is thus a major source of disturbance to the U.S. economy. Furthermore, we have entered a period of what from the point of view of rational decisionmaking can only be considered a grotesque process of budget cutting under the Gramm-Rudman Act. If that act goes into full effect, there will be an enormous amount of human dislocation and for no higher purpose than to save our government—the executive and the legislative branches taken together—the task of rationally bringing the budget back into balance.

Foreign trade comes third as a source of dislocation and hence required adjustment in the U.S. economy, well below technological change and government spending. We also have some experience in adjusting to the impact of changing patterns of trade. In the last half century Japan was the first successful NIC. It is worth recalling that in 1953, well after the period of postwar reconstruction, Japan's per capita income was only $350. In today's prices that would be a shade over $1,000, or a bit more than half of South Korea's current per capita income. Over the last thirty years Japan has moved to a point where its per capita income is equal to that of the United States at an exchange rate of $1 equals 157 yen, and it is considerably higher than Britain's per capita income.

The rapid growth of Japanese manufacturing output, and its changing composition, has been a source of dislocation both for the United States and for other countries. We saw first the emergence of a strongly competitive textile industry, then steel, followed by automobiles and consumer electronic products. But the dislocations that strongly competitive Japanese exports have created, although discomforting to those in the industries feeling the competitive pressures, have not been disastrous. Overall, the U.S. economy has adapted. Indeed, some of the growth of Japanese exports has been in response to changes in the pattern of U.S. demand, as in the case of small automobiles after the second oil price increase, or even have created new U.S. demand, as in the case of video tape recorders.

Japan was an economically large country relative to most of today's NICs. It might well be the case that if all the 130 developing countries together were to emerge as newly industrializing countries over the next fifteen to twenty-five years, there would be a major problem of dislocation. But we can count on the inappropriateness of economic policies in many of these countries to spread that process over a half to three-quarters of a century, if not longer. As long as the pace of change remains on the scale that we have seen, the U.S. economy, which is remarkably flexible, can and will adapt to it without major difficulty.

Incidentally, it has become a journalistic cliché to say that the pace of change in the U.S. economy has been accelerating. I do not believe that there is any evidence for that; on the contrary, it is highly doubtful that the pace is accelerating. The phrase about taking in each other's wash is a century old. The observation that the pace of change has been accelerating is also a century old, going back to the rapid changes of the nineteenth century. In fact, the U.S. economy has been in a process of rapid transformation for over a century now. New industries have been created—steel, the electrical industry, the chemical industry—in the course of a couple of decades. I do not believe that the pace of required change—the rate at which we have to adapt the labor force, for example, or change the structure of output—has accelerated from what it was forty or eighty years ago. It has been and remains rapid, but acceleration suggests an ever increasing speed.

We tend to forget how rapidly our agricultural sector declined. From 1947 to 1957 the decline in U.S. agricultural employment was 25 percent, and a further 35 percent decline in the ten years from 1957 to 1967. The decline in manufacturing employment over the decade from 1973, a strong year, to 1983, the employment low point following the 1982 recession, was only 9 percent, and manufacturing employment has increased 5 percent since then. There is of course continual change within the pattern of both agricultural and manufacturing employment, but there also was change in those sectors twenty or forty years ago. The question of whether change is actually accelerating is a subject that deserves further research, but there appears little evidence that acceleration has occurred.

My final point is that as the NICs mature economically, their problems and their outlook will become similar to those of the advanced industrialized countries. As a result, it will be both necessary and desirable to integrate them more fully into the economic framework of the advanced industrialized countries. That means several things, some that are negative from the point of view of the NICs. It means that they will lose their special privileges as developing countries—"special and differential treatment," as it is called in United Nations language. It means the eventual loss of discriminatory tariffs in favor of their products under GSP. It means not only getting off the list of eligibility for IDA loans—all the NICs have graduated from that list already—but eventually becoming ineligible even for World Bank loans. It means that they will have less and less claim on foreign assistance. One by one, as the NICs become technically more advanced, we will worry about transfers of their high technology to potential adversaries, particularly the Soviet Union. This concern will require bringing them into a cooperative framework, and above all it means bringing them into the extensive system of consultation, which is not always action oriented but involves an intense exchange of information among advance industrialized countries. This process of adaptation is one that the United States, the other advanced countries, and the NICs should all strive for together.

COUNTRY PROFILES

4 BRAZILIAN-BASED REFLECTIONS
Debt, Stabilization, and Growth

Edmar Lisboa Bacha

This is an interim assessment, written in September 1986, of the Brazilian experience with external and domestic adjustment to the debt crisis of the 1980s. Rather than a revision of facts and figures, what follows calls attention to some salient features of this important Latin American case.

We first review the external shocks of the early 1980s and the external adjustment that followed. Attention is then shifted to the difficulties of domestic adjustment. The monetary reform program of February 1986 is reviewed next. The chapter concludes with a brief discussion of the country's economic perspectives.

SHOCKS AND EXTERNAL ADJUSTMENT

The Brazilian economic miracle, which started in 1968, was interrupted in 1973 by a combination of the first oil shock with domestic capacity limitations (Bacha 1980). There followed a period of Brazilian-style adjustment, in which GNP growth was kept at 7 percent per year through an intense state-led import substitution program, financed by a sizable accumulation of external debt (Bacha and Malan, 1987). The second oil shock combined with the Volcker interest rate shock to take 5 percent off Brazil's GDP (Bacha 1986).

During 1980 the country saw its external sources of credit shrink, but rather than go to the IMF at year end it opted to implement a stiff deflationary program of its own making (Bacha 1983a). Brazil was halfway through this program when the debt crisis erupted in September 1982 on the wake of the Mexican moratorium. This time there was no escape from the IMF, which oversaw the application of its standard stabilization package to Brazil for nearly two years starting in early 1983 (Bastos Marques, 1987).

On the trade front, the adjustment to the external shocks worked very well. Exports increased from $20.1 billion in 1980 to $27.0 billion in 1984, while imports contracted from $22.9 billion to $13.9 billion. As a consequence, the trade balance shifted from a negative $2.8 billion in 1980 to a positive $13.1 billion in 1984. This was partly achieved through recession. Thus, manufacturing output fell by 11 percent between 1980 and 1984. But structural change was also important. The export coefficient (exports over GDP) went up from 8.0 percent in 1980 to 12.3 percent in 1984, while the import coefficient declined from 9.2 to 5.5 percent during the same period (Carneiro 1986). This successful transformation in the trade position was guaranteed by both structural and relative-price measures. Thus, the emphasis on import substitution investment in oil since the early 1970s allowed an increase in the share of domestically supplied oil in total domestic consumption from 20 to 40 percent between 1980 and 1984. At the same time, a significant devaluation of the real exchange rate, by 18 percent between 1980 and January 1985 (CEMEI/FGV 1986), propelled the desired short-term supply and demand adjustments.

The improvement of the trade figures was sufficiently strong to allow Brazil in 1984 to start paying the interest bill on its foreign debt without new money. In fact, interest payments went up from $6.3 billion in 1980 to $10.1 billion in 1984. Nonetheless, Brazil's current account, which was a negative $12.8 billion in 1980, shifted to a positive figure of $166 million in 1984. On a flow basis, the external adjustment was thus completed in 1984, and this explains why Brazil could drag its feet on IMF's demands for additional domestic adjustment.

The successful completion of the external adjustment on a flow basis did not mean that Brazil's debt problem was solved. On the contrary, as a proportion of exports, interest payments were higher in 1984 than in 1980 (37.3 percent as compared to 31.3 percent).

The ratio of net debt over exports, on the other hand, was up to 3.0 in 1984 from 2.3 in 1980 (Carneiro 1986). In other words, Brazil was able to solve its external liquidity problem, but the debt overhang continued to cast a heavy shade over its future economic perspectives. Particularly telling is the situation of fixed investment, which fell from 21.8 to 16.4 percent of GDP from 1980 to 1984.

EXTERNAL ADJUSTMENT, DOMESTIC MALADJUSTMENT

In contrast to its successful external adjustment, Brazil's domestic accounts worsened considerably in the reference period. Just before the inception of the IMF program, Brazil's inflation was running at 100 percent per year. By 1984 it stood at 220 percent. Similarly, the nominal public sector deficit ratio to GDP went from 15.8 percent in 1982 up to 23.3 percent in 1984.

The need for additional domestic adjustment was recognized in Brazil. But controversy raged with the IMF over the nature, sequence, and dosage of the required medicine. As viewed from Brazil (and more vocally by the economists who were then in opposition to the military regime), observed domestic maladies were in good measure a consequence of the successful external adjustment performed by the Brazilian economy since the early 1980s. We consider inflation first and then the budget deficit.

The Inflation Conundrum

Chronic inflation has been as important a part of Brazil's economic life as coffee beans used to be of its past. The most impressive thing about Brazilian inflation was not so much that it was high but that it did not accelerate rapidly, as both the Phillips curve and the German hyperinflation would lead one to believe would happen. In fact, Brazilian economists of different persuasions were convinced that the country's virulent inflation had little to do with excess demand theories, of either the monetarist or the Keynesian variety. After a series of failed attempts at controlling Brazilian inflation through monetary stringency, even the IMF finally conceded that in Brazil demand contraction was a very inefficient way of reducing inflation because of the widespread backward-looking indexation schemes that character-ized most nominal contracts in the country. Econometric exercises by Brazilian economists agreed in that a 10 percent increase in excess capacity would provoke a 10 percent reduction of inflation (Modiano 1985; Cysne 1985). This is in line with the Phillips curve results for the United States. However, the United States would start from a inflation plateau of 10 percent per year, while Brazil's hovered around 220 percent per year. Hence, increasing unemployment by 10 percent would eliminate U.S. inflation but would reduce Brazil's to only 210 percent in one year.

The situation was one in which all economic agents, after a long learning period, had developed a myriad of formal and informal indexation arrangements as the most rational way to act in a context of chronic inflation. In such a situation, the most important reason that inflation was 220 percent in any year was that it was 220 per-cent the year before. Sure enough, liquidity had to come from some-where, and the place from where it usually came was the government budget deficit. But the latter normally would expand in step with inflation, for the simple reason that government taxes and expendi-tures both tended to increase uniformly when prices speeded up. Thus, starting from a situation with a positive deficit, the monetary base would tend to follow passively the ups and downs of the infla-tion rate, as determined by supply shocks and indexation practices.

Experience showed that Brazil's inflation shifted up in steps. A rough description of nearly twenty years of inflation is as follows. From 1968 to 1973, inflation stabilized at 20 percent per year. As a consequence of the first oil shock, inflation went up to 40 percent in the 1974–79 period. The second oil shock, together with the December 1979 maxidevaluation, set a new inflationary plateau of 100 percent for the 1982 period. Finally, the February 1983 maxi-devaluation and a food supply shock made inflation shoot up to 220 percent in the 1983–85 period.

With some oversimplification, the mechanics of this process can be described briefly. Indexation was widespread but not perfect. Wages, in particular, were held down by the rule of 100 percent backward indexation at fixed six-month intervals. At any particular month, roughly one-sixth of the wage bill was due for readjustment. The exchange rate was a crawling peg, which went up daily according to the last month's inflation rate. (These minidevaluations were at times superseded by a mididevaluation, as in the second quarter of 1985, or more rarely by a maxidevaluation, as in December 1979 or February 1983.) Industrial prices responded swiftly to domestic wage and import price pressures, with roughly constant mark-ups. It was the lagged wage adjustment that made inflation jump to a new plateau, rather than accelerate continuously, when a supply shock occurred, as caused by OPEC, a crop failure, or a maxidevaluation.

In this context, maxidevaluations are inflationary—but they work. Costs go up, but the relative attractiveness of exporting or replacing imports increases. Industrialized Brazil reacts as expected, expanding exports and replacing imports. The trade balance improves at the cost of a higher inflationary plateau. This had been the experience of Brazil since the mid-1960s. The conclusion is unavoidable that inflation jumped from 100 to 220 percent per year mostly as a consequence of the February 1983 maxidevaluation, which was forced on the government by the need to produce the megatrade surpluses of the subsequent periods.

The Budget Deficit

Consider now the question of the public-sector deficit. There are many facets to it. Undoubtedly, the Brazilian government spends big and badly, as governments are prone to do in the south as well as in the north. However, the IMF (in the September 1986 tentative Mexican agreement) has now recognized the inadequacy of trying to monitor nominal budget deficits in conditions of high inflation. As Brazilian economists continuously insisted with the Fund, the relevant concept is the inflation-corrected budget deficit (Bacha 1983b). Looking at the problem from this perspective, the figures show that real government absorption did go down during the adjustment process. In constant 1984 cruzeiros, total federal government expenditures fell from 35.1 trillion in 1980 to 33.8 trillion in 1984. Excluding debt service and transfers to state and municipalities, spending declined from 21.5 trillion in 1980 to 19.9 trillion in 1984. A similar picture is revealed for the state enterprises. Their total spending in 1984 cruzeiros fell from 90 trillion in 1980 to 87.5 trillion in 1984. Excluding debt service, the spending of state enterprises dropped from 86 to 77 trillion in the same period (Brasil 1986).[1]

Unfortunately, a uniform series is not available on the fiscal expenditures that appear on the so-called Monetary Budget (which is an aggregation of the accounts of the Central Bank and Banco do Brasil). It is in this budget that most of the public-sector debt service, both domestic and foreign, is taken care of. But consider the following qualitative argument. Since the early 1980s the Brazilian government offered the private sector the opportunity to prepay its foreign debts through the deposit of an equivalent amount in cruzeiros to a special account at the Central Bank. Facilities also existed to provide subsidized domestic credit to private firms anxious to get rid of their foreign currency–denominated debts. The propensity to use these facilities increased enormously after 1982 as the real devaluation of the cruzeiro significantly raised the cost of carrying foreign debt. Thus, foreign currency deposits in the Monetary Authorities were equal to the monetary base in December 1982; in the following period, the ratio between them changed markedly. During the second half of 1984, the foreign currency deposits in the Monetary Authorities were nearly three times as high as the monetary base.

As the private firms deposit in the Monetary Authorities the cruzeiro equivalent of its foreign debt, the Brazilian government loses the opportunity to finance itself through the inflation tax. In fact, the government exchanges with the private sector an interest-free cruzeiro liability for an interest-paying dollar liability. When it extends cheaper domestic credit to replace private foreign debt, the government loses future revenue to the tune of the negative interest rate differential embedded in this subsidized financial intermediation. In both cases, the government budget is burdened by new expensive financial obligations while helping the private sector to cope with the crisis. Thus, the February 1983 maxidevaluation hit the public sector not only because it already held the lion's share of the country's external debt but also because it effectively nationalized a good part of the external debt of the private sector.

Additionally, the suppression of the country's access to the international financial market was clearly a case of too much too fast. In 1982 foreign savings represented 5.7 percent of Brazil's GDP; two years afterwards, it was nil. The government tried to adjust its spending, but that was not nearly enough. In addition to the higher real cruzeiro cost of the foreign debt, taxes were eroded by the recession, while public sector prices were being held down to avoid burdening private-sector costs even more. Private-sector employment also went down; consequently, the political pressures increased to expand public-sector employment. In the end, budget deficits failed to decrease as required and could not be financed from abroad. Rather than throwing its net on the sea of international financial markets, the government was forced to go fishing in the small ponds of the domestic financial market. Domestic interest rates soared, the private sector was crowded out, and an untenable financial situation became manifest once the government proved unable toward the fourth quarter of 1984 to continue repressing public-sector wages as a means of controlling its deficits.

The critical nature of Brazil's budget deficit is revealed by the fact that in 1985 the federal government paid $12 billion in foreign and domestic interest. This is equal to no less than one-half of its total tax intake. The fact that noninterest spending was not larger than the tax intake itself was of little help, except to ensure that the value of the government nonmonetary liabilities would grow by no more than the interest rate on its outstanding debt. Both social spending and government infrastructure investment are well below requirements. Hence, the fiscal crisis of the Brazilian state poses an unusual challenge for economic policymakers in the near future.

THE CRUZADO PLAN

The monetary reform program, known as the cruzado plan, which was implanted in February 28, 1986, derived from the conception that inertia was the single most important explanation for Brazil's high inflation rate. Neither Keynesian gradualism nor monetarist shock treatment were up to the task of dealing with inertial inflation because both were based on demand contraction, a very indirect and costly way to break the social contracts sustaining inflationary inertia. A radical rupture with the past, through a comprehensive monetary reform program, was required to cope with the problem (Arida and Lara-Resende 1985; Lopes 1986). Four interrelated sets of measures were adopted: the introduction of a new currency, a "neutral" conversion rule for all nominal contracts, the elimination of short-term financial indexation, and a general price freeze. The new currency, the cruzado, was introduced with a fixed dollar value and with an initial value equal to 1,000 times the old currency, the cruzeiro.

The neutrality in the conversion of all nominal contracts had the purpose of replicating in a stable currency the equilibrium income and financial wealth distribution generated in the context of a depreciating currency. This required that the value of such contracts in cruzados was made equal to the average real value in cruzeiros. Consider, for example, the critical problem of wage conversion. By law, wages were readjusted every six months, in proportion to the cost of living increase that had occurred since the previous adjustment. With inflation running at 105 percent per half year (as in the September 1985 to February 1986 period), it can be shown that the average real value of the wage was equal to 71 percent of its peak value. Moreover, at any moment in time each wage-earning group was at a particular point of its own wage cycle, depending on the date of the group's last wage readjustment. Thus, at the time of the monetary reform, for each wage-earning group (as defined by the month of its last readjustment), a different conversion factor was determined in such a way as to maintain the rule of converting all nominal contracts according to their average real value in the old currency.[2]

Consider now the problem of preserving neutrality for debt instruments with fixed nominal interest rates. Supposedly, the parties of this contract shared an inflation expectation at the time in which this contract was signed, which was based on currently observed inflation rates. With the sudden elimination of inflation, a corresponding deflator needed to be adopted for these interest rates in order to preserve neutrality in the relationship between creditors and debtors. This was achieved by converting future cruzeiros into cruzados at a daily depreciating rate, equal to the observed inflation in cruzeiros during the three previous months. By contrast, debt contracts with a monetary correction or indexation clause (plus a real interest rate on top of it) had their values updated according to the price-level change observed between the date of their last readjustment and the day of the reform, also ensuring a neutral conversion of capital values. Afterwards, however, no additional monetary corrections were allowed for short-term financial instruments.

The outlawing of short-term indexation was combined with the fixing of the exchange rate between the cruzado and the dollar and with the daily devaluation of the cruzeiro vis-à-vis the cruzado to guarantee that government debt service would stop increasing with inflation. (Less than 20 percent of the indexed domestic debt was longer than one year, which was the period beyond which indexation was preserved.) Thus, inflation would no longer feed onto itself as under the cruzeiro, merely because of its effect on higher nominal interest payments on outstanding government debt.

Finally, a general price freeze was adopted to force an immediate change in price expectations, on the theory that such coordination function could not possibly be provided by a regularly functioning market mechanism in which inflationary expectations had become as entrenched as in Brazil. In Tobin's (1981) apt analogy, inertial inflation can be compared to a football match that is being watched with everyone standing up. It is useless to sit down by oneself, but all would benefit from a joint decision to sit down simultaneously. A temporary suppression of the rules of the game through the adoption of a general freeze should thus be in everyone's interest.

The cruzado plan worked extremely well in its first six months, producing very low rates of inflation, very high rates of economic growth, and an improved income distribution. This experience suggests that expansionary stabilization is a real possibility and not only a heterodox economist's daydream. However, excess demand, supply bottlenecks, and price distortions are accumulating rapidly. Thus, adjustment measures will need to be taken before a steady return to market-determined pricing can be made.

ECONOMIC PERSPECTIVES

The Brazilian economy is booming again, after the recession interlude of 1981–84. Viewed from a distance, the country would seem to have been able to combine the best of all possible worlds, simultaneously achieving record rates of GDP growth, inflation stabilization, and steady trade surpluses.

However, it is not all roses. Fixed investment rates are well below required for the maintenance of 7 to 8 percent GDP growth, which Brazilians are aiming for. The fiscal position of the state is very shaky, even without the required expansion of social expenditures and infrastructure investment. Firms' complaints against the freeze and violations thereof are increasing. Labor unions' wage demands are hardly in consonance with a regime of price stability. Consumers' lines at food stores are increasing, and supply shortages mounting. Some of these problems are short-term and require the introduction of aggregate demand control measures and the establishment of a consensual incomes policy in lieu of the price freeze. Others are medium term and require both a fiscal reform and an alleviation of the burden of external debt service. The Brazilian government will need to tackle current short- and medium-term economic problems with new innovative domestic and foreign initiatives.

NOTES

1. The price index used to deflate these series was the Vargas Foundation general price index.
2. This implied that the wage-earning groups that had recently received a half-year readjustment had their wages converted at a rate of less than 1,000 cruzeiros per cruzado. In part to soften the negative political impact of this reduction of nominal wages, a general 8 percent wage bonus was added to the average real wage of the previous semester. This bonus seems to have been at least partially responsible for the consumption boom of the following months.

REFERENCES

Arida, P., and A. Lara-Resende. 1985. "Inertial Inflation and Monetary Reform in Brazil." In *Inflation and Indexation: Argentina, Brazil, and Israel*, edited by J. Williamson, pp. 27–45. Washington, D.C.: Institute for International Economics, distributed by MIT Press.

Bacha, E. 1980. "Selected Issues on Recent Brazilian Economic Growth." In *Models of Growth and Distribution for Brazil*, edited by L. Taylor, pp. 17–48. Oxford: Oxford University Press.

_____. 1983a. "Vicissitudes of Recent Stabilization Attempts in Brazil and the IMF Alternative." In *IMF Conditionality*, edited by J. Williamson, pp. 323–40. Washington, D.C.: Institute for International Economics, distributed by MIT Press.

_____. 1983b. "The IMF and the Prospects for Adjustment in Brazil." In *Prospects for Adjustment in Argentina, Brazil, and Mexico*, edited by J. Williamson, pp. 323–40. Washington, D.C.: Institute for International Economics, distributed by MIT Press.

_____. 1986. "External Shocks and Growth Prospects: The Case of Brazil, 1973–89." *World Development* 14(8) (August): 919–36.

Bacha, E., and P. Malan. 1987. "Brazil's Debt: From the Miracle to the Fund." In *Democratizing Brazil*, edited by A. Stephan. Princeton, N.J.: University Press.

Bastos Marques, M.S. 1987. "FMI: a experiência brasileira recente." In *Recessão ou Crescimento: O FMI e o Banco Mundial na América Latina*, edited by E. Bacha and M. Rodriguez. Rio de Janeiro: Paz e Terra.

Brasil/República Federativa. 1986. *I Plano Nacional de Desenvolvimento da Nova República*. Brasília: Secretaria de Planejamento da Presidência da República.

Carneiro, D.D. 1986. "Stabilization Policies and Long-Run Adjustment: The Brazilian Experience in the Eighties." Paper prepared for the UNU/WIDER Project on Stabilization and Adjustment Programmes and Policies. Rio de Janeiro: PUC/RJ. Mimeo.

CEMEI/FGV. 1986. *Banco de Dados Nacionais e Internacionais*. Rio de Janeiro: Centro de Estudos Monetários e de Economia Internacional, Fundação Getulio Vargas.

Cysne, R.P. 1985. *Política Macroeconômica no Brasil, 1964/66 e 1980/84*. Rio de Janeiro: Fundação Getúlio Vargas.

Lopes, F. 1986. *Choque Heterodoxo: Combate à Inflacão e Reforma Monetária*. Rio de Janeiro: Editora Campus.

Modiano, E. 1985. "Salários, precos e câmbio: multiplicadores dos choques numa economia indexada." *Pesquisa e Planejamento Econômico* 15(1) (April): 1–32.

Tobin, J. 1981. "Diagnosing Inflation: A Taxonomy." In *Development in an Inflationary World*, edited by M.J. Flanders and A. Razin, pp. 19–29. New York: Academic Press.

5 MEXICO
Growth with Structural Change in the Presence of External Shocks

Pedro Aspe Armella

As Carlos Díaz-Alejandro (1984) stated in his paper, "Latin American Debt, I Don't Think We are in Kansas Anymore," the balance of payments has been fundamental in determining the real development of Latin American economies since 1982. In his work, Díaz-Alejandro makes an exhaustive analysis of the causes that led up to the 1982 financial crisis and how the Latin American economies have endured it. He placed special emphasis on the enormous adjustment effort that these countries have had to make in order to meet their foreign debt obligations. This chapter is a case study of Mexico, in which some of the problems presented by Díaz-Alejandro are dealt with in greater detail: its foreign debt burden, the external shocks to the Mexican economy, the deterioration in its terms of trade, and its policies to promote exports and structural change.

It isn't news that Mexico's economy is in crisis and that the foreign debt burden is considerable. In contrast, very little is known about how during the last four years the country has used a broad process of industrial reconversion and the reduction of trade protection to adjust its economy, to introduce profound structural changes, and to increase efficiency in both the public and private sectors.

This ambitious task, which even in normal circumstances would be extremely complex, becomes enormously difficult in Mexico's case. The collapse of the oil market, the heavy burden of the foreign debt,

31

and the damage inflicted by the 1985 killer earthquakes constitute a particularly adverse context for determining economic policy.

This chapter summarizes recent economic behavior, the objectives and achievements of economic policy in the last few years, and especially the measures that have been adopted to improve the linkages between Mexico and the international economy and describes the prospects for the coming years.

MEXICO'S PARTICIPATION IN
THE WORLD ECONOMY

Mexico ranks eleventh in the world in population and thirteenth in territory and total output. Nevertheless, Mexico's share of world trade has been relatively low and traditionally concentrated in a few products. In 1984 Mexico accounted for 1.38 percent of total world exports, ranking eighteenth among exporting nations and twenty-eighth among importers, with 0.61 percent of total imports. The composition of its exports reflects the development of the country's economy: In 1950, 58 percent of total exports came from the farm sector, 32 percent from mining, and only 10 percent from manufacturing. In 1974 manufactured goods accounted for more than 50 percent of exports, while farm products represented 30 percent, and the share of mining was only 17.5 percent.

The importance of oil began to increase in 1975. Mexico's share went from 1.2 percent of total exports in 1973 to a peak of more than 80 percent in 1982. Mexico's low share of world trade (outside of oil) can be explained mainly by its domestically oriented development strategy, which was based on import substitution. This process, begun in the 1930s with the manufacture of consumer goods, provided high rates of growth for almost four decades. After the growth potential of this stage was exhausted at the end of the 1970s, the country progressed to the substitution of intermediate and capital goods.

Paradoxically, between 1973–82 the financing of this strategy was increasingly based on foreign loans, at the same time in which oil exports began to generate new income. By 1979 Mexico had become one of the world's most important oil producers, and by 1983 it was the fourth largest exporter in the world and the greatest outside the Persian Gulf.

In financial markets, Mexico's importance has also been growing in recent years. A foreign debt of more than $100 billion (the second highest in the world after Brazil) has given the country a major role in the international financial system and in the strategy to solve the debt problem of developing countries.

THE FOREIGN SECTOR OF THE MEXICAN ECONOMY: THE EFFECTS OF THE DEBT, INTEREST PAYMENTS, AND OIL EXPORTS

The need to achieve an adequate balance in the economy's foreign sector has become one of the main restrictions to growth. Due to its strong orientation toward the domestic market and its heavy dependence on imported inputs, any acceleration in the economy has traditionally been accompanied by a deterioration in the trade balance.

In recent years, the current account balance has been strongly linked with the trend in oil prices and foreign interest rates. With oil exports of 1.35 million barrels a day and a more than $100 billion foreign debt, the effect of oil and debt on current account income and outflows is decisive.

In 1976 oil exports accounted for only 6.8 percent of current account income. Its importance began to increase after that year, and by 1980 it had become Mexico's leading source of foreign exchange. In 1982, 58.8 percent of foreign exchange earnings on current account came from oil, and until 1985 it continued to produce around 50 percent. The recent fall in oil prices worsened an external situation that, since 1981, has been uncommonly unfavorable for the country. With the decline in the price of oil and other export products, Mexico's terms of trade have deteriorated 63 percent since 1980 and 40.1 percent during 1986 alone.

The size of the foreign debt and the recent developments in the oil market have weakened the position of the foreign sector to such an extent that foreign interest payments represented almost 56 percent of export earnings during 1986 and around 35 percent of current account income. In total, between 1982 and 1985 interest payments surpassed the incredible figure of $44 billion.

To understand how Mexico became so heavily indebted, it is important to consider the expectations that prevailed regarding oil prices and real interest rates. The rise in the country's debt level surprisingly (and paradoxically) parallels its emergence as an important oil producer. At the end of 1976 foreign obligations totaled $26.1 billion, but by 1981 the amount had soared to $78.0 billion. In the same period, the value of Mexico's oil exports went from $563 million to $14.6 billion. The sharpest increase in the debt occurred in 1980 and 1981, precisely the same years in which oil earnings also registered their highest gains.

One must remember that both Mexico and its creditors assumed at that time that the debt service would be guaranteed by ever growing oil earnings, originating in the upward trend in prices (as had occurred in previous years) and with expectations that they would reach levels of $50 to $70 per barrel by the mid-1980s. This assumption, of course, was wrong, but in the meantime it produced an overindebtedness in terms of the country's ability to pay.

Another important factor explaining the high debt level was the trend in real interest rates. Between 1976 and 1980 these rates were very low (fluctuating between 0.3 and 2.3 percent), which made foreign indebtedness attractive. However, in 1981 the rate jumped to 8.8 percent and has remained high ever since. In 1981 it was thought, again incorrectly, that the increase was transitory, but, of course, the facts have proven otherwise.

Errors in forecasting oil prices and real interest rates, in turn, produced other errors in the management of aggregate demand and the peso exchange rate. Regarding the former, expansionary policies were sustained in 1981, when actually recessive measures were called for, while the exchange rate was allowed to become overvalued as the internal rate of inflation increased faster than the rate of depreciation.

RECENT DEVELOPMENTS IN THE
MEXICAN ECONOMY

The accelerated growth of the Mexican economy between 1979 and 1981 worsened many of the productive sector's structural problems. With growth based on increased government spending and expanded public sector activities, the fiscal deficit also began to rise. Similarly with growth oriented toward the domestic market and with the peso overvalued, there was a continuous deterioration in the current account balance. Mexican industry's lack of competitiveness, together with its strong dependence on imported inputs, contributed to the disequilibrium in the foreign sector, at the same time that insufficient domestic saving increased the dependence on external financing. The forecasting errors mentioned above added to these problems, and when combined with very unfavorable conditions abroad, produced a severe economic crisis in 1982, the first symptoms of which were felt by mid-1981.

This domestically produced crisis was characterized by two disequilibrium conditions: The first, short-term in nature, required frank and immediate attention, while the second, predominantly structural, would require several years of constant effort to overcome. In response to this evaluation, the National Development Plan 1983–88 established a short-term strategy based on the following premises:

1. Reduction of the disequilibrium in public finances.
2. Reduction of the external disequilibrium.
3. Increase in domestic savings.

The National Development Plan's strategy for attacking structural problems was based on correcting fiscal, monetary, and external disequilibria through the following policies:

1. A structural reform of public spending, which meant reducing the overall size of the public sector and reorienting spending toward high-priority socioeconomic activities;

2. A structural reform of public sector receipts, including tax revenue and public sector prices, to correct distortions, eliminate subsidies to higher income groups, and to achieve a more efficient and equitable tax system; and

3. A structural reform of foreign trade protection mechanisms, in order to achieve a greater (and especially qualitatively better) participation in international trade, gradually reducing the country's dependence on oil and on foreign credit.

This strategy began to produce results: Employment levels were maintained, and there was an upturn in the economy by the end of 1983, a trend that strengthened during 1984 and the first half of 1985. Inflation was reduced to half its 1982 level. Between 1983 and 1985 the total public sector deficit decreased from 18 percent of GDP to 9.9 percent, despite growing interest payments, as spending in goods and nonfinancial services was reduced by 9 percent of GDP.

The balance of payments improved substantially, and the relative weight of the debt decreased. This progress was registered under adverse conditions in external markets, reflected in a 15 percent fall in the terms of trade up to 1985 and a sharp increase in foreign interest rates in 1984.

By the end of 1985, when the economy was beginning to accelerate the process of structural change, two unforeseeable events—the tragic earthquake and the unprecedented decline in oil prices—complicated the consolidation of efforts made between 1983 and 1985 and underscored the economy's vulnerability and its dangerous dependence on oil exports. The combined effect of these two events had a cost of more than 10 percent in GDP and a fall of close to one-fourth of total exchange income, leading the country to a new crisis, now clearly external in origin.

This new and unexpected crisis has produced the following actions:

1. Restrictive monetary and credit policies using a 100 percent bank reserve requirement, which brought about a net inflow of private capital from abroad of almost $2.5 billion during the year and caused a 25.7 percent reduction in the real supply of money;

2. A greater depreciation in the controlled exchange rate to promote nonoil exports and limit imports and to avoid a greater deterioration in the current account balance and protecting international reserves; this policy achieved a 41 percent increase in nonoil exports and a 13.5 percent fall in imports during 1986;

3. A deferral of public sector spending in goods and nonfinancial services that reduced outlays by 14.7 percent in real terms during 1986;

4. The implementation of a policy to increase public sector nonoil income that increased receipts by 1.2 percent in real terms in the year.

These policies enabled the economy to absorb temporarily the oil shock internally. The social cost, however, was very high: The inflation rate doubled, and the recession deepened. Because it is neither equitable nor possible for the country to continue to absorb the entire impact of the shock, Mexico has proposed to solve the debt problem through the principle of coresponsibility with the nation's creditors.

The Program of Recovery and Growth, which aims at the reactivation of the economy in conditions of price, exchange, and financial stability, was implemented in order to address these changed external conditions. This program proposes a renegotiation with creditors to assure the availability of resources required for the country's development and internally encourages domestic savings and the acceleration of structural changes in order to make economic recovery compatible with a reduction in inflation levels. Mexico's present strategy emphasizes economic growth as a requirement to pay its debt and obtain better terms from its international creditors. Regarding inflation, it recognizes that Mexico has implemented domestic spending cuts so large that the possibility of generating inflation via demand is virtually nil, particularly since the public-sector operational deficit is small and manageable and that the goal is to eliminate it.

In negotiations with the IMF, the underlying premise was the need to reactivate the economy so that it would grow at an annual rate of between 3 and 4 percent in 1987 and 1988, under conditions of stability. The IMF's acceptance of this premise represents a significant change in its policy orientation. The agreement with the IMF budgets the external resources required for reaching the targeted goals, isolating the economy from possible external shocks due to oil price changes. This will be achieved through a mechanism that automatically compensates exchange losses if the average price for Mexican crude drops below $9 per barrel.

Another point of enormous importance in the agreement with the IMF is its recognition of the significant adjustments undertaken during the last four years, unparalleled in recent economic history. This point was fundamental because Mexico could not accept further adjustments similar to those already instrumented.

TRADE RELATIONS WITH
THE UNITED STATES

Trade with the United States is of primary importance to Mexico because it represents 64 percent of Mexico's trade. For the United States, Mexico is its third-largest trading partner (after Canada and Japan), accounting for about 5.6 percent of U.S. trade. Border trade, both in goods and services, is also substantial. In addition, in-bond industries are growing in importance, as are the increasing number of undocumented Mexican workers in the United States. Consequently, export promotion strategy must take into account recent developments in the current trade situation with the United States and the perspectives and changes in U.S. trade policies.

Trade between the two countries has fluctuated sharply in the course of this decade, due principally to the increase of Mexican oil exports in the first years and the Mexican economic crisis beginning in 1982. Trade increased considerably in 1980–81, dropped in the following two years, only to recover slightly in 1984–85, reaching a total of $21.8 billion last year. The balance was favorable to the United States until 1981. Beginning in 1982 Mexico had surpluses due largely to the contraction in its imports. The highest surplus was in 1983 ($7.3 billion), declining to $4.4 billion by 1985.

Mexican exports to the United States increased during the period from 1980–84. In 1985, despite a small drop relative to 1984, they totaled $13.1 billion. By trade categories, Mexican exports have tended to diversify. Although oil represented more than 45 percent of total exports to the United States in 1983, in 1985 it had declined to 37 percent, while the sale of machinery and transport equipment, manufactured goods, and chemicals increased so that they now account for almost 45 percent of total exports.

Mexican imports from the United States have shown an important contraction, dropping from $12.1 billion in 1980 to $8.6 billion by 1985. By trade categories, imports have been concentrated in machinery and transport equipment (46.5 percent of total imports in 1985) and in manufactured goods.

Mexico has been one of the main beneficiaries of the U.S. Generalized System of Preferences (GSP). Mexican exports under the GSP increased markedly, growing from $509 million to $1.2 billion from 1980 to 1985. Nevertheless, Mexico's use of GSP has been declining. In 1980, 24.5 percent of total exports were tariff free; in 1984 the figure had dropped to 20.7 percent. This is the result of the growing proportion of exports excluded under the Discretionary Graduation and Competitive Need Clauses, as well as of administrative reasons.

Between 1980 and 1985 the Competitive Need Clause led to the exclusion from GSP benefits of 271 Mexican products, with an estimated value of $10.1 billion. In total, Mexico uses only 1,600 of the 3,000 categories considered under the GSP, and these, in turn, are highly concentrated in a few products. The 1984 Trade and Tariffs Law carries a provision for reviewing the effects of the GSP on U.S. trade. It is anticipated that many Mexican goods will be affected by the revision because restrictive measures have already been proposed. In the last few years, Mexico has been negotiating with the U.S. government to reach an agreement that will solve our bilateral trade problems. The April 1985 signing of the Understanding on Subsidies and Countervailing Duties was an important step in this direction.

Despite the fact that the bilateral agreement with the United States represents important advantages for Mexico, these are diminishing with the recent protectionist trends in U.S. commercial policies. Quotas have been applied to Mexican steel, sugar, and textile exports; duties have been levied on products previously exempt; nontariff barriers have been set up to protect U.S. agricultural markets, especially fruits and vegetables, such as through regulations and delaying practices; and countervailing duties have been imposed for alleged subsidies. Additionally, the proposed 1986 Trade Practices Reform Act envisions the levying of compensating duties on imports from countries that use supposedly subsidized natural resources. If approved, this legislation would gravely affect many Mexican exports. The protectionist threat notwithstanding, the U.S. market offers great potential for increasing and diversifying Mexican exports. Because Mexico accounts for only 3.4 percent of all U.S. imports, excluding oil, it is certainly feasible to increase Mexican exports to the United States.

THE REDUCTION OF PROTECTIONISM AND MEXICO'S DECISION TO ENTER THE GATT

To foster greater linkages of the Mexican economy with foreign markets and to encourage the industrial sector's reorientation toward exports, Mexico has taken decisive action to reduce the level of protectionism of its markets. In November 1985 Mexico announced its intent to join the GATT, concluding negotiations on July 25, 1986, with the formal signing of the Protocol of Accession. This decision is consistent with the policy of promoting a greater participation in world trade, increasing exports, and making the nation's industrial sector more competitive.

Entrance into the GATT means increased certainty for Mexican exporters by opening foreign markets and providing greater security from unjust trade restrictions, such as guaranteeing access to the right of petition and other mechanisms to resolve trade problems and protect exporters from the imposition of one-sided measures. Other actions to promote exports include the introduction of incentives, facilities for using imported components through reexport mechanisms, quick financing at competitive rates through the use of internal letters of credit, rapid drawback of indirect taxes, and simplified export procedures.

Mexico has initiated a process to reduce protection to more reasonable levels in an effort to promote efficiency in the productive plant through greater exposure to international competition. Traditionally our protective measures were carried out primarily through import quotas and licenses. The combination of quantitative restrictions and highly varied tariff levels resulted in imbalances in the degree of protection given different sectors and thereby distorted the allocation of resources. The most protected sectors were basically those that substituted capital intensive imports, while some sectors with export potential were left unprotected.

To correct this strong anti-export bias in the trade protection system, beginning in July 1985 measures were implemented to reduce the protection given by import licenses and to use tariffs more intensively. At the beginning of that year, 65 percent of the general import duty classifications, accounting for 84 percent of the value of imports, required import licenses. By December progress had been made in reducing the level of import protection: Fully 89.6 percent of the import categories, representing 65 percent of the value of imports, did not require import licenses. In April 1986 a process of gradual tariff equalization and reduction was initiated to provide more uniform levels of trade protection and thereby reduce the anti-export bias.

The maximum tariff should be 30 percent by the end of 1988, and the process of import license elimination will be continued, retaining them only where strictly necessary. By the end of this adjustment period, Mexico will have a tariff structure compatible with both an adequate opening of the domestic market and reasonable levels of protection for the productive plant

COMPETITIVENESS OF MEXICAN INDUSTRY
AND ITS EXPORT POTENTIAL

Mexican industry expanded notably in the postwar period. Manufacturing production rose at rates of 6.3, 8.3, and 7 percent in the last three decades, higher than that of the economy in general. Due to the type of industrialization model adopted, the principal source of growth has been the rapid expansion of domestic demand, especially in the 1950s and 1960s, while exports barely accounted for 2 to 3 percent of total industrial growth in the period. Consequently, manufactured exports have played a small role in industrial growth. At the beginning of the last decade manufactured exports barely represented 4 percent of industrial output and less than 1.5 percent of GDP.

Exaggerated protectionism led to low growth in productivity. Although at the world level productivity increments generated between 20 and 30 percent of production increase, in Mexico gains in productivity contributed less than 1 percent of the overall growth in output in the 1970–80 period. Compared to other countries, Mexico's industry has become increasingly less efficient in the use of existing production techniques and new technologies. At the same time, the distortions in the relative factor prices have led to the use of capital-intensive technologies. Protectionism resulted in low efficiency and international competitiveness. Only about half of industrial activity in Mexico is internationally competitive, while one-fourth is in an intermediate range, and the rest is totally lacking in competitive capacity.

Because opening up the economy will affect the most protected and inefficient industries, the process will be gradual and selective to maintain strategic branches and permit the modernization of others. It would be absurd to deny that modernization has its costs, but the benefits to the economy of reducing protectionism must also be considered. Mexican industry will have access to raw materials and inputs at internationally competitive prices and quality, produce in greater volume, take advantage of economies of scale, and utilize fully its comparative advantages.

One example of the possibilities offered by the international market, and by the U.S. market in particular, are the in-bond industries. In 1980 earnings under this heading, came to $770 million and increased to $1.29 million in 1986. Employment generated by in-bond industries has shown notable growth in contrast with the low rate in the rest of the manufacturing sector. Between 1982 and 1986 the number of jobs practically doubled, going from 127,000 to 240,000. Furthermore, by combining imported inputs with Mexican products and labor, Mexican industry has been able to increase its exports. Under this system, nearly $1.3 billion were generated during 1986, representing about 20 percent of nonoil manufactured exports.

THE INTERNATIONAL CONTEXT AND MEXICO's INDUSTRIAL RECONVERSION

It could be said that the process of world industrialization has led to a gradual and permanent transfer of the production of increasingly complex products from the more developed to the relatively less developed countries. In past decades, the textile industry was transferred; now it is steel, shipbuilding, and the automotive industry.

For the developed countries, this has meant the decline or even disappearance of some productive sectors and increased unemployment in others. Few countries have confronted the challenge with integrated programs for industrial reconversion. The majority have given in to internal pressures and limited their response to an increase in protectionism, an attitude that only postpones and increases the cost of the inevitable adjustments.

The developing countries have adapted more easily, especially those recently industrialized that constantly see their exports barred by the protective practices of the more advanced nations. Until a few years ago, the newly industrialized countries had based their participation in international trade chiefly on cheap labor and, to a lesser degree, on their natural resources and geographic location. It was precisely these factors that recently allowed Mexico to start a new process of interaction with the world economy and that have transformed it into the fourth-largest supplier of manufactured goods to developed countries.

However, increasing automation jeopardizes the advantages of cheap labor in addition to the growing competition of still cheaper labor in relatively less developed countries. Reduced freight rates have nullified in part the advantages of geographic location; and in many cases, technological advances have eliminated the advantages once provided by natural resources. Energy-efficient production techniques have diminished the advantage of cheap energy, and the appearance of new materials have displaced older ones such as copper.

All this makes it imperative for Mexico to adopt and adapt innovative technologies that raise competitiveness and improve the use of the country's resources. This, in turn, requires an accelerated reduction in trade barriers, greater flexibility to the productive sector, and reduced government regulations to encourage technological change and innovation.

Foreign investment, with its technological contributions, will play an important role in this process. To this end Mexico is actively promoting foreign investment from medium and small foreign firms. Within the context of the foreign investment legislation, greater participation by foreign capital in auto parts and mining, among other industries, is under study.

The modernization of Mexican industry is all the more urgent in view of its relative lag with respect to its principal competitors: the newly industrialized countries of Southeast Asia. These countries adopted export promotion policies at a more propitious time, the first twenty-five years of the postwar period, when trade and the world economy were registering an unprecedented expansion. Many countries are carrying out industrial reconversion processes that will increase their productivity and result in more competitive world trade. Mexico will have to compete in this world, relying more on innovation and the development and incorporation of technological improvements than on traditional advantages.

Structural change of the productive system is advancing in this aspect. Government-owned industries, important producers of goods and services, are striving to increase efficiency through technological change, the elimination of obsolete production lines and expensive plants, and training and retraining of its labor force. In the first stage attention is being focused on the steel, shipbuilding, railroad, fertilizer, sugar refining, and fishing industries. Industrial reconversion programs have been implemented in these sectors in order to improve their productivity and efficiency. In addition, disincorporation (that is the sale, liquidation, or merging) of nonstrategic and nonpriority public entities has been initiated.

The restructuring of the private sector's industrial plant will be promoted by greater exposure to foreign competition, by pricing of input and capital goods closer to international levels, and by support for new investments, for the acquisition and development of technology, and for training its workforce. As a result, it is reasonable to foresee a growing and diversified participation of Mexican exports in world markets.

CONCLUSIONS

Caught up in the greatest external shock in its history, Mexico is carrying out a wideranging process of economic transformation that complements the macroeconomic adjustments implemented between 1982 and 1986. The objective is to create a self-generating process of growth, through increased exports, in order to generate adequate levels of foreign exchange for imports and to fulfill financial obligations.

It is fallacious to think that the external debt can be paid with greater austerity. The decline in living standards and the prospect that the recession could deepen cancel that option. It would also affect U.S. industry because every dollar paid in interest has as its counterpart a reduction in Mexican imports from the United States.

Economic growth with structural change represents the only viable strategy in economic, social, and political terms that will allow Mexico to fulfill its international obligations. Favorable commercial and financial support will help create the conditions that ensure a more rapid response to the strategy. This, in turn, will lead to adequate growth rates and price and exchange rate stability. The increase in exports will provide the foreign exchange to service the debt, while the burden of the debt will be lightened in the sense that its importance relative to GDP will diminish and interest payments will be a smaller portion of foreign exchange income.

Job creation cannot be put off. Although Mexico has considerably reduced its population growth rates (from 3.3 percent in 1973 to 2.0 percent in 1986), the number of persons reaching working age is at historic levels in the late 1980s (about 1 million people per year) as a result of the high birth rates registered at the end of the 1960s and the beginning of the 1970s.

Mexico has forged an economic policy that should resolve its internal problems. Maintaining this effort requires adequate external financing to complement domestic savings. For this reason, Mexico will continue its policies of negotiating new resources and further reductions in the costs of its foreign debt and will keep on fighting for better access to its exports. Only with higher exports will Mexico be able to resolve the dilemma between growth and servicing the debt.

REFERENCES

Aspe, Pedro. 1986. "Charting Mexico's Progress." *Wall Street Journal*, Aug. 8.

Castillo, V., Gustavo Del. 1986. "Del Sistema Generalizado de Preferencias a un acuerdo bilateral de comercio." *Comercio Exterior* 36(3) (March): 230-40.

"Change and Continuity in OECD Trade in Manufactures with Developing Countries." *The OECD Observer*, No. 139 (March): 3-9.

Díaz-Alejandro, Carlos F. 1984. "Latin American Debt: I Don't Think We Are in Kansas Anymore." *Brookings Papers on Economic Activity*. Washington, D.C.: Brookings Institution.

Kahn, Herman. 1979. "World Economic Development: 1979 and Beyond." New York: Morrow Quill.

Laumer, Helmut, and Wolfgang Ochiel. 1986. "Adaptation des structures industrielles: L'Example Japonais." *Problèmes Economiques* 9 (September): 22-31.

6 TRADE STRATEGY AND INDUSTRIAL POLICY IN TAIWAN

Kuo-shu Liang and
Ching-ing Hou Liang

The economic conditions of Taiwan, the Republic of China, during the early postwar period were similar to those in many resource-poor, low-income developing countries. It was overpopulated, and the natural rate of growth of its population exceeded 3 percent per annum. The domestic market was small. The inordinate military needs competed with development projects for scarce resources. The economy suffered from chronic balance-of-payments deficits and a violent inflation (Jacoby 1966: 118; Lin 1973: 30–31).

As can be seen in Table 6–1, manufacturing activity accounted for 11 percent of NDP in 1952, while 38 percent of NDP originated in the primary sector. Exports accounted for 8 percent of GNP, and the percentage share of manufactured exports in total exports was only 7.6 in 1955. In such an environment, the commitment to development by the government was a matter of necessity. The industrial policy in Taiwan has had to cope with problems to encourage investment and accelerate the structural transformation.

This chapter attempts to examine the contribution of industrial policy to rapid postwar economic development, as exemplified by the experience of the Republic of China. It briefly highlights the success of export-led industrialization in Taiwan and then describes the challenges that the economy faces in the 1980s and examines the role of industrial policy for achieving growth and productivity gains

Table 6-1. Major Economic Indicators, 1952–86.

	1952	1955	1960
A. Computation of per capita income			
GNP (NT$ million at 1981 prices)	145,824	188,801	261,223
Population (thousand persons)	8,128	9,078	10,792
GNP per capita (NT $1,000 at 1981 prices)	17.1	19.9	23.4
B. Percentage shares in NDP (at current prices) at factor cost by industrial origin			
Primary production	38.01%	34.61%	35.10%
Manufacturing	10.84	13.80	16.83
Social overhead[a]	8.90	9.64	9.86
Services	42.25	41.95	38.21
C. Percentage shares in GNP			
Government current revenue	23.56	24.59	23.77
Government saving	5.47	5.08	4.01
Total domestic saving	15.38	14.63	17.86
Gross capital formation	15.40	13.40	20.30
Exports	8.07	8.28	11.30
Imports	14.21	12.62	18.86
D. Percentage share of manufactured exports in total exports			
Manufactured exports (NT$ billion)[b]	–	0.14	1.69
Manufactured exports/Total exports	–	7.6	28.2

	1952–55	1955–60	1960–65
E. Compound annual growth rates			
GNP (at 1981 prices)	9.0	6.7	9.5
GNP per capita (at 1981 prices)	5.3	3.3	6.3
Index of manufacturing output	16.8	11.1	13.8
Total exports (at 1981 prices)	4.4	11.9	21.6
Employment			
Total	2.0	2.2	2.2
Manufacturing	4.3	4.6	3.6
Agriculture	0.5	0.9	0.1
Real wages			
Manufacturing	5.8	-0.9	5.6
Prices			
GNP deflator	10.7	8.6	2.8
Wholesale price index	8.4	9.1	2.1

a. Includes construction; electricity, gas, and water; transport, storage, and communications.

b. Includes SITC categories 5 through 8.

Sources: Directorate-General of Budget, Accounting and Statistics (DGBAS), *National Income of the Republic of China* (Taipei: various years); DGBAS, *Monthly Bulletin of Labor*

Table 6-1. continued

1965	1970	1975	1980	1985	1986
410,422	654,345	995,706	1,645,875	251,858	2,495,397
12,628	14,676	16,150	17,805	19,258	19,455
31.7	44.9	62.2	93.3	117.7	128.9
29.26%	19.41%	16.18%	10.26%	7.54%	7.17%
20.14	26.43	29.28	34.23	36.04	39.00
11.34	12.68	14.57	15.82	14.03	13.19
39.26	41.48	39.97	39.69	42.39	40.64
20.06	22.68	23.36	24.25	22.64	20.49
2.40	3.46	7.04	7.96	5.50	4.27
20.82	25.71	26.96	32.74	33.10	37.44
22.83	25.69	30.81	34.32	17.57	16.30
18.73	29.72	39.50	52.97	55.17	58.90
21.75	29.77	42.82	54.18	40.94	39.81
7.78	43.60	163.53	628.08	1,109.30	
43.3	74.0	81.3	88.2	90.7	

1965-70	1970-75	1975-80	1980-85	1952-85
9.8	8.8	10.6	6.5	8.6
7.2	6.7	8.4	4.8	6.0
20.6	13.3	15.0	6.9	13.8
22.7	15.9	16.7	9.0	15.1
4.0	3.8	3.5	2.6	2.9
9.0	10.2	7.5	3.1	6.1
-0.8	+0.03	-5.3	0.3	-0.7
6.6	8.3	8.6	5.3	5.1
4.8	11.7	8.9	3.7	7.1
1.9	12.6	8.9	0.8	6.1

Statistics, Republic of China (Taipei: various years); Council for Economic Planning and Development, *Taiwan Statistical Data Book* (Taipei: various years); Department of Statistics, Ministry of Finance, *Monthly Statistics of Exports and Imports, The Republic of China* (Taipei: various years); Overall Planning Department, Council for Economic Planning and Development, *Research Report No. (66) 120.119* (Taipei: July 1977).

in rapidly changing economic environments. A brief conclusion follows.

EXPORT-LED INDUSTRIALIZATION IN TAIWAN

The reconstruction of the Taiwan economy began in earnest in 1949, following the relocation of the central government on the island. Economic development from the end of World War II through the 1950s was characterized by efforts to promote both growth incentive in the agricultural sector as well as import-substituting industrialization.

A broad base for economic development was laid by land reform, which was carried out during 1949–53 (Tang and Liang 1973: 116– 17). The positive role played by the agricultural sector in Taiwan sharply constrasts with the experiences of many other less developed countries, where the lack of agricultural development acted as a drag on industrial and general economic development.

The prewar agricultural and industrial production level was, by and large, restored during the years 1948–51, and the U.S. economic aid was resumed in June 1950 after the outbreak of the Korean war. Taiwan had benefited from a substantial aid program. A total of more than $14 billion (U.S.) had been appropriated over the period 1951–65, amounting to $10 per capita a year. Aid played an important role in helping to control inflation in the early 1950s. In addition, were it not for U.S. aid, Taiwan's trade gap would have become a serious factor limiting its economic development during the period. U.S. aid broke this bottleneck by augmenting foreign exchange resources and sustaining the import of necessary inputs that complemented domestic labor and other investment components. The share of U.S. aid imports in total imports had remained above 30 percent until 1961 but declined rapidly thereafter (Liang and Lee 1974: 296–99).

The diversification and expansion of industrial production placed primary emphasis on the domestic market. The government adopted a multiple exchange rate system and strict import controls during this period. Such measures increased the profitability of import substitution industries and were partly responsible for the doubling of manufacturing production during the period 1950–58. Changes in the relative importance of the primary sector and manufacturing reflect the expected structural transformation as a concomitant of economic development. By 1960 manufacturing activity accounted for 17 percent of NDP. The compound annual growth rate of manufacturing employment exceeded 4 percent throughout the 1950s.

The simple and relatively easy phase of import substitution, however, appeared to have reached its limit in a relatively short period in a narrow, protected domestic market. It was recognized that only an outward-looking or export-oriented industrialization strategy could sustain a high rate of economic growth in such a small island economy as Taiwan, and a series of policy reforms were undertaken during 1958–61. Overvalued currency was devalued, and the complicated exchange rate structure was simplified and finally unified in June 1961. Laws and regulations governing investment and imports were liberalized. The emphasis of trade strategy shifted from strict import controls to export promotion. The economic indicators in Table 6-1 clearly reveal that economic performance in the 1960s and early 1970s improved notably compared with the 1950s.

The growth of manufactured exports, coupled with rising domestic demand, accelerated the pace of industrialization. The compound annual rate of growth in the index of manufactured output, rising at 11 percent during the period 1955–60, accelerated to 21 percent during the period 1965–70. As the growth of manufactured output accelerated, the share of manufactured products in total exports rose from 28 percent in 1960 to 77 percent in 1970. Moreover, the rapid development of labor-intensive export industries permitted economic growth to be more labor absorptive and equitable. Employment and real wages in manufacturing revealed a clear trend of accelerated increase in the 1960s and the early 1970s. Manufacturing employment rose 9 percent a year in 1965–70, while real wages increased at a rate of 6.6 percent. Taiwan is also one of the few developing economies that achieved an impressive growth record with relative price stability in the 1960s.

Between 1952 and 1985, the volume of exports grew at an average annual rate of 15.6 percent (Table 6-1), accompanied by continuing shifts in the composition of exports. As shown in Table 6-2, in the first half of the 1950s two staples, sugar and rice, dominated Taiwan's exports, accounting for more than 70 percent of the total. The share of these commodities had fallen to less than 1 percent by 1985, and their place was taken by manufactured goods.

Table 6-2. Major Export Commodities, 1953-85 (percentage).

	1953	1955	1960	1965	1970	1975	1980	1985
Agricultural products								
Rice and paddy	10.6%	23.3%	3.1%	9.1%	0.1%	—	0.3%	—
Bananas	2.4	3.1	3.7	10.8	2.2	0.4%	0.1	0.1%
Processed agricultural products								
Sugar	67.2	49.9	44.0	13.1	3.2	5.0	1.2	0.1
Tea	5.3	4.4	3.7	2.0	0.9	0.4	0.1	0.1
Canned pineapple	1.9	4.2	4.8	3.8	1.4	0.3	0.1	—
Canned mushrooms	—	—	—	4.3	2.2	0.9	0.5	0.2
Canned asparagus spears	—	—	—	2.3	2.4	1.5	0.7	0.2
Manufactured products								
Plywood	—	0.1	1.5	5.9	5.5	2.5	1.9	0.8
Textiles	0.1	0.9	11.6	10.3	13.0	11.5	8.2	7.1
Cement	0.7	—	0.7	1.9	0.8	0.1	0.1	0.3
Clothing and footwear	0.8	1.4	2.6	4.9	19.9	16.4	14.4	12.6
Plastic products	—	—	—	2.6	5.1	6.5	7.4	8.6
Electrical machinery and appliances	—	—	0.6	2.7	12.8	14.7	18.2	21.0
Machinery	—	—	—	1.3	3.4	3.6	3.8	4.0
Transportation equipment	—	—	—	0.4	0.9	2.2	3.2	4.1
Metal products	—	—	0.6	1.1	2.0	2.5	4.4	5.8
Basic metals	0.8	1.6	3.7	3.6	4.6	2.3	2.0	2.5
Total exports	100.0	100.0	100.0	100.0	100.0	100.0	100.0	100.0

Source: Republic of China Inspectorate General of Customs, The Trade of China (Taipei: various years).

The leading manufactured exports have been electrical machinery and appliances (mainly telecommunications equipment), clothing and footwear, textiles, and plastic articles. Over the years 1965–85 rapid growth was achieved in exports of electrical machinery and appliances, transportation equipment, and metal products. Structural changes in the pattern of exports over the period reflect a growing importance of higher value-added products.

In the meantime, the decline of traditional agricultural exports was accompanied by the emergence of new export-oriented agricultural products, of which canned mushrooms and asparagus spears were the most notable examples in the late 1960s. The emergence of these new export crops was largely stimulated by the provision of incentives and government aids, including the availability of overseas market information, as well as technical assistance.

Taiwan provides an example of an economy capitalizing its comparative advantage and reaping the gains from trade as illustrated by the traditional theory of international trade. On the whole, Taiwan's exports were of low capital and skill intensity. However, factor intensities varied considerably in different export markets. Although exports to developed countries were relatively labor intensive and of low skill intensity, exports to less developed countries were relatively capital as well as skill intensive. The resulting pattern of trade conforms to expectations, as Taiwan's factor endowments place it in an intermediate position between developed and less developed countries (Liang and Liang 1978; Lee and Liang 1983: 310–83).

Taiwan provides an example of a highly successful export-led industrialization. The expansion of manufactured exports has contributed not only to efficient industrialization, by permitting specialization according to comparative advantage and stimulating technological improvement, but also to higher living standards. It improved income distribution through the expansions of employment in manufacturing that pulled workers from low-paying agricultural jobs to higher-paying manufacturing employment and helped to raise wages. It is noteworthy that female workers played an important part in the economic development of Taiwan as the rapid growth of labor-intensive export industries induced the large-scale entry of women, mostly young and unskilled, into manufacturing.

The industrial and trade policies aimed at reducing domestic distortions and encouraging labor-intensive production for export have created profitable opportunities and thereby encouraged capital accu-

Table 6-3. Key Indicators of Financial Deepening, 1961–85.

	1961–65	1966–70	1971–75	1976–80	1981–85
1. Ratio of M_{1B} to GDP (%)	12.4	15.5	20.2	27.0	29.1
2. Ratio of M_2 to GDP (%)	28.5	37.8	49.8	65.9	86.8
3. Change in wholesale price index (%)	2.1	1.9	12.6	8.9	0.8
4. Interest rate on one-year deposits (%)	12.9	9.8	10.9	10.9	9.8
5. Real return on holding one-year deposits (%)	10.8	7.9	-1.7	2.0	9.0
6. M_2 at 1981 constant prices (NT$ billion)	79.7	189.1	425.9	921.5	1,844.6
7. Net assets of domestic banks as percentage of GDP (%)	33.4	42.0	54.4	78.2	77.6
8. Ratio of net private national saving to national income (%)	9.7	12.3	17.0	16.3	18.9
9. Government bonds outstanding as percentage of GDP (%)	1.8	4.2	2.4	1.6	2.2
10. Corporate bonds outstanding as percentage of GDP (%)	0.2	0.3	0.3	1.3	1.8
11. Market value of stocks outstanding as percentage of GDP (%)	20.0[a]	8.6	12.1	14.8	14.5

a. 1962–65. The stock market was established in 1962. M_{1B} and M_2 are averages of monthly figures. M_{1B} = Net currency issued + checking accounts + passbook deposits + passbook savings deposits. M_2 = M_{1B} + quasi-money. M_2 at 1981 constant prices is deflated by the wholesale price index.

Sources: DGBAS, Commodity-Price Statistics Monthly, Taiwan District, the Republic of China (Taipei: various years); Economic Research Department, The Central Bank of China, Financial Statistics Monthly, Taiwan District, the Republic of China (Taipei: various years); DGBAS, National Income of the Republic of China (Taipei: various years).

mulation and financial deepening. Table 6-3 provides key indicators of Taiwan's success in financial deepening. *Financial deepening* means an accumulation of financial assets at a pace faster than accumulation of nonfinancial wealth (Shaw 1973: vii).[1]

The most important measure aimed at financial growth was to offer savers a positive real rate of return. Thus, financial deepening advanced progressively as the wholesale prices stabilized in the 1960s. The M_2/GDP ratio increased from 28.5 percent in 1961-65 to 37.8 percent in 1966-70. M_2 deflated by the wholesale price index, which represents the real lending capacity of the organized banking sector (McKinnon 1973: 114), grew 2.4 times during the period. The strengthened liquidity position provided an important base from which credit expansion of the commercial banks could proceed. The net assets of domestic banks as percentage of GDP increased from 9.7 percent in 1961-65 to 12.3 percent in 1966-70. The relative price stability contributed not ónly to the financial growth observed but also to the rise in the measured net private savings.

It can be noted that corporate bonds and market value of stocks outstanding as percentage of GDP have not revealed an increasing trend during the period under review. One of the principal characteristics of corporate finance in Taiwan is a low proportion of bond financing and a correspondingly heavy dependence on bank credit.

Broadly speaking, inward orientation that expands manufacturing industries oriented toward domestic market tends to set in motion many forces that can have adverse impacts on efficiency and growth over the longer term—namely, high protection, price distortions, the prevalence of sellers' markets, domestic inflation, financial shallowing, social tension, and discouragement of foreign private investments caused by strict controls on imports and foreign exchange payments. Conversely, placing greater importance on export competitiveness by making increased use of price mechanism and reducing price distortions is indicative of outward orientation. With a quicker payoff in terms of productivity, labor absorption, export earnings, and financial deepening, outward orientation would be the more desirable strategy (de Vries 1967: 11-14, 46-47, 55-56). A viable industrialization scheme must go beyond import substitution and gain access to markets abroad on a competitive basis. Firms that must live with foreign competition must change the product composition of exports in response to changes in world market conditions, whereas inward orientation entails establishing a more rigid economic structure.

TRADE STRATEGY AND INDUSTRIAL POLICY IN THE 1980s

From the beginning of the export drive in the early 1960s until the middle of the 1970s, outward-looking policies for industry and trade were essential for the steady growth and remarkable structural transformation of the Taiwan economy. In addition to the outward-looking development strategy, the climate conducive to the conduct of business was created by such factors as a strong and stable political leadership, reasonably well-educated and hardworking labor force, weak labor organization, the mutual trust between the government and industry, and the commitment of the pragmatic bureaucracy to accelerate economic development.

The turbulent decade of the 1970s witnessed, however, two oil shocks in late 1973 and in 1979. The recovery of the economy after the first oil shock was rapid and could be primarily attributed to the timely implementation of the economic stabilization program in the early 1974, the continuous growth of manufactured exports with increased proportion of exports being directed to the oil-producing countries (see Table 6-4), and the high rate of gross domestic capital formation through major government investment projects in infrastructure and heavy and petrochemical industries.

The second oil shock unfortunately aggravated the widespread adverse effects. The growth rate of the GNP and the volume of exports declined sharply. Slow growth in the industrial countries reduced the demand for manufactured goods. The export competitiveness eroded as the value of the U.S. dollar, to which the NT dollar was tied, appreciated. Protectionist sentiment resulted in higher and widespread trade barriers. Rising real wages threatened Taiwan's ability to compete with new exporters of labor-intensive products. Meanwhile, the prices of many products produced by the domestic heavy and petrochemical industries remained high relative to world market prices. Stagnant demand for exports, high real interest rates, lower profits, low capacity utilization in many industries, and uncertainties eroded business confidence. As a consequence, the real growth rate

Table 6-4. Exports to and Imports from the United States, Japan, the European Economic Community, and OPEC as Percentage of Total Exports and Imports, 1952-85.

Year	United States		Japan		EEC		OPEC	
	Exports	Imports	Exports	Imports	Exports	Imports	Exports	Imports
1952	3.45	46.98	52.59	31.02	5.17	5.88	2.59	0.03
1955	4.07	47.76	59.35	30.35	5.69	5.97	8.13	6.97
1960	11.59	38.05	37.80	35.35	6.10	8.42	10.98	6.40
1965	21.33	31.65	30.67	39.75	10.00	7.37	2.22	4.14
1970	38.08	23.88	14.58	42.85	9.52	8.33	4.52	4.79
1975	34.34	27.76	13.07	30.44	13.83	11.46	8.59	13.98
1980	34.12	23.69	10.97	27.13	14.16	8.06	9.52	23.61
1981	36.10	22.48	10.96	27.97	11.46	7.50	8.82	23.40
1982	39.45	24.16	10.73	25.31	10.77	9.68	9.18	20.79
1983	45.11	22.90	9.86	27.54	9.86	9.33	7.21	20.39
1984	48.82	22.96	10.46	29.34	9.03	8.72.	5.10	17.80
1985	48.08	23.61	11.26	27.60	8.67	9.91	4.86	16.82

Source: Republic of China Inspectorate General of Customs, The Trade of China (Taipei: various years).
Notes: The European Economic Community comprises Belgium, Denmark, France, Federal Republic of Germany, Greece, Ireland, Italy, Luxembourg, the Netherlands, and United Kingdom. OPEC (Organization of Petroleum Exporting Countries) comprises Algeria, Ecuador, Gabon, Indonesia, Iran, Iraq, Kuwait, Libya, Nigeria, Qatar, Saudi Arabia, United Arab Emirates, and Venezuela.

of gross fixed capital formation fell sharply from 15.7 percent in 1980 to 3.7 percent in 1981 and even became negative in 1982 and 1983.

The Taiwan economy in 1984 experienced once again simultaneous rapid economic growth and price stability as a result of a booming export trade. The growth rate of real GNP rose from 7.9 percent in 1983 to 10.5 percent in 1984. The wholesale price index rose only 0.48 percent over the previous year, and the consumer price index slipped 0.03 percent. However, it has to be noted that the growth rates have shown a clearly decreasing trend since the latter half of 1984 because the U.S. demand has been flattening. The growth rate of real GNP fell to 4.7 percent, and export value in NT dollars increased only 1.5 percent in 1985. The year 1985 was somewhat disappointing from the viewpoint of economic growth. Many industries appeared to experience difficulties and revealed structural weakness in addition to problems reflected by cyclical downward movements in economic activities.

The economy of the Republic of China is presently at a crossroad, and current structural problems are basically the result of the success of past development efforts. Real wage rates have risen considerably since the 1970s, and the era of relatively stable real wage rates and unit labor cost appeared to have come to an end (see Table 6–5).

Higher labor cost, slow growth, and low inflation made it difficult for businesses to make profits. Companies that took on heavy debts to invest in real estate in the hopes of making quick and easy profits have been in trouble. The shift to slower growth and stable prices now demands that businesspeople reexamine and reshape their production, financing, investment, and marketing strategies. Drastic measures are needed to cut costs, control quality, diversify products, and manage debts to stay competitive. Capital spending plans must be geared to increase productivity and quality rather than to expand capacity.

In addition, the rising costs of pollution and environmental degradation and the poverty of public services and welfare activities can no longer be ignored. The government must restructure its policy to give greater priority to pollution control, consumer protection, and social welfare improvement. Government-business relations in the 1980s will certainly be less advantageous for business compared to previous decades.

Table 6–5. Average Annual Percentage Changes in Wages, Labor Productivity, and Unit Labor Costs in Manufacturing, 1952–85.

	1952–55	1955–60	1960–65	1965–70	1970–75	1975–80	1980–85	1952–85
Money wages	16.11	9.42	8.04	11.19	21.01	17.95	9.4	12.6
Consumer prices	9.90	9.52	2.39	4.36	12.20	8.67	3.9	7.1
Real wages[a]	5.65	–0.07	5.52	6.54	7.85	8.54	5.3	5.1
Labor productivity	11.51	6.26	9.89	10.37	2.73	8.25	3.5	7.0
Unit labor costs[b]	4.60	3.16	–1.85	0.82	18.28	9.70	5.9	5.6

a. Money wages divided by the index of urban consumer prices.

b. Difference between rate of change of money wage and rate of change of labor productivity. Labor productivity is calculated by dividing output index by employment index.

Sources: Council for Economic Planning and Development (CEPD), *Taiwan Statistical Data Book* (Taipei: various years); CEPD, *Adjusted Statistics of Manufacturing in Taiwan Area* (Taipei: 1st Quarter 1952–4th Quarter 1976); CEPD, *Adjustment of Labor Force, Unemployment and Employment by Sectors in Taiwan Area* (Taipei: 1952–77); Ministry of Economic Affairs, *Taiwan Industrial Production Statistics Monthly* (Taipei: various years); Directorate-General of Budget, Accounting and Statistics (DGBAS), *Commodity-Price Statistics Monthly* (Taipei: various years); DGBAS, *Monthly Bulletin of Labor Statistics* (Taipei: various years).

Although the increasing complexity of the economy demands greater decentralization of economic decisionmaking, industry has not always been in a position to effect adjustments unaided. Many firms have been unsure about how to improve their technological base. The role of industrial policy is to provide information on the direction of changes in industrial structure, help remove structural rigidities, coordinate with macroeconomic policies to assist industry adapt to new conditions and perform more efficiently, and promote the flow of resources to activities where they can be most productively employed (Jaffe 1984: 11).

The government has recognized that new directions are imperative. In May 1985 it created the Economic Reform Committee to undertake a review of the economy, identify existing constraints on new growth opportunities, and make proposals to modernize the legal and institutional framework of the entire economic system and restructure the economy. Whether the economy of the Republic of China can successfully restructure its industry and attain the high rate of economic expansion that it experienced in the past will depend to a great extent on ensuring technology transfers, reforming financial system, diversifying export markets, and liberalizing imports and foreign exchange control to reduce the risks of protectionism.

The Significance of Technology Transfers in Export-Led Industrialization

Using a modified form of the Cobb-Douglas production function, the Council for Economic Planning and Development estimated that the rate of exogenous technical progress was 4.5 percent per annum during the period 1962–78. It dropped to 2.9 percent per annum during the period 1979–81. Technical progress is an indispensable determinant of sustained economic growth. The economy has been beset with difficulties, however, caused by the slowdown in the rate of technical progress in recent years.

By far the most important determinant of technical progress is the continuous inflow of foreign technology through imported capital goods. Modern technology is embodied in machinery and equipment imported from abroad. Export-led industrialization encourages a more rapid rate of capital formation and technical progress by financing the imports of capital goods through rapid export expansion. It also produces learning effects to local entrepreneurs in developing marketing and design capabilities. The pace of export-led industrialization will, in turn, be facilitated by technical progress (Lee 1981: 12–13, 128). From this standpoint, the government and industry leaders have felt uneasy about the recent decrease in the investment in and import of machinery and equipment.

Table 6–6 shows overseas Chinese and foreign investment during the period 1978–85. The contribution of direct foreign investment to exports has not been important in the Republic of China apart from a few manufacturing sectors such as electronics and electrical appliances and to a lesser extent chemicals (Ranis and Schive 1985: 106).

Export-oriented foreign firms appeared to use more labor-intensive techniques than their local counterparts in the same industry (Schive and Yen 1982). Given the mobile nature of export-oriented direct foreign investment, investing firms adapt their techniques to local circumstances to take full advantage of low labor costs. The transfers of technology normally focus on training within the firm as well as outside, extending to the suppliers of inputs and users of final products. Taiwan Singer showed how direct foreign investment helped local firms improve the quality of parts supplied and the sewing machine industry in general (Ranis and Schive 1985: 124–29).

Increasing emphasis on technology transfers is both an opportunity and a necessity. The interesting feature of figures in Table 6–5 is

Table 6–6. Overseas Chinese and Foreign Investment, 1978–85 (*U.S. $ million*).

Year	Investment in Arrival	Reinvestment of Profits	Total
1978	$ 68	$ 23	$ 91
1979	69	51	120
1980	109	62	171
1981	87	60	147
1982	79	46	125
1983	112	50	162
1984	121	88	209
1985	254	67	321

Source: Investment Commission, Ministry of Economic Affairs, *Statistics on Overseas Chinese and Foreign Investment, Technical Cooperation, Outward Investment and Outward Technical Cooperation, Republic of China* (Taipei: various years).

the discontinuation of past trends in the changes in real wages and labor productivity. The rise in labor productivity accelerated and unit labor costs remained unchanged or even declined in the 1960s. This undoubtedly strengthened the competitive edge of Taiwan's labor-intensive manufactures in the world market. However, the absolute size of the agricultural labor force began to decline in 1969 as outflow rate accelerated in the late 1960s. The era of relatively stable real wage rates and unit labor costs came to an end. Failure to recognize the dynamic nature of comparative advantage would freeze capital, labor, and other scarce resources in industries where opportunities are declining and lead to the neglect of advantageous new export opportunities.

The government cannot avoid serious adjustment problems when some major industries lose international competitiveness. For instance, the textile and clothing industries have exemplified many of the issues involved in trade between the industrial countries and the newly industrializing countries. Quantitative restrictions on imports have encouraged producers to move into higher value-added fashionable products to maintain export earnings despite restrictions on import volume. However, the continued viability of the industries has been at stake. Outdated technology and skill have hindered progress in bleaching and dyeing. Success in producing fashionable textiles requires a sensitive response to shifts in consumer preferences, ability to produce in small lots with very tight delivery schedules, and precise quality controls. These are not easy tasks. The recent adjustment problems have intensified because structural rigidities have been reinforced by trade frictions.

Some of the defensive measures taken in the past during the recession years to provide special assistance to the companies in trouble resulted in the perpetuation of an inefficient allocation of productive resources and aggravated problems of overcapacity. The government policy must be more adjustment-oriented and encourage industry to be more responsive to new challenges and opportunities. A number of traditional labor-intensive industries—such as cotton textiles, footwear, toys, and canned foods—must improve competitiveness through modernization, phasing out of excess capacity, and shifting to new product lines.

Although traditional industries in trouble can pose significant policy problems, perhaps the most important and difficult task is to develop the climate in which new industries can prosper. The present industrial policy has been striving to restructure the economy by switching the focus of industrial development from unskilled-and-labor-intensive manufactures and capital-and-energy-intensive heavy and chemical industries to high-technology areas. Strategic industries include machinery manufacturing and information and electronics industries. These industries are skill intensive and relatively low capital intensive and energy saving. In addition, they support the automation of other industries and accelerate the economy's rate of increase in productivity. They will be next in line for the achievement of a high rate of export expansion as the growth of experience and capacity in manufacturing permits the economy to move beyond simple labor-intensive types of production.

It should be noted that to foster the growth of machinery and electronics industries and expand their share of world trade are not an easy tasks. Unlike process industries such as cement, steel, and chemicals, where production is machine paced and the technology embodied mainly in imported equipments, machinery is skill-intensive and requires a longer learning period. Moreover, the operation scales of most firms in Taiwan are small. Most firms produce a wide spectrum of products instead of concentrating on a few parts and components. As a result, they are poorly suited for the efficient production of machinery. Productivity has also been hampered by a high turnover of labor. In most cases, products are imitated due to the lack of the R&D capability. The supplies of materials such as special steels, ceramics, and electronics still lag behind. Machinery produced by small companies is being sold without credit, and the after-sales services are inadequate.

The electronics industry is tightly ruled by technological change, and local producers are still very much in the business of assembling components and computer peripherals, with high-technology inputs being imported. Some producers may not be able to survive unless they enter into close subcontracting with the major international corporations. Most software is provided by hardware vendors that devote little attention to developing software packages.

Concerted efforts should be made to promote a successful development of the strategic industries. Incentives to the strategic industries take the form of extending low-interest loans, the right to retain earnings of up to 200 percent of paid-in capital, and the right to delay the start of its five-year income tax holiday by up to four years. The government is also encouraging the establishment of ven-

Table 6-7. Approved Technical Cooperation Projects and Royalty
Payments, 1978-85.

Year	Approved Technical Cooperation Projects	Royalty Payments (U.S. $ million)
1978	110	$ 52
1979	133	69
1980	143	86
1981	124	95
1982	144	99
1983	141	95
1984	168	122
1985	197	151

Source: Investment Commission, Ministry of Economic Affairs, *Statistics on Overseas Chinese and Foreign Investment, Technical Cooperation, Outward Investment, and Outward Technical Cooperation, Republic of China* (Taipei: various years); Central Bank of China, *Balance of Payments, Taiwan District, The Republic of China* (Taipei: various years).

ture capital firms to help promote high-technology ventures and technical upgrading. However, adequate financial mechanisms, such as adding the share of unlisted ventures in the over-the-counter securities market, are needed to stimulate the provisions of risk capital for new ventures.

Table 6-7 indicates a generally increasing trend in approvals of technical cooperation projects and royalty payments in recent years. Technical cooperation provides an important channel for the transfer of technology. In order to move faster in capturing a share of the world market for high-technology products in the 1980s, the government has set the target for R&D spending by the government and public and private enterprises at 1.2 percent of GNP by 1985 and 2 percent by 1989 (The Executive Yuan 1982: 32). However, national R&D expenditures still remained at a low level, as is shown in Table 6-8.

High-quality manpower with basic academic training in science and technology is Taiwan's most important and most abundant resource. Many foreign-invested firms in Taiwan have reaped substantial rewards in energy saving, materials substitution, upgrading of manufacturing processes, and equipment design and modification resulting from research, development, and engineering work by Chinese scientists, engineers, and technicians (Li 1983: 4).

Table 6-8. National R&D Expenditures as Percentage of GNP, 1978-84.

Year	National R&D Expenditures as Percentage of GNP
1978	0.30%
1979	0.42
1980	0.55
1981	0.76
1982	0.70
1983	0.73
1984	0.99

Source: National Science Council, *Survey of R&D Activities, Republic of China* (Taipei: various years).

The Hsinchu science-based industrial park began operation in September 1981. Its establishment is a bold step taken by the government to lead industry into the domain of high technology. The park will span 2,100 hectares centered around two national universities, technology research institutes, and research laboratories. Investors in the park are provided with land and buildings at low rentals and guaranteed a five-consecutive-year tax holiday within the first nine years of operation, import duty exemption, and freedom to structure capital and repatriate profits. The operation of the park has contributed to the return-flow of overseas Chinese talent. Computer components, telecommunications equipment, carbon fibers, laser equipment, and biochemical products have already been produced.

All these efforts broaden the industrial base, expedite the transfers of technologies, and restructure industry and exports in favor of high value-added products. However, a transition away from highly labor-intensive products to skill-intensive products is not an easy process. It is difficult to keep up with the rapid technical progress in these products and to compete in markets dominated by oligopolistic producers in industrial countries.

Technology transfers in high-tech areas are risky. A system of socializing risk must be developed, with the government assuming a portion of the risk by providing government-financed training, some R&D funds, and start-up capital as well as encouraging collaboration among university research centers and business. The expanded technological research cooperation will optimize scarce skilled personnel and facilities and reduce the costs both financially and intellectually by providing a mechanism for pooling research efforts. At the same time, macroeconomic measures must complement industrial policy that takes into account the important microeconomic differences among different sectors. The Economic Reform Committee has recommended that business and personal income taxes be cut that interest rates be reduced, and that the central bank conduct foreign exchange market intervention to avoid unduly affecting international price competitiveness and dampen seasonality. It also recommended tax simplification, relaxation of foreign exchange controls, reduction of the average nominal tariff rates to 15 to 20 percent by 1991, replacement of the positive list with a negative list of commodities subject to import controls as well as of activities eligible for overseas Chinese and foreign investment, abolishment of such performance requirements as exporting a minimum portion of a foreign company's output or using a certain amount of local components, financial deregulation, and a fundamental reform of the financial system. The major objective of these recommendations is to achieve a better functioning market economy. An open and competitive domestic economy makes manufacturers fit and lively, encourages small firms to grow big, attracts multinational firms to secure the benefits of technology transfers, and restructures the industrial base to make industries more income elastic and high value-added.

An interesting case is the recent attempt of the government to encourage foreign direct investment, promote a more efficient production of lower-priced cars, and enlarge the components-industry base for the domestic market as well as internationally. There are indications that the incentives provided for foreign investment become less effective the greater their complexity and the more frequently they are altered. The direct foreign investment in countries that have followed a more open development strategy has been in general more in line with the country's comparative advantage (The World Bank 1985: 129).

Reforming the Financial System, Diversifying Markets, and Liberalizing Import and Foreign Exchange Restrictions

The experience of Taiwan confirms that the industry and trade sectors have to be dynamic and government policies have to be flexible

Table 6-9. Key Indicators of the Significance of Export Surplus 1980-85 (*percentage*).

	1980	1981	1982	1983	1984	1985
Export surplus/GNP	-1.21%	2.08%	5.26%	8.98%	11.44%	14.23%
Export surplus/Exports	-2.28	3.97	10.39	16.66	20.06	25.80
Foreign assets of the Central Bank/Imports	12.63	24.48	44.42	54.95	66.97	99.12

Sources: Directorate-General of Budget, Accounting and Statistics (DGBAS), *National Income of the Republic of China* (Taipei: various years); Central Bank of China, *Balance of Payments, Taiwan District, the Republic of China* (Taipei: various years).

Notes: Exports surplus, GNP, and exports are based on the data of national income statistics, while imports are based on the customs data. Foreign assets of the Central Bank are the twelve-month averages.

to deal with the internal and external challenges. The success of outward-oriented industrialization has resulted in the growing export surplus. As is shown in Table 6-9 export surplus as percentage of GNP widened from -1.2 percent in 1980 to 14.2 percent in 1985. The foreign reserves held by the Central Bank of China amounted to almost one year of imports in 1985.

An export surplus represents more domestic savings than domestic investment or a positive net foreign investment, which is unusual for a newly industrializing country. In fact, Taiwan exports its savings in very large amounts to the United States to help finance the U.S. budget deficits, notwithstanding that the quarrel over the trade imbalance continues.

The gross domestic investment was only 17.9 percent of GNP, while gross national savings amounted to 32.1 percent in 1985, generating a huge export surplus. The difference between domestic savings and investment has been accumulated mainly in the form of short-term foreign financial assets. The Republic of China is still a newly industrializing country that has to maximize the static and dynamic allocative efficiency, and yet as much as 13.7 percent of GNP was transferred abroad and not utilized for domestic economic activities in 1985. One reason for transferring huge domestic savings abroad may be an inadequate and out-of-date financial regime that has failed to function as an efficient intermediary between savers and investors.

The Cathay financial scandal has clearly demonstrated that the failure of financial institutions has serious repercussions that extend far beyond the financial sector. Because the process of market restructuring and regulatory reform have remained incomplete, the Economic Reform Committee recommends financial deregulation and a fundamental reform of the financial system.

The essential functions of financial regulation consist of ensuring the soundness of the financial system while providing an individual financial institution with the maximum possible freedom to foster efficient allocation of financial resources by promoting competition and innovation. Just like driving on a freeway at a high speed, the driver has to strictly obey the traffic regulations and constantly check the brake and the safety belts to ensure safety. However, a car made of very thick steel plate will be slower, although safer, than some others. By the same token, financial regulation has to attend to market discipline, as well as the cost of excessive regulation.

The Economic Reform Committee recommends easing restrictions that have proved unnecessary or counterproductive. The regulations should place more emphasis on enforcing market discipline and sticking to the principle of sound banking. It recommends improving the bank examination process, streamlining the regulatory structure, strengthening capital requirements, improving disclosure, and reinforcing reporting requirements.

The Banking Law and the Central Bank Law stipulate that the Central Bank prescribes the ceiling of bank deposit rates and approves the range of bank lending rates as proposed by the Bankers' Association. Not surprisingly, controls spawned evasions and innovations. Corporations circumvented lending rate floors by issuing commercial paper and bankers acceptances to fund large sums in the money market at rates lower than the bank deposit rates under the current situation of excess liquidity caused by a huge export surplus, high domestic savings, and underinvestment. The Economic Reform Committee recommends not only reducing bank rates to bring them in line with the market clearing equilibrium levels but also revising the Banking Law, the Central Bank Law, and other regulations governing interest rates to completely deregulate bank rates in due course.

Most of the domestic banks are state owned and subject to the onerous regulations of numerous government agencies. Bank staff becomes less respected by government bureaucracy and politicians alike. The most troublesome regulations are very difficult standards and procedures for writing off bad loans. Small mistakes can cost a loan officer an administrative penalty in the civil service appraisal system; he or she also may be liable to repay bad loans. The Economic Reform Committee recommends enacting a special law governing state-owned banks with minimum state interference so that banks avoid resembling a government bureaucracy. Bank regulation should be based on the banking laws applied to both government banks and private banks. The government exercises its authority only in the capacity of shareholders. The Economic Reform Committee also recommends allowing the entry of new private banks to promote competition and avoid the excessive concentration of banking power.

In order to equip the financial system to meet the challenges of financial deregulation and international competition, the Financial Subcommittee recommends enacting a law governing mergers and conversions of financial institutions that will restructure the financial system. Financial institutions should be allowed to apply for mergers or conversions in the future, if these changes (1) improve efficiencies and strengthen sound banking, (2) exploit economies in providing financial services but avoid interrupting credit facilities for the medium and small business sectors as well as excessive concentration of financial powers, and (3) provide adequate protection of the interests of shareholders.

Because the gains to the economy as a whole from the development of money and capital markets are considerable, the Economic Reform Committee recommends diversifying high credit-standing instruments in the money market, establishing prudent criteria to evaluate the credit rating of the issuing companies of commercial papers and bankers acceptances, allowing the new entry of bills finance companies, improving the interbank market functions, making a clearer definition of the responsibilities of the Securities Exchange Commission and the Stock Exchange, adopting rules to clearly define fair trading practices, strengthening the supervision of brokers and traders and monitoring market behavior for irregularities, and improving accounting and disclosure requirements for listed companies.

The foreign exchange market in Taiwan has been composed almost exclusively of nonspeculative exporters and importers and covered interest arbitrageurs. Financial transactions in foreign exchange are still very limited. Ronald McKinnon (1979: 143) points out that such a market is inherently unstable. Exchange rates can move continuously in one direction.

It should be noted that, with a huge trade surplus, there exists a pressure for the NT dollar to appreciate against the U.S. dollar because the supply of foreign exchange exceeds its demand. In order to avoid having the NT dollar appreciate further against the U.S. dollar, the Central Bank has been discretely intervening to steady the NT dollar. The ceiling on the cumulative foreign exchange long position held by the authorized banks was removed in August 1984 to alleviate upward pressure on the NT dollar as well as to make the authorized banks' portfolio management become more sophisticated. However, the accumulation of foreign exchange has exposed banks to foreign exchange risk.

With regard to geographical concentration, Taiwan's exports to the United States amounted to almost half of its total exports in 1985 (see Table 6-4) and have been heavily concentrated on textiles, footwear, machinery (mainly machine tools), and miscellaneous manufacturing. Taiwan has also been the largest beneficiary of the U.S. Generalized System of Preferences; $3.2 billion of its product gained duty-free entry to the United States in 1985. Because of the danger of U.S. protectionism, Taiwan has to change the composition of its exports and diversify its markets by seeking other important trade partners.

Broadly speaking, the relative importance of domestic supply and foreign demand in determining the rate of growth of a country's exports will vary according to its share in the export market. The greater the country's share the more probable that its exports will grow more or less in line with the growth in foreign import demand for the product it exports. The smaller its share, the more important is its ability to produce for export at prevailing world prices (Maizels 1968: 168). The need to expedite the diversification of its markets and product composition is evident if Taiwan is to sustain its recent rate of export growth.

Market diversification, the state of the world economic environment, and prevailing limitations on trade by the industrial countries all argue in favor of a trade and industrial development strategy that supports a balanced and widespread expansion of exports from a broad array of manufacturing subsectors—not a sudden large spurt in a few traditional exportables that are important sources of employment in industrial countries. Participation in the international division of the production process begins by revising domestic content regulations that raise the costs of domestic production and limit a firm's choice among inputs. Sectoral diversification of exports could proceed with a substantial increase in intra-industry trade. For instance, firms can specialize in certain kinds of machinery and equipment and import others—produce cars and particular varieties of electronic consumer appliances and import parts and components for assembling (World Bank 1984: xii). Emphasis on intraindustry trade through increased import liberalization and an expansion of exports on a broad front would diffuse the tensions that spring up when trade is one-sided and resources would be used more efficiently according to the nation's comparative advantage.

Import and foreign exchange controls and restrictions have been relaxed considerably in recent years. The Republic of China has been under heavy pressure from the United States to take drastic market-opening measures to reduce its trade surplus with the United States. The government has lowered tariffs in many commodities targeted by the United States and eliminated a controversial duty-paying scheme. The Reagan administration also has pressured the Republic of China to adequately protect intellectual property rights and ease restrictions on the operations of U.S. banking, insurance, film, beer, wine, and cigarettes firms in Taiwan.

Taiwan's strong balance-of-payments position would permit trade liberalization and the substantial easing of foreign exchange controls. The Economic Reform Committee recommends freer transactions of gold and replacing the burdensome and ineffective customs requirements of reporting gold carried by tourists into the country with the imposition of import duty on gold bullion. It also recommends the replacement of the prior licensing or approval system with a reporting system to simplify the procedures for commodity imports and exports as well as for miscellaneous overseas payments of firms within a certain limit. Forward cover facilities are recommended to include services and capital transactions. In addition, it recommends allowing authorized banks to act as conduits for placing funds of domestic customers into offshore investment and issuing foreign-currency CDs.

The appropriate new exchange rate will be influenced by the mix of those policies aimed at opening the domestic market to more imported goods and foreign investment, even though the purchasing-power-parity effective exchange rate indexes will serve as a base to identify the direction of the change. However, the government has the tendency to overstate the steps that it has taken to liberalize imports. Restrictions apply to particular sources of origin, the status of applicants, and also the reluctance of the lower ranks of bureaucracy to give up discretionary powers with unjustifiable reinterpretation of the policies that they are charged with enacting. In order to avoid the disruptive effects of substantial exchange rate revaluation, to appease protectionist pressure and, to improve the country's standing with the United States, trade and foreign exchange liberalization is required.

Tariff structure should not be adjusted fragmentarily under renewed foreign pressure. The government should make serious attempts to revise and simplify the entire tariff structure with a clear conception of the economic rationale in view (Lee and Liang 1982: 322-32). In addition, liberalization of import restrictions and reform of the tariff structure should be carried out on the basis of a program made public in advance to minimize the adjustment costs to firms. Trade liberalization will lower the cost of exports by reducing prices of imported machinery and raw materials, provide a spur for improvements in productivity, trigger accelerated adjustment among industries that compete with imports, and lead to better treatment for exports in foreign markets through bilateral negotiations to obtain mutual concessions with selective protectionism. The liberalization of foreign exchange control will stimulate more efficient use and increase the demand for foreign exchange, alleviating upward pressure on the NT dollar. As pointed out by Ronald McKinnon (1984: 479), liberalization of the capital account of the balance of payments comes last, following the liberalization of foreign trade and the domestic capital market. With a huge export surplus, Taiwan has to make better use of its foreign exchange earnings for foreign investment abroad.

A number of enterprises in the Republic of China make overseas investments and run multinational businesses. Local enterprises' activities in outward investment have gradually expanded since the late 1970s. A company undertakes foreign investment to extend foreign markets due to limited local markets, to maintain competitiveness in the international marketplace in the face of constantly rising local wage rates that make the manufacturing of standardized products at home less competitive, and to avoid tariff and nontariff barriers proliferating in the current environment of heightened international trade protectionism. Outward investment is mainly in electric appliances, chemicals, and textiles in the United States and Southeast Asian countries. The emergence of the multinationals in the Republic of China is a recent phenomenon. Foreign investments in manufacturing appear to be an effective method of heading off protectionist action in the United States and other markets.

Finally, the rapid growth in world trade in the 1960s and the early 1970s has now been replaced by slow growth and increasing protectionism in industrial countries against manufactured exports from developing countries. As growth slowed in industrial countries, fewer new jobs were created. It has become increasingly difficult to resist the pressure from those industries that have been in secular decline.

Countries that facilitate structural adjustment permit a liberalized attitude toward trade policies, while countries that refuse to let their economic structures adjust are forced into protectionist actions. Selective protectionism is often applied arbitrarily and with rather more vigor to the diplomatically weak than their trade offenses may actually justify (Turner and McMullen 1982: 264). The EC's Generalized System of Preferences (GSP) scheme excluded Taiwan, quotas were sometimes unilaterally determined, and the market access of the Taiwanese products to the EC has been on terms inferior to those covering the goods from other countries. As shown in Table 6–10, quota restrictions are applied extensively to Taiwan's textile exports. The Reagan administration has asked Taiwan to freeze textiles shipments at their 1985 level for three years from 1986 through the end of 1988 and to restrain voluntarily machine-tool exports.

The policy of protectionism is both inefficient and costly to industrial countries. The effects are at least threefold (Jenkins forthcoming; Turner and McMullen 1982: 151–52; "Costs and Benefits of Protection" 1985: 18–23):

1. It creates a scarcity value that is added to the cost of goods, so that domestic consumers pay higher prices for imports. The cartel pricing transfers the wealth from consumers of the importing nation to authorized suppliers of the exporting nation. Many studies clearly show that the cost of the restraints outweighed the value of jobs saved. It also encourages bureaucratic regulation and control and foreshadows a long-term decline in economic viability.

Table 6-10. Export Values of Taiwan's Textiles Subject to Quota
Restrictions 1980-85 (*U.S. $1,000*).

	1980	*1981*
Exports to the United States		
Total exports	$1,269,296	$1,496,820
Exports subject to quota restrictions	1,152,820	1,373,442
Quota restrictions coverage (%)	90.8%	91.8%
Exports to the European Economic Community		
Total exports	$424,535	$459,651
Exports subject to quota restrictions	377,450	359,341
Quota restrictions coverage (%)	88.9%	78.2%
Exports to Canada		
Total exports	$115,161	$146,382
Exports subject to quota restrictions	100,895	131,530
Quota restrictions coverage (%)	87.6%	89.9%

Source: The Taiwan Textile Federation.

2. It insulates the domestic industry from price competition to
    some extent, but the domestic industry usually does not reap the
    anticipated benefits because higher prices encourage the entry of
    unrestricted new exporters and imports from the more restricted
    sources were replaced by imports from other suppliers.

3. It creates an incentive for foreign producers to improve the qual-
    ity of their products and aim for higher value added per unit ex-
    ported, thus causing foreign producers to compete more directly
    with manufacturers in industrial countries that traditionally pro-
    duce high-quality products. Hence, domestic producers may find
    that they now face an increase rather than a decline in competi-
    tion from imports in the high-quality ranges. Because the quota
    increases the relative cost of low-quality imports, there will be an
    incentive for domestic producers to manufacture the low-quality
    goods previously imported.

All these protection-induced effects have tended to undermine the
objectives of import control. Given the economic losses to industrial
countries involved, a preferred policy would be to eliminate bilateral
quotas and rely on tariff protection, accompanied by an adjustment

Table 6-10. continued

1982	1983	1984	1985
$1,635,430	$1,864,389	$1,537,272	$2,414,885
1,442,418	1,708,079	2,267,392	2,223,872
88.2%	91.6%	89.4%	92.1%
$450,852	$424,342	$404,545	$394,685
352,834	334,577	343,243	330,817
78.3%	78.9%	84.9%	83.8%
$140,458	$178,080	$209,271	$217,569
116,856	148,316	185,231	187,540
83.2%	83.3%	88.5%	86.2%

program for labor, although adjustment is never easy and requires considerable political courage.

The economic performance of the Republic of China is determined by the pace of its export growth, which, in turn, depends to a great extent on market conditions in the industrial countries. The easing of protectionism in these countries will be a welcome blessing. If protectionist sentiment persists, all countries will suffer, but nations heavily reliant on trade will find that they are the big losers.

SUMMARY AND CONCLUSIONS

The major findings of this study may be summarized as follows:

1. From the beginning of the export drive in the early 1960s, outward-looking policies for industry and trade have been essential for the rapid growth and remarkable achievement in the structural transformation of the Taiwan economy. Taiwan provides an example of an economy following its comparative advantage and reaping the gains from trade illustrated by the traditional

theory of international trade. The rapid expansion of labor-intensive manufactured exports contributed to efficient industrialization by permitting specialization according to comparative advantage and stimulating technological improvement. It also improved living standards as well as income distribution through the creation of new productive employment and a rapid increase in real wage rates.

2. The economy of the Republic of China is presently at a crossroads, and the current problems of structural adjustments are the result of the success of past development efforts. Whether the economy of Taiwan can successfully restructure its industry and attain the high rate of economic expansion that it experienced in the past will depend to a great extent on ensuring technology transfers, reforming the financial system, diversifying export markets, and liberalizing imports and foreign exchange control to reduce the risks of protectionism.

3. The most important lesson that emerges from this study is that trade strategy and industrial policy have to be adjustment-oriented and coordinated with macroeconomic policies to help improve the efficiency and flexibility of the industry and trade sectors to meet internal and external challenges. Industrial policy must be foresighted and should not simply be reactive to situations that have gotten out of hand. It is necessary to create an open and competitive domestic economy to make its manufacturer robust in order to expedite the restructuring of industry, and to make better use of the country's comparative advantage to maintain continued growth and the country's competitive edge. At the same time, protectionism will make much-needed structural adjustment less costly.

4. Taiwan and Korea are often mentioned as the most successful cases of export-led industrialization. It is interesting to note that both economies have much in common. Both possess well-educated and hardworking labor forces. Neither is endowed with abundant natural resources. Both underwent a lengthy development process under the colonial rule of Japan, during which they accumulated considerable investments in infrastructure and education. Both inherit a Confucian tradition emphasizing the values of education, frugality, and kinship ties. Both face hostile regimes and have to maintain a high level of military spending. In recent years both have been under intense pressure from the United

States to open their markets at a much more vulnerable development stage than that of Japan when it began to liberalize. Fast actions on trade liberalization will help reduce the trade gap between both countries and the United States, but Japan may benefit more than the United States. The development of high-tech and high value-added industries, through private initiative and accelerated technology transfers from abroad, is the cornerstone of both Taiwan's and Korea's hopes for sustained high growth. Despite these similarities, a few differences between them have become evident. First, Korea has accumulated a large external debt, while Taiwan has kept its debt service ratio around 4 percent since the 1970s and has emerged as a net creditor with a very high rate of national savings. It may be said that Taiwan has run too great a trade surplus and accumulated too much in foreign exchange reserves, while investing too little in the industrial modernization and economic infrastructure. Second, Korea is dominated by large conglomerates patterned after the Japanese Zaibatsus, while the Republic of China is a country of small and medium enterprises. Korea has been attempting to adopt a more balanced policy to promote healthier medium business sector, while Taiwan's major concern is to encourage small and medium businesses to grow big. However, other than such structural defects as local enterprises being generally run by individuals or families and financial regimes remaining inflexible and conservative that hinder the exploitation of scale economies, small and medium businesses are more adaptable, help to keep market competitive and the entrepreneurial spirit alive, as well as reduce income inequality (Lau 1986: 10). Eager young entrepreneurs and well-educated engineers may help Taiwan promote the transition of the economy to high-tech areas, if the government takes adequate measures to assist these ventures by providing capital and developing marketing capabilities.

NOTES

1. Table 6-3 provides some indicators of Taiwan's progress in financial deepening by computing changes in the ratios of financial instruments outstanding as a percentage of GDP. GDP is used as the denominator because national wealth statistics are unavailable. In a steady state, capital stock must grow at the same rate as output.

REFERENCES

Balassa, B. 1985. *Change and Challenge in the World Economy.* London: Macmillan.

"Costs and Benefits of Protection." 1985. *The OECD Observer,* No. 134 (May): 18-23.

de Vries, V.A. 1967. *Export Experiences of Developing Countries.* Baltimore, Md.: Johns Hopkins Press.

The Executive Yuan. 1982. *Science and Technology Development Program.* Taipei, Republic of China.

Jacoby, N.H. 1966. *U.S. Aid to Taiwan: A Study of Foreign Aid, Self-Help, and Development.* New York: Praeger.

Jaffe, I. 1984. "Industrial Policies: Responses to a Common Core of Problems." *The OECD Observer,* No. 130 (September): 11.

Jenkins, G.P. Forthcoming. "Costs and Consequences of the New Protectionism: The Case of Canada's Clothing Sector." In *Canada in a Developing World Economy: Trade or Protection.* Oxford: Oxford University Press, North-South Institute/World Bank monograph.

Lau, L., ed. 1986. *Models of Development: A Comparative Study of Economic Growth in South Korea and Taiwan.* San Francisco: Institute for Contemporary Studies Press.

Lee, Eddy, ed. 1981. *Export-Led Industrialization and Development.* Singapore: Maruzen Asia.

Lee, T.H., and Kuo-shu Liang. 1982. "Development Strategies in Taiwan." In *Development Strategies in Semi-Industrial Economies,* edited by B. Balassa et al., pp. 310-83. Baltimore, Md.: Johns Hopkins University Press.

Li, K.T. 1983. "Development of Science and Technology in the Republic of China." *Industry of Free China* 59 (1) (January): 4.

Liang, Kuo-shu, and Teng-hui Lee. 1974. "Process and Pattern of Economic Development in Taiwan." In *The Economic Development of East and Southeast Asia,* edited by Shimichi Ichimura, pp. 269-346. Honolulu: University Press of Hawaii.

Liang, Kuo-shu, and Ching-in Hou Liang. 1978. "Export Expansion and Economic Development in Taiwan." Paper presented at the Conference of the Asian Studies on the Pacific Coast, Anaheim, Calif., June 9.

Ling, Ching-yuan. 1973. *Industrialization in Taiwan, 1946-72: Trade and Import-Substitution Policies for Developing Countries.* New York: Praeger.

Maizels, A. 1968. *Exports and Economic Growth of Developing Countries.* London: Cambridge University Press.

McKinnon, R.I. 1973. *Money and Capital in Economic Development.* Washington, D.C.: Brookings Institution.

_____. 1979. *Money in International Exchange: The Convertible Currency System.* New York: Oxford University Press.

_____. 1984. "The International Capital Market and Economic Liberalization in LDC's." *The Developing Economies* 22 (4) (December): 479.

Ranis, G., and C. Schive. 1985. "Direct Foreign Investment in Taiwan's Development." In *Foreign Trade and Investment: Economic Development in the Newly Industrializing Asian Countries*, edited by W. Galenson, pp. 85–137. Madison, Wis.: University of Wisconsin Press.

Schive, C., and R.S. Yen. 1982. "Multinational Corporations and Host Country Technology: A Factor Proportion Approach in Taiwan." Discussion Paper Series No. 82–01. Council for Asian Manpower Studies. Mimeo.

Shaw, E.S. 1973. *Financial Deepening in Economic Development*. New York: Oxford University Press.

Tang, Anthony M., and Kuo-shu Liang. 1973. "Agricultural Trade in the Economic Development of Taiwan." In *Trade, Agriculture and Development*, edited by G.S. Tolley and P.A. Zadrozny, pp. 115–46. Cambridge, Mass.: Ballinger.

Turner, L., and N. McMullen. 1982. *The Newly Industrializing Countries: Trade and Adjustment*. London: George Allen & Unwin.

World Bank. 1984. *Korea: Development in a Global Context*. Washington, D.C.: World Bank.

_____. 1985. *World Development Report 1985*. New York: Oxford University.

7 THE KOREAN PERSPECTIVE ON TRADE RELATIONS WITH THE UNITED STATES

John T. Bennett

Korea has grown very rapidly over the last twenty-six years. Much of that growth was directly due to foreign trade, particularly exports to the United States. The record of the U.S. relationship with Korea is important because of current trade frictions and because it offers some lessons for other countries. Understanding on both the Korean and the U.S. side, however, affects not only the economic aspect of the relationship but also the security and the political dimensions, which in the eyes of most people are of even greater significance.

The Korean perspective on trade has been shaped by its unique historical experience. Hence, it is necessary to look at the historical development of the Korean economy and then to look at changes in the wider international scene. These provoke some comments on the present frictions with the United States, on Korea's prospects, and on some of the domestic problems that Korea faces—its large foreign debt, the concentration of economic power, and so on.

HISTORY OF THE KOREAN ECONOMY

Korea's growth is not new. We do not have data for the period before the Japanese annexation, and the country was largely rural then, but there seems little doubt that the economy grew at least as fast as the population.

81

There was some development during the period of Japanese annexation as well. New technology and investment laid a foundation for the industrial development that occurred thereafter. The Japanese, themselves quite poor then, exploited the Korean economy as thoroughly as they could, so that Koreans benefitted little or not at all at the time and felt justifiably aggrieved about their political and social mistreatment. But many Koreans experienced industrial labor and began to learn the skills that it requires. Some Koreans learned management skills as well. Thus, as a by-product of a draconian regime, some abilities important for future development were acquired.

Development was slow after independence in 1945 and was set back by the Korean War in 1950. The armistice in 1953 allowed the beginnings of reconstruction, but the rate of growth in GNP over the next nine years, 4 percent, was little more than that in population. From 1962–85, however, real growth averaged more than 8 percent, and there was only one year, when a set of particularly adverse events occurred, that it actually declined. Per capita GNP rose to about $2,000 in 1984 from $100 in 1962 (Mason 1980).

How was this remarkable development managed? Scholars have suggested several explanations, which I have grouped as follows:

1. Good economic policy and implementation,
2. Historical and cultural factors,
3. Existence of the Japan model, and
4. Unique adaptations such as contract manufacture.

Elements of truth exist in all of these explanations, so that one must end up being skeptical of any single simple explanation. It is also necessary to recognize that had Korea not been resource poor and densely populated, it probably would not have chosen the export-led strategy but rather the import-substitution strategy that most developing countries have adopted. Finally, of course, Korea would have been able to do nothing with an export-led strategy, had not the United States and the free world promoted growing international trade and international capital movements.

GOOD ECONOMIC POLICY

Korea started out with the right national goals for development. It sought full employment and growing incomes. These not only contributed to individual welfare but to political support for the government and national military strength—the latter both directly in what Korea could afford to spend on its defense and indirectly in persuading the United States to pledge assistance in case of attack and in impressing many Third World nations that the south was worthy of great respect, perhaps even providing a model for them.

It was also recognized that a high rate of investment and saving were necessary for rapid growth, as well as appropriate selection of projects, so that the investment was both profitable and efficient. These questions are also closely related to policies determining interest and exchange rates.

Economists make much of the policy choices because those are the issues on which they speak with authority. Within fairly narrow limits, Korea got them right over the years. But at least some other countries have probably done that part of the development task as well and have not prospered.

Implementation was a second aspect of Korea's development that many emphasize as crucial. (*Korea's Competitive Edge*, by Yung Whee Rhee et al., gives perhaps the best account of both policy formulation and implementation.) This took the form of an elaborate reporting system, culminating in monthly meetings of senior businesspeople, ministers, and the president. Such frequent high-level attention has the effect of bringing problems to the attention of those who can solve them and of disciplining subordinates to make ever greater efforts by keeping them constantly under surveillance. Such close interaction between business and government would be ineffective, if not impossible, in many countries, but cultural values held by Koreans make it acceptable there. Indeed, what we see is a Korean family, writ large as the whole nation, working together to improve its welfare.

HISTORICAL AND CULTURAL FACTORS

Korea's Confucian history and values, the Japanese annexation, and the continued threat from the north are all seen as decisive influences on Korea's economic development. We have alluded to the importance of cultural values in permitting government and business to work closely together. This really stems from the Confucian values that project Korea's homogeneous population as a single family (not entirely incorrectly, since for example, 26 percent of Koreans are named Kim), with the president (earlier the king) as the father. The family, not the individual, is considered the measure of merit—what is good for the family, that is, the nation, is good.

Family values—harmony, deference to seniors, and mutual obligation for family members to help one another—are considered the models for conducting all relationships. Departures from the model are frequent enough in day-to-day experience, just as lapses from good behavior are common in other societies, but that is all they are—lapses. The model has produced a highly disciplined labor force, willing to work hard for long hours (more than fifty hours a week on average) and responsibly—its ability to master new technology is a measure of the dedication it brings to the work place.

The historic experience of Japanese annexation and devastating invasion before that have on the one hand strengthened national solidarity and on the other made Korea a ferocious competitor in world trade. The sense of wishing to outdo the Japanese is without doubt a powerful motivation, particularly since the Japanese themselves have been economically successful.

The Korean War is the most recent, and for some, the best explanation of Korea's economic emergence. Security is certainly a strong motivation, based on the fact that as many as 10 percent of the south's then 20 million people died and that a third of the reproducible capital stock was destroyed. Seoul, to give just one example, was fought through on four different occasions—leaving very little standing.

The sense of solidarity that the war experience still conveys can never be fully appreciated by those who did not share it. In any case, it further legitimizes and reinforces the already powerful role of government in the economy.

THE JAPAN MODEL

Although Korea might have discovered the export-led strategy on its own, it made the choice much easier because Japan had already blazed the trail. This was important in two respects. It proved that the export-led strategy could work and could produce spectacularly rapid growth.

The Japanese experience also produced some practical lessons that Korea followed. The use of industrial strategy—early emphasis on light industry, later diversification into heavy industrial products and chemicals, and the acquisition of technology from abroad—were all used by Japan and probably borrowed from it. Having said that, of course, there were earlier models from Europe and the U.S. experience. Japan was simply closer both geographically and in time.

The Japan model also included some other policies that were adopted by Korea. These were stringent controls on imports in general and protection for infant industries in particular. The logic for the former was to reserve scarce foreign exchange for only the most important imports. (This point may seem trivial but for the fact that many other developing countries try to allocate foreign exchange for essentials in principle, but in practice fail.) Infant industry protection allows labor and management to learn by guaranteeing them the domestic market, in effect subsidizing their education through an indirect tax on consumers. To be successful, however, it requires a domestic market large enough to allow the infant to grow and achieve economies of scale that ultimately make it world competitive.

Korea is reluctant to admit its use of the Japan model, particularly now that it is often accused of being a second Japan and engaging in unfair trade. It needs therefore to be recognized that Korea has recently departed from the earlier model and is well on the way to becoming a free trader. This does not mean, however, that all of the old policies will be abandoned.

Although Korea used infant industry protection, it was unable to achieve world competitiveness in many products. Its domestic market was simply too small to attain economies of scale. It had therefore to try to achieve it by exporting from the beginning. Automobiles were a case in which it failed to do so for many years, and as a result, buyers paid very high prices in the protected domestic market.

Saving its limited foreign exchange also meant that Korea paid high prices for what it could produce as substitutes for the prohibited imports. This was particularly true of luxuries, such as cosmetics, whose prices were exorbitant and quality low.

Korean economists long recognized the price that their country paid for import restrictions. They were particularly incensed by some of the decisions to invest in heavy industry made in the 1970s. The assassination of Park Chung Hee, the major proponent of that investment, allowed the costs to be reassessed and the policy reversed.

CONTRACT MANUFACTURE

Although contract manufacture—the Korean company producing on order from a foreign company, usually U.S.—is not widely recognized as a model for development, it played a particularly important role in the early days of Korea's growth. Contract manufacture evolved from market forces. Individual U.S. buyers began looking abroad for cheaper sources of goods, notably shoes and clothing but also stuffed toys, wigs, and many other products. The list has now expanded to a wide variety of industrial as well as consumer items, including most notably electronic products, steel, ships, autos, and computers. More new items will be added as Korea's manufacturing skill grows.

Contract manufacture allowed Korean businesspeople to concentrate on what they knew best, running the labor force and supervising the manufacturing process. On the other hand, marketing was in the hands of the buyer. Technology, if it was not already available, was also often provided through the buyer. Finally, finance was supplied with the sale; most were made under a letter of credit that was usable as security for a bank loan equal to roughly 80 percent of the value of the sale.

Thus, contract manufacture became an alternative for Korean business to both foreign investment and to the typical business arrangement, in which a product is sold out of inventory through a complex wholesale and retail structure. Elements in this pattern have changed in many industries, but the basics are still widely used, as evidenced by the fact that few Korean consumer goods are sold in the United States under Korean brand names. It has proven highly flexible and economic. Korean companies have moved rapidly to more complex technology and to higher value-added products. They have also financed their businesses on very favorable terms.

INDUSTRIAL STRATEGY

Korea's economic strategy has followed most of the lines already suggested in the previous discussion. It has, however, changed in recent years in response to the growth in the size and complexity of the economy. Partly this was motivated by the mistakes that became obvious after the second oil shock. But there is also implicit in this a belief that the Korean government's decisionmaking process had been corrupted by too close a government-business relationship.

Korean economists have long been concerned about the decisions made in the 1970s. It was always clear that as a small economy Korea had to make choices and that errors were difficult to hedge against. A minimum commitment had to be made to an industry, or economies of scale could not be obtained; but minimum commitments made it difficult to achieve sufficient diversification and thus to avoid overdependence on some products and markets.

What is evolving—the process continues—is greater reliance on the market mechanism but considerable government involvement in the business decision process. Thus, Korea adopted a new Industrial Development Law, effective July 1, 1986, replacing most of the old laws that governed Korea's major industries. Under this law, the government retains the power to decide what industries are to be favored and what to be phased out, as well as whether new entrants will be allowed and what tax and lending incentives, if any, are to be granted.

The law establishes an Industrial Development Screening Committee made up of businesspeople, academics, and researchers from the think tanks. The objective in using such a committee is to broaden the base for decisions and make them more professional and less bureaucratic or political. Newspapers report this committee has already recommended that autos, heavy construction equipment, marine diesel engines, and heavy electric equipment be treated as promising industries and that textiles and alloy steel be considered for phase-out.

The committee also recommended that new entrants be barred from all of the enumerated industries. This issue has become most pressing in the case of autos, where Samsung and Chrysler had already agreed on a joint venture but the government turned it down, at least until 1989. Korea faces the problem of having too much invested in any particular industry, a downturn which might carry the whole economy with it. The committee recommendations still need to be reviewed by the government. Moreover, because the law is so new, some experience will be needed before an assessment of its effects will be possible.

The government remains hostage to past errors. The banking system was used to channel credit to target activities, and some of these have become losers. The government has been trying to make the banks competitive and free profitmaking businesses, but their non-performing loans to overseas construction and to shipping companies would weaken them, perhaps fatally, without continued government support. The alternative would be to have the banks take the losses, a politically difficult step. In any case, it would not alter anything real—the existing productive capacity would still be used, as long as it retained some value.

Although industrial strategy comes down to deciding to go with one or another product, some more general rules have also guided Korean behavior. Perhaps the most important relates to the choice of technology and how it should be acquired.

Because Korea started behind other countries in manufacturing, it has been able to acquire technology that was being abandoned in the advanced countries. This made it cheap and easier to master than leading technology.

The ease with which Korea could acquire technology has also meant that it should not waste time or money in research and development. Thus, expenditure on R&D has been low in the past, and even that was not particularly productive.

An initial R&D effort was, however, important in creating the foundations for R&D that will sustain Korean growth in the future. This is the case for two reasons. First, acquiring advanced technology from abroad becomes increasingly difficult. Second, trading technology has become important—for example, the ability to trade one microchip design for another may be critical to staying in the forefront of computer development.

At a deeper level, however, Korean R&D will be crucial to sustaining a high rate of growth. Coming from behind, Korea had a seemingly endless supply of technology that it could acquire from abroad. Its rate of growth was therefore determined by the rate of investment and the rate at which it could master the new technology, which was very fast indeed. Once it reaches the leading edge of technology, however, the development of new technology will determine the rate of growth. Japan is perhaps an object lesson—its rate of growth is down because, among other reasons, it must depend much more on its own technological efforts. Korea has begun to face the same problem. Thus, Korea will follow the same path—of trying to overcome the bottleneck constraining its growth by increasing its R&D sharply in the coming years.

OTHER PROBLEMS

Korea has other economic problems. These include the need to adjust continually to the flow of labor out of agriculture and into the cities. In the past, this has resulted in an excessive flow to Seoul, in the view of many making the city overcrowded.

Education remains a very important value in Korea. Providing expanded public facilities is a commitment of the Korean government, but cost continues to limit what actually is made available.

Similarly, welfare programs are widely desired, yet their cost is beyond Korea's capacity at current levels of income. Fortunately, family ties remain powerful, so that family members can usually be relied on to care for the unfortunate who cannot care for themselves. Nevertheless, it is no longer simple, as the nuclear family replaces the extended family in urban areas, as mobility separates branches of the family, and as the sense of mutual obligation weakens. The demand for public welfare improvements will thus be a growing factor in future economic and political programs.

Improving education carries with it a special problem as well—providing jobs that utilize the additional skills. Korea has generally had a surplus of skilled and educated workers at any given time, so that this has not slowed the country's growth. However, the supply of university graduates currently appears to exceed the creation of appropriate jobs, creating both an economic and a social problem.

Still another problem has been the distribution of income and wealth. The emergence of the large company groups (*chaebol*) symbolizes the issue because they seem to have grown with government help and have become a key element in government industrial policy. However, although a few families have benefitted enormously, by themselves they do not account for much of the observed change in income distribution.

Income distribution has worsened and improved in phases over a long period of time but started in Korea at a pretty reasonable level, following land reform and the universal devastation of the Korean War. The best assessment is that equality of opportunity is quite good—starting with access to education and the general absence of prejudice among Koreans. People can rise using their talents, and meritocracy remains an apt description of Korean society. Nevertheless, Korean cultural values that disdain wealth, power, and inequality focus popular attention on this aspect of public policy. Government has a constant problem compromising this with other goals.

Labor relations, trade unions, and wages provide a last set of public issues that remain only partially resolved in Korea. Although trade unions exist and account for more than 12 percent of wage employment, their power is sharply limited (Economic Planning Board 1986). Nevertheless, wages have kept pace with the country's development and for prolonged periods were a source of inflation. Government has tried to influence the average wage bargains by indicating what would be noninflationary increases that accorded with productivity improvements. However, in times of skill shortages the market really determined the wage, and at other times political uncertainty lessened government's ability to influence wage negotiations.

Working conditions and employer-employee relations remain a problem in Korea, in part because traditional arrangements and understandings about their mutual obligations are changing. A new understanding and new institutions will be needed to facilitate communication, a role that trade unions can play. However, unions have yet to establish their legitimacy in the eyes of the broad Korean public and their confrontational role in negotiation conflicts with traditional Confucian values about harmony in the community.

Government has sought to fill the vacuum as well, enforcing minimum acceptable behavior among employers and setting up new institutions—that is, labor-management councils in each plant. But performance has been uneven and insufficient to prevent labor actions that Koreans consider a breakdown in healthy industrial relations. Outsiders who have taken doctrinaire positions about how Korea should organize its institutions have not helped the process. Still, most Koreans would probably agree that existing institutions are not the final answer.

TRADE PROBLEMS

Because trade is so important to Korea, it has been very worried about protectionism, particularly in the all-important U.S. market. It had thought that its steps to open its own markets would blunt most demands, but the size and persistence of the U.S. trade deficit and its probable cause, the U.S. budget deficit, have made U.S. manufacturing uncompetitive in world markets and even at home. The resulting political pressures are extreme, and although the Reagan administration has generally been opposed to protectionist measures, it has made concessions at the margin and has failed to reduce the budget deficit. In the final analysis, the United States has emerged as the largest debtor in the world and faces the prospect that at some point, foreigners will cease to be willing to lend it additional funds. Whether this is accompanied by a flight from the dollar and its collapse must be a matter of concern for all.

The administration response to congressional protectionism has been a heightened campaign of market opening, focusing on the major U.S. trading partners, including Korea. The Korean government has responded positively after some hard bargaining. Most recently, it agreed to extend the protection of patents, copyrights, and trademarks, although its past record on such protection was widely considered to be above average in the world. It also agreed to allow U.S. insurance companies to sell in the Korean market and announced that it would start importing cigarettes as the first step in opening up the tobacco market. Most important, it has held to the schedule of market opening steps that it had previously announced.

Both the administration and the Congress seem unaware that the net inflow of foreign capital has accounted for the high dollar in recent years. This happens because the dollar rises sufficiently to create a current account deficit equal to the demand for dollars from foreign investors. Most Americans have apparently also failed to see the connection between the inflow of capital and the federal budget deficit. The continued growth of the deficit and no certain progress on cutting it in the future has kept foreign capital coming in and the trade deficit high. This will continue to be so until the budget deficit decreases or until foreigners decide they have invested enough in the United States.

One unfortunate consequence of U.S. pressure on market opening measures has been to alter their image. Korea's economists had previously argued that they were good for Korea, but that perception is not now widely shared. Instead, they are generally believed to be costly concessions unfairly extracted by a large power. The change will undoubtedly slow future liberalization, although the government remains committed to it.

To some extent, Koreans perceive U.S. pressures as a response to its own failure to improve its productivity and to increase its low savings and investment rate. They also believe that U.S. business has been less aggressive in selling to Korea than the Japanese, citing the fact that Japan has gotten most of the benefit of market opening measures already taken. Many Americans share those views, but in fact the high dollar often makes the profitability of exports and additional investment unattractive.

PROSPECTS

Korea's economic prospects remain very good in the foreseeable future. Although the current world expansion has gone on for longer than most, there seem to be no signs of its actual demise. Korea, in the meantime, is in the midst of a boom, benefitting from continued world growth and a number of fundamentals—the rise of the yen and lower interest rates and energy prices.

Other positive elements include the development of new competitive export products, especially automobiles and parts and computers. These seem to ensure growth in Korea's exports for some time to come.

Over the long run, Korea might expect trouble in maintaining earlier growth rates because of problems acquiring new more advanced technology. Nevertheless, there seems to be plenty of outmoded technologies available from the developed countries that will keep Korea growing well into the future, even should its own research and development prove less successful than expected.

Protectionist measures in the developed countries could reduce export growth overall, but Korea can adapt by adjusting its exchange rate and continuing to diversify its product mix to minimize the impact. In any case, protectionist measures cushion an industry but will not reduce the trade deficit because the exchange rate effects of protectionist measures make them self-defeating.

Korea does remain vulnerable to problems managing its large foreign debt, but they are likely to arise only should the world economy deteriorate badly. It seems improbable that the advanced countries, most importantly the United States, would not act to prevent that from happening.

Finally, it is clear that the United States cannot go on running a current account deficit and increasing its debt indefinitely. Adjustment to a sharply lower U.S. trade deficit will make it hard for Korea to increase its exports. It is possible to do so by taking market share from other countries. The alternative would be to increase its exports to other countries, most likely in the Pacific Rim countries. Non-Japan Asia is already Korea's second market, more important than Japan. Proximity, price, and product mix make them natural trading partners.

CONCLUSION

Korea's situation, history, and cultural traits have all formed its distinctive character. When Americans form their views of Korean actions, they need to be aware of what drives Korea and how far it has come. Its future seems solid, a continuation of past trends, to the extent that outside forces will allow them to go on. Certainly, Korea's goals and its success in achieving many of them appear admirable in the eyes of most Americans. The relationship has therefore been one of mutual benefit that should continue despite the normal frictions associated with growing trade, competition, and the need to adjust to one another.

REFERENCES

Economic Planning Board. 1986. *Korea Statistical Yearbook.*
Mason, E.S. 1980. *The Economic and Social Modernization of the Republic of Korea.* Cambridge, Mass.: Harvard University Press.
Rhee, Yung Whee, et al. 1984. *Korea's Competitive Edge.* Baltimore, Md.: Johns Hopkins University Press.

8 THE SCENE IN SINGAPORE

Tommy Koh

WHO ARE THE NICs?

The economic literature offers no satisfactory definition of a newly industrializing country. It is easier to say who they are than what they are. The countries most often described as the newly industrializing countries are the four dragons or tigers from Asia—South Korea, Taiwan, Hong Kong, and Singapore; the ABM group of Latin America, Argentina, Brazil, and Mexico; and Israel and India. Another group of countries forms the second tier of the newly industrializing countries. The group consists of the four ASEAN countries—Thailand, Malaysia, the Philippines, and Indonesia; Chile, Colombia, and Peru from Latin America and Pakistan from South Asia.

What do these countries share in common? They are developing countries that are working out of poverty and on their way to becoming industrialized countries. All have made impressive progress in their development, in their industrialization, and in their per capita income. Beyond that, they are a rather heterogenous group of countries. Not all of them have a high per capita income. Indeed, many of the OPEC countries, which are not regarded as newly industrializing countries, have higher per capita incomes than the NICs. A high per capita income is therefore neither a necessary nor a sufficient characteristic of a newly industrializing country. Although all are considered to be significant exporters of manufactured goods, the share of manufactured exports as a percentage of their total exports varies widely, ranging from a high of 95 percent in the case of South Korea to between 20 and 40 percent for the ABM group (Turner and McMullen 1982).

THE NICs AND THE INTERNATIONAL DIVISION OF LABOR

The progress made by the newly industrializing countries during the past two decades is a reflection of the liberal international economic order that the world has enjoyed since the end of World War II. The economic order is founded on the twin pillars of the Bretton Woods Agreement and GATT. In spite of all its imperfections, the present order has enabled countries to escape poverty by taking advantage of the international division of labor. The NICs have been able to sell their goods and services by acquiring a comparative economic advantage in certain sectors. As a rule, they have started with developing such labor-intensive industries as textile and apparel and footwear. They have moved on to the higher value-added, more capital-intensive intermediate industries such as steel, shipbuilding, consumer electronics, office machines, and automobiles. When further progress is made, and as skills and wages rise correspondingly, the NICs should shed the labor-intensive and low value-added industries that were developed during the first phase of their industrialization. Some, such as Korea and Brazil, already compete in the lower end of the high-tech industries, while others, such as Singapore, make components and peripherals for the high-tech industries in the West.

INDUSTRIALIZATION STRATEGY

All the NICs have not based their industrialization on the same strategy. Hong Kong and Singapore have retained their traditional character as free ports. Their industries are protected neither by tariffs nor quotas. The other NICs have adopted strategies that combined export promotion and import substitution. In the early 1960s South Korea and Taiwan turned away from import substitution policies. They liberalized imports, unified and decontrolled exchange rates, and initiated programs to encourage exports. Brazil also adopted an export-oriented policy in the late 1960s. Argentina and Mexico followed in the late 1970s. India never shifted course and continued to adhere to a policy of import substitution. Under Rajiv Gandhi, there are signs to suggest that India may be reconsidering its policy. Following the oil shock of 1973 South Korea and Brazil reversed course and tilted toward import-substitution policies. In recent years, however, South Korea has initiated adjustment measures including the liberalization of import restrictions. Brazil and Mexico, because of their debt crisis and the need to generate surpluses to service their debts, have adopted aggressive export policies and discouraged imports.

HEADING TOWARD SLOWER GROWTH?

In the decade between 1973 to 1984, the four Asian NICs—Korea, Taiwan, Hong Kong, and Singapore—achieved a real growth rate of between 7 and 8 percent. During the same decade, Brazil and Mexico grew at the slower rate of between 4 and 5 percent. Nevertheless, 1985 may have been a watershed year, and the NICs may be entering a new phase of slower growth. In 1985 South Korea, Taiwan, and Hong Kong grew only at between 2 and 4 percent. Singapore actually suffered a decline of 1.7 percent in its economy (World Bank 1986).

THE NICs AND INTERNATIONAL TRADE

According to a study by GATT, six of the NICs were among the top twenty exporters in world merchandise trade in 1984. Taiwan, which ranked twenty-seventh a decade earlier, had moved into the twelfth position, accounting for 1.6 percent of the value of world exports. South Korea, which ranked thirty-fifth a decade earlier, had moved into the fourteenth position, accounting for 1.5 percent of the value of world exports. Hong Kong, which ranked twenty-fourth a decade earlier, had moved into the fifteenth position, accounting for 1.5 percent of the value of world exports. Brazil, which ranked nineteenth a decade earlier, had moved into the sixteenth position, accounting for 1.4 percent of the value of world exports. Mexico, which ranked forty-first a decade earlier, had moved into the nineteenth position, accounting for 1.3 percent of the value of world exports. Singapore, which ranked twenty-third a decade earlier, had moved into the twentieth position, accounting for 1.3 percent of the value of world exports (General Agreement on Tariffs and Trade 1985).

If the NICs have become major exporters in world trade, have they also become major importers? According to the same GATT study four of the NICs were among the top twenty importers in world merchandise trade in 1984. South Korea, which occupied the twenty-ninth position in 1973, had moved to the twelfth position, accounting for 1.5 percent of the value of world imports. Singapore, which was in the twenty-fourth position in 1973, had moved to the fifteenth position in 1984, accounting for 1.4 percent of the value of world imports. Hong Kong had moved from the twenty-second to the sixteenth position, accounting for 1.4 percent of the value of world imports. Taiwan had moved from the thirty-first to the twentieth position, accounting for 1.1 percent of the value of world imports.

Three inferences can be drawn from the above statistics. First, the statistics confirmed the proposition that dynamic suppliers are also dynamic customers. Second, the four Asian NICs—Korea, Taiwan, Hong Kong, and Singapore—are importing as much as they are exporting and are therefore behaving as good members of the international trading system. Third, the Latin American NICs—Brazil and Mexico—appear to have much more protected markets than the Asian NICs. This probably accounts for the fact that although Brazil and Mexico are among the world's top twenty exporters they are not among the top twenty importers.

THE NICs AND GATT

It is difficult to generalize about the attitude of the NICs toward GATT and toward the new round of multilateral trade negotiations. Singapore's attitude toward GATT is very positive. We recognize, of course, that GATT has many imperfections. For example, its coverage is inadequate as is its dispute settlement mechanism. We also acknowledge, with regret, that an increasing percentage of world trade is being transacted outside the framework of GATT. Nevertheless, we attach great importance to GATT because the relatively open trading system that we have enjoyed for the past forty years would have been impossible without it.

ATTITUDES TOWARD THE NEW ROUND

There is no unanimity in the attitude of the NICs toward the new round of multilateral trade negotiations. Countries such as Singapore support the new round, whereas Brazil and India remain opposed to it. In my view the NICs should support the new round. Their prosperity is vitally dependent on the continued access of their exports to the markets of the developed countries. There are strong forces in all the developed countries demanding the imposition of barriers against imports. The coalition of interests that supports free trade in the developed countries is weaker today than it has ever been in the postwar period. A new trade round is therefore in the interest of the NICs because it may succeed in holding back the tide of protectionism and in lowering the existing barriers to free trade.

The NICs should not be opposed to putting everything—the labor-intensive industries, the intermediate industries, high-technology industries, agriculture, and services—on the negotiating table. There must be a mutuality of interest for the new round to succeed. If the NICs are interested in the labor-intensive industries and the intermediate industries, they must accommodate the interest of the developed countries in the high-technology industries and in services. Indeed, a probable outcome of the negotiations would be that the developed countries agree to keep open their markets for the manufactured exports of the NICs in exchange for the NICs' agreeing to open their markets to the high-technology exports and services of the developed countries.

U.S. POLICY TOWARD THE NICs

The United States should not shut out the manufactured exports of the NICs. Imports of consumer goods from the NICs is in the interest of U.S. consumers. Such imports have helped to reduce the rate of inflation in the United States. The export earnings of the NICs have enabled them to become customers for U.S. exports. In 1982, 44.9 percent of U.S. exports of machinery and transport equipment went to the developing countries. In the same year, the developing countries also accounted for 61.4 percent of U.S. exports of construction machinery, 59.8 percent of electrical devices, and 54.9 percent of telecommunications equipment. The pattern of trade between the United States and Singapore is a good illustration of this thesis. From 1970 to 1983, a period of fourteen years, the United States enjoyed a trade surplus with Singapore each year ("New Awareness" 1984).

Do imports from the NICs threaten the jobs of U.S. workers in competing industries? During the past five years, the U.S. dollar has appreciated between 40 and 100 percent against the currencies of the other ten major industrialized countries. The overvalued dollar has been the principal cause of making U.S. industries uncompetitive in the world market. Many of the U.S. industries that have lost jobs to foreign competition are the mature industries that have lost or are losing their comparative economic advantage and are in a state of decline anyway. These industries are faced with four choices: innovate, automate, emigrate, or terminate. An industry that is losing its competitive edge to foreign competitors can, through innovation or automation, increase its productivity and thereby recover its competitive edge. I am told by a friend in the Department of Commerce that as a result of innovation and automation, one of the factories owned by Goodyear succeeded in increasing its productivity tenfold or by 1,000 percent. If the mature industries do not or cannot recover their competitive edge through innovation or automation, they are faced with two stark alternatives—either to emigrate or to allow the plant to fail. In the event that plants in the mature industries are shut down, the United States can do a good job in retraining and otherwise assisting the workers who are laid off for employment in other growth industries.

Do the NICs demand access to the markets of the developed countries but remain highly protective of their own markets? Do the NICs indulge in unfair trade practices? If these allegations are true, isn't the United States justified in retaliating against the NICs by imposing tariffs and quotas against their exports?

Not all the NICs are alike, and it is necessary to differentiate them. For example, Hong Kong and Singapore are practically free ports. They do not subsidize their industries. They do not protect their industries against foreign competition by imposing tariffs, quotas, or other more devious devices. Their markets are open to the exports of all countries in the world. I shall quote only one statistic to illustrate my point. In 1984, 96 percent of U.S. exports entered Singapore without duty or quota. By contrast, only 25 percent of Singapore's exports entered the United States duty free (Staff Studies Mission 1987). On the other hand, some other NICs are highly protective of their own markets. Instead of erecting barriers against the exports of those NICs that are protectionist or that indulge in unfair trade practices, it would be better for the United States to demand that they dismantle their barriers and stop their unfair trade practices. The U.S. demand that all countries must compete on a level playing field is a fair one.

A number of senators have cosponsored a bill, the GSP bill (S.1867), which would have the effect of graduating Hong Kong, Taiwan, Korea, and possibly other NICs from GSP eligibility. I am not sure why the cosponsors of the bill are not satisfied with the U.S. GSP contained in the 1984 Trade and Tariff Act. The 1984 Trade and Tariff Act extended the U.S. GSP for a further period of eight and one-half years. The act, however, envisages both country graduation and product graduation. A country that attains a per capita income of $8,500 will be graduated. The act requires that the president complete within two years a general review that determines which products from which countries are sufficiently competitive. In those instances where the determination is affirmative, lower competitive need limits, set at 25 percent and $25 million, will be applied. Otherwise, the current limits of 50 percent and $57.7 million will continue to apply. The renewed program will place considerable emphasis on the extent to which the beneficiary countries are offering adequate market access to U.S. exports, protecting U.S. intellectual property rights, eliminating trade-distorting investment practices, and ensuring various worker rights. It is unclear why the U.S. Congress wants to alter a program that it enacted only a year ago and before it has been fully implemented. It also appears unfair for the Senate GSP bill to target Hong Kong for graduation. Hong Kong is, after all, one of the world's two fairest trading nations. It is a model that should be held out for other NICs to emulate. Hong Kong should therefore be rewarded not penalized for its good behavior. It also appears unfair to single out the Asian NICs for graduation because they are not saddled with huge debts. Prudent financial management should be rewarded and not punished.

Finally, the United States has an economic, strategic, and ideological stake in the success of the newly industrializing countries. It is no accident that none of the NICs is a communist country. In the battle for the hearts and minds of the world's peoples—between democracy and the free enterprise economic system on the one hand and communism and the centrally planned economy on the other—the West has an ideological stake in the success of the NICs. If the NICs succeed, the West can use them as examples for the rest of the Third World. I would also observe that coincidentally, the Asian NICs are either allies or friends of the United States. Because of their economic progress, they are able to devote a substantial share of their GNP to defense and thereby assist the United States in maintaining stability in East and Southeast Asia.

REFERENCES

General Agreement on Tariffs and Trade. 1985. "Prospects for International Trade." Reference no. GATT/1374. Geneva: GATT.

"New Awareness of U.S.-Third World Ties Wins Converts in Free Trade." 1984. *National Journal*, September 22, p. 1759.

Staff Studies Mission. 1987. *U.S. Trade Relations with Asia.* Report prepared for the Committee on Foreign Affairs. Reference no. 68-021. Washington, D.C.: U.S. Government Printing Office.

Turner, Louis, and Neil McMullen, eds. 1982. *The Newly Industrializing Countries: Trade and Adjustment.* Winchester, Mass.: Allen & Unwin.

9 ECONOMIC DEVELOPMENTS IN CHINA AND SINO-AMERICAN RELATIONS

Robert F. Dernberger

Economic relations between the United States and China are not the only considerations determining the political relations between these two major economies that lie opposite each other on the rim of the Pacific. Yet economic relations are a central issue in Sino-U.S. relations and deserve the special attention given them in this chapter. The time and space available, however, preclude a detailed analysis of those economic relations here. Rather, our purpose is limited to briefly laying out major features of economic policy developments in China today, the role played by the foreign sector in those developments, and the specific problems within the foreign sector that influence Sino-U.S. relations. We conclude with a few arguments concerning economic developments in China that are believed important in determining Sino-U.S. relations in the future but that may be considered debatable or uncertain at the present time.

CHINA'S PROGRAM OF ECONOMIC REFORM

Unlike most other developing countries and territories in Asia, since the mid-1950s China has been an Asian example of a Soviet-type, centrally planned economy. With abundant resources and excess supplies of labor, the use of the Soviet-type economy to do what it does best—to mobilize resources by means of forced savings for the extensive creation of new production facilities, especially in the heavy industrial sector—yielded one of the highest average annual growth rates in national income among all the developing countries and territories over the past three decades. Unfortunately, this statistical success was accompanied by another attribute of the Soviet-type economy: The high rates of growth in gross material output were matched by equally rapid increases in inputs, and there was limited evidence for a process of sustained or true economic modernization, such as increases in efficiency and productivity; the introduction of innovations on a regular basis and significant technological change throughout the economy; and steady increases in the standard of living, a true test of successful economic development.

The neglect of specialization and efficiency over a prolonged period meant that the Chinese lost their comparative advantage in agricultural production, while the neglect of nonproductive investments in social overhead capital and infrastructure created serious shortages in these areas. These problems are often found in other Soviet-type economies but were made worse in the case of China due to both poor central planning (that is, concentrating on targets for key items and neglecting supply-and-demand conditions for other commodities) and an attempt to implement impractical or counterproductive Maoist economic principles (that is, equitable distribution of income, self-sufficiency, and eliminating markets, material incentives, and other "vestiges" of capitalism). By the mid-1970s the Chinese economy was well within its production possibilities frontier, and there was no basis for believing that the problem was cyclical rather than secular.

The Deng/Zhao leadership was fully aware of the unfavorable comparison between China's economic development and that in many of the other countries of Asia by the time they emerged as the head of the new post-Mao leadership coalition. As a result, they have overseen the adoption and implementation of an extensive program of economic reforms. The package of economic reforms are just that—a great number of very diverse individual policy innovations, many on an experimental basis; they are not a collection of uniform and integrated policies adopted on the basis of a well-defined master plan, nor is that their purpose. Quite simply, the Chinese are feeling their way to a new and unique Chinese-brand of socialism.

Yet, given our assignment, we must try to capture the essence of the economic reform program rather than emphasize its tremendous diversity and lack of uniformity or consistency. In basic terms, these reform policies represent a rejection of the big-push development strategy (Stalin's development strategy) in favor of a balanced-growth development strategy (Bukharin's development strategy). Even more emphatically, the economic reforms reject the Maoist economic principles in favor of establishing a socialist commodity economy with markets and material incentives, specialization, and the division of labor, as well as greater involvement in the world economy.

As for systemic reforms, ultimate objectives and the actual steps to be taken to achieve those objectives are much less easily identified or defined at the present time. Essentially, systemic reform got started in the agricultural sector, as much due to local initiative as to central direction, focusing on the contract responsibility system that had been experimented with in the early 1960s. Eventually, the central leadership judged this reform to be a success and now claims it as their own "correct policy" for the solution of China's agricultural problem. At the present time, production decisions and income allocations are made within the basic unit—the household—subject to its share of the welfare fund contributions, the agricultural tax payments, and the quota deliveries assigned by the state planners. The apex of the collective system, the commune, is being done away with and replaced by the reestablished unit of local government, the township. Some collective activities remain at the village level, run by the old brigade-level cooperative or by new voluntary associations of peasant households. As for the assigned quotas of output to be sold to the state, that system is being replaced by negotiated, advanced-purchase contracts between the household and state purchasing agencies. Finally, markets, sideline activities, village private businesses, and cooperative and state industries at the local level are flourishing in the rural areas.

On the basis of this very popular and successful reform of the agricultural sector, reform of the urban-industrial sector became official party policy at the end of 1984. Still being introduced, the attempt is being made to decentralize decisionmaking to stimulate local initiative and skills for promoting greater efficiency and productivity throughout the industrial sector. For this purpose, each enterprise is to be removed from the budget and is now responsible for its own profits and losses, paying a profits tax to the state. Investment funds can come from self-provided funds, bank loans, and loans from the state. Labor can be hired and fired by the enterprise, and enterprises can go bankrupt. Private and cooperative enterprises can exist and compete with state enterprises. Private commerce and trade are to be allowed to promote competition, while mandatory plans and uni-lateral budget grants for investment are to be limited to sectors and enterprises producing essential commodities.

In the area most relevant to our purposes in this chapter—the search for technological change and increases in productivity and efficiency—the Deng/Zhao leadership has rejected the pursuit of autarkic development of the economy in isolation from the world economy. Compared with the past, the Chinese have clearly opened their economy, seeking significantly higher levels of trade, foreign loans, and even direct foreign investment. The decentralization of decisionmaking also has been adopted in the foreign trade sector, allowing some local enterprises and units of government to negotiate directly with the foreigner. As a result, the demand for imports great-ly exceeded the supply of exports, and, therefore, attention in both China and the West has focused on the policy reforms having to do with foreign loans and investment as a way of offsetting this deficit in the current account and to more effectively transfer modern tech-nology to China.

Foreign loans—especially cheap, concessionary loans from inter-national financial institutions (The World Bank, IMF, and so forth)—are being obtained by the central government and included in the budget as a revenue item. In addition, Chinese banks, local govern-ments, investment companies, and even individual enterprises have, on occasion, been allowed to borrow directly from abroad, especially from foreign banks and in foreign money markets—that is, by selling bonds abroad. Foreign investment in joint-ventures, partnerships, coproduction facilities, and in a wide variety of arrangements has been allowed and encouraged. Direct investment in wholly owned foreign subsidiaries, especially in those areas where the Chinese econ-omy does not produce the product domestically, lacks similar up-to-date production techniques, or the investment provides a service largely for foreign visitors, are also allowed and encouraged. Finally, foreign banks have been allowed to open branches in China and re-ceive deposits and provide consulting services, although the Chinese authorities have not allowed these offices to engage in normal credit operations within the domestic economy.

The Chinese authorities, of course, exercise tight controls over these new foreign sources of investment financing, but their desire to utilize this source is reflected in their attempt to encourage the initiative of local authorities to promote a more rapid transfer of modern technology from abroad in newly created foreign investment parks and special economic zones (SEZs). Specific regions and cities have been allowed to negotiate foreign loans and investments directly with the foreigner, granting the foreign investor various financial concessions as inducements for investing in China. The four SEZs along the coast and Hainan Island have been granted the broadest powers in this regard, but fourteen cities were declared open to the foreign investor with only slightly more stringent regulations imposed by the central authorities. The province of Guangdong and Fujian (where many families have relatives living in Southeast Asia and overseas) also have been given some freedom to negotiate foreign loans and investment in these provinces.

This very brief and sketchy review of the economic reform program must suffice but should convey the accurate impression of the range and dramatic change involved in the economic reform program. The current political leadership has made a serious commitment to seeing the economic reform program through, and we can expect the process of new regulations and policy statements to continue. Announced regulations and policy statements in Beijing, however, cannot be interpreted as actual policy implementation or results. How effectively have these reforms been implemented, and what has their impact been on economic performance?

THE IMPLEMENTATION AND IMPACT OF THE ECONOMIC REFORMS

There is much debate over the extent to which support for the reforms is uniform throughout the top leadership and at lower levels of the bureaucracy and the extent to which opponents have blocked their effective implementation. There is always considerable slippage between policy announced in Beijing and their implementation at the local level, and the economic reforms are no exception. In addition, various members of the top leadership are not in complete agreement with every aspect of the reform program, especially the opening of the economy, despite the general consensus in support of the need for economic reform. Attempts to modernize China by opening the economy have been tried and have failed at various times over the past century, and potential opponents in the future may well rally around an attack on the extent to which the economic reform program involves dependence on the foreigner and foreign influences. Whether or not his followers will have built up their political base to sustain the economic reforms in the face of opposition after Deng dies is yet to be tested, but Deng has displayed remarkable skill in securing critical appointments and promotions within the political and bureaucratic system to significantly increase the chances of continued economic reform in the post-Deng period.

A different type of problem involves the quality of the human inputs—their skills, values, and behavior. Some of the Maoist principles drew on traditional Chinese values, and personal relations have always been more important than regularized, impersonal decision-making rules in business management. Modern management skills are in short supply, and bureaucrats in China will find it difficult to administer economic policies without becoming directly involved in the operations of the economic unit concerned—despite instructions to do so. In other words, the success of the reforms is tied up with the transformation of the Chinese management class—both political and economic management. That transformation will take time, and much of the present problem in implementing the economic reforms is related to the pace of this transformation. To identify this problem as opposition to the economic reforms, however, is incorrect. This problem should be alleviated as skills and experience are acquired and the older generation, born and raised in the Soviet-type economy, retires.

It has been pointed out above that the degree to which the economic reform program is identified as a Western solution to China's economic problem may well reduce support for that program in the future, and, unfortunately, some of the new managerial class sought to staff the economic and political bureaucracy exhibit values, behavior, and dress that are readily identified as Western. In fact, many of this class are being trained in the West or in China by Westerners. This problem of "spiritual pollution" that draws on memories of the sad history of China over the last century is not now as serious as it could be, largely due to the economic success of the economic reforms or—more properly stated—the widely held perception of their success.

Both aggregate output and the standard of living for both rural and urban residents have increased significantly in the post-1978 period. Between 1978 and 1985, national income increased by 8.8 percent a year (State Statistical Bureau 1986: 41), while in 1978–84 per capita income increased by 9.3 percent a year for peasants (State Statistical Bureau 1986: 576) and by 4.1 percent for nonagricultural families (State Statistical Bureau 1986: 582). Cited by both Chinese and outside observers as "the results" of the economic reform program, there can be little doubt that this empirical evidence is the source of considerable support for and encouragement to the advocates of the reform program. Yet serious econometric analyses of these statistical results and common sense indicate other factors are at work as well. First of all, the Chinese economy was in terrible shape in the mid-1970s, and the return to power of any rational government, eliminating the worst excesses and stupid mistakes of their predecessors, would lead to considerable improvement in the economy. Good weather and higher prices for output didn't hurt either. Thus, it is not surprising that the one attempt to decompose the sources of growth in agriculture that I am familiar with assigns the introduction of the systemic changes credit for about 40 percent of the increase in output in 1978–84, but the contribution of this one-time change declines over time and explains little of the increase in output by the year 1984 (Lin 1985). In fact, by 1984 most of the increase in output in the agricultural sector comes from the rapid expansion of rural industry, not traditional agricultural activities.

The urban-industrial sector, compared with the rural sector, involves a considerably greater degree of interdependence and diverse levels and sources of administrative controls. Thus, coordinating the decentralization of decisionmaking in this sector is a rather complicated problem, and most units of production find that they have gained some freedom to determine their output and allocation of that output, greater authority over their labor force and capital, and access to greater amounts of retained earnings. At the same time, there remain many administrative controls, plan targets for many outputs, and central distribution of many critical inputs. In some cases, central authorities' control over the running of the enterprise has been transferred to local authorities, who are able to exercise more direct and greater administrative control than the central authorities were ever able to achieve in the past. Quite simply, although there has been a considerable decentralization of decision-making in the economy and a significantly greater role played by markets and market prices in those decisions, the Chinese have a long way to go before achieving true market socialism, and the present system is permeated with contradictions and opposing forces.

As for results, most econometric studies of the available data indicate that investment and increases in inputs remain the dominant explanation for increases in outputs. Energy and transport bottlenecks remain at critical levels. The existing mix of planning and central controls versus markets and local decisionmaking heavily favors the central authorities. Yet as a result of their attempt to decentralize decisionmaking and allow greater revenue sharing and retained earnings at the local level, the central authorities have simply lost control over some major activities; investment, imports, wages and bonuses, bank loans, house building, and so forth. This has led to inflation, budget deficits, and balance of payments problems—all problems commonly associated with Western capitalist countries and claimed to have been eliminated in China under socialism.

In fact, the economic reforms have created a serious dilemma, an opening of Pandora's box by the leadership. For example, by allowing local units to retain a larger share of revenues and earnings at the local level, local units have reacted to this opportunity with a vengeance and have accumulated a large pool of funds outside the control of the central authorities, using those funds for investment in projects that create employment and produce goods in demand locally. These small-scale, local enterprises are less efficient than the state-run, large-scale enterprises. Thus, the macrostatistics fail to show a dramatic improvement in profits and productivity.

To remedy this situation—that is, to make local decisions serve national rather than just local interests—two additional reforms are needed. Otherwise, the reform program remains incomplete. For decisions to be rational (in terms of national interests and economic efficiency at the macrolevel), prices must be rational. Much of China's price system still relies on administratively determined and fixed prices. Although real price reform has been repeatedly postponed, the Chinese reformers have tried to carry out a partial reform by having three prices for many commodities—the state's fixed price, a price that can be adjusted within limits, and a market price. This creates a real struggle, the buyer desiring to buy from the state at the fixed price, while the seller tries to sell on the market. In other words, the local unit tries to get its inputs within the state sector and dispose of its output in the market sector; the state tries to achieve the opposite result.

A second problem is the need to introduce true competition among units of production by opening up trading channels and transport—that is, by breaking down the administrative barriers to free trade that exist throughout China. Not only do the Chinese lack the material facilities for the free flow of commodities throughout the economy, local resistance to eliminate the administrative barriers that protect local enterprises or to attempts by the state to close down inefficient or unnecessary enterprises from the "national interest" point of view is quite strong. Having just won the ability to finance their own local industrial projects, local authorities and cooperatives as well as individuals have done so, and the results far exceeded the level of planned investment. Thus, local industry is the fastest-growing sector in the economy, responsible for a significant share of the impressive growth rate. These enterprises have provided rapidly expanding employment opportunities in the rural sector and are responsible for a significant amount of the increases in per capita incomes. The state authorities will find it very difficult to close these enterprises in the name of increasing efficiency, eliminating duplication and waste, and opening local enterprises to outside competition.

As for the attempt to open the Chinese economy to greater involvement in foreign trade, that reform also was more successful than intended. Foreign trade has grown rapidly—more rapidly than national income—and China's foreign trade dependency ratio therefore has increased. Between 1978 and 1985 exports increased by 14.9 percent a year, but imports increased by 17.4 percent, very large import surpluses being generated in 1979 and 1985 (*Statistical Yearbook of China* 1986: 481). If converted into domestic currency at a true purchasing power parity exchange rate, the foreign trade dependency rate would be exceptionally high for a continental economy of China's size and level of per capita income.

Although never abandoning the open economy policy, each period of decentralization and relaxed control over foreign trade has resulted in a rapid increase in imports and an import surplus that was getting out of control, leading to the reimposition of strong central control over foreign exchange allocations and imports. With a few key commodity categories—such as textiles, petroleum, and raw materials—still dominating China's list of exports, growth in import demand runs far ahead of foreign exchange earnings in the current account in the balance of payments. The threat of this secular import surplus is a serious problem that faces the advocates of economic reform in China and is a major reason that they place so much emphasis on the need for foreign investment.

The attempt to diversify the domestic sources of investment financing to complement moves to decentralize decisionmaking throughout the economy has generated local funds and investments well above the reformers expectations. Nevertheless, attempts to secure foreign loans and investment to facilitate acquisition of foreign technology at a rate more rapid than current foreign exchange earnings from exports would allow appear to have fallen far short of expectations, hopes, or needs. The initial surge of enthusiastic borrowing from abroad has been muted as the Chinese soon discovered that cheap, concessionary loans were not available on a scale large enough to underwrite a large portion of China's investment program, and the increases in outpayments of interest and principal on commercial loans soon caught up with the borrowing of new money. Thus, foreign loans rose to a peak in 1981, accounting for almost 7 percent of the state's financial revenue and over one-fifth the value of budget allocations for capital construction investment in that year (Dernberger forthcoming: tables). Since then, however, their annual level has declined to the point where foreign loans account for less than 2 percent of budget revenue and about 5 percent of capital construction in the state sector. The Chinese have not made significant use of commercial credit as a source of investment financing; this source accounted for only 6 percent of total foreign loans and investment in 1979–85.

A key feature of the open-economy policy is the attempt to obtain direct foreign investment. Thus far, however, most foreign investment has been in the form of money—that is, foreign loans. Of the $21.5 billion U.S. in foreign investment the Chinese utilized in 1979–85, 72.6 percent was accounted for by foreign loans. Furthermore, of the $4.6 billion U.S. of direct foreign investment, much of that was cooperative and joint ventures with overseas Chinese in processing industries in which the Chinese had already mastered the technology involved—if not modern managerial and operating procedures. Direct foreign investment made thus far by non-Chinese has been concentrated in the offshore oil projects and in hotels and other service industries serving foreigners in China. Chinese criticism of the SEZs and open cities argues that the Chinese investment required has exceeded the foreign investment obtained, little new technology is being brought to China, and rather than promote exports and the earning of foreign exchange, the products of these projects are finding their way into the domestic market to compete with domestic products. Despite the significant publicity given to foreign direct investment projects being discussed or suggested by the Chinese, direct foreign investment remains less than 5 percent of China's total investment.

CONCLUDING ARGUMENTS

There are several important conclusions explicitly stated or implicit in the above discussion or based on analyses of contemporary developments in China presented elsewhere that should serve as guides to policy formation in regard to U.S. relations with China in the future.

1. China is a growth economy where rather impressive growth rates in aggregate output are commonly observed. Yet these alone do not signify successful economic development. In fact, several decades of impressive growth rates with limited increases in productivity and the standard of living led the current leadership to reject past policies and introduce a significant program of economic reforms.

2. The economic reforms are an attempt to partially decentralize economic decisionmaking and control over resources, while retaining considerable central authority over the economy. They allow market forces to play a significant role within the basic context of a planned economy and open the economy to greater foreign trade and investment, while protecting domestic producers from foreign competition. In short, this partial reform tries to develop a true mixed economy in a step-by-step manner. Yet the very partial and staggered means by which the reforms are introduced means that their negative aspects cause delays in proceeding with the reforms, and the failure to proceed with complementary and necessary further reforms means that those already introduced do not achieve their desired effects. Considerable attention has been paid to how dramatically the reforms already introduced have changed the Chinese economy and how far the Chinese have gone in introducing economic

reforms; much more important to the success of the reforms is how much farther they must go to make the reforms work. Efficiency and productivity have improved, but serious imbalances and inefficiencies remain.

3. In assessing support for the reforms, political and administrative opposition and lack of skills are cited as major problems, while the economic results are cited as a major argument in favor of the reform. Yet the transformation of the party and bureaucracy will not happen overnight. The progress made by Deng and his followers, thus far, is truly remarkable and has considerably reduced this threat to the reforms. The economic results, as favorable as they have been or are perceived to have been, are not as encouraging as they may seem. When everyone's income is rising, things are fine. But when the rate of increase slows and inflation eats into real income gains, while growing inequality of incomes becomes more noticeable and leads to considerable differences in styles of living, support for the reforms may wane. As the one-time increase in output and incomes due to institutional changes, higher prices, changing product mix, and so forth wears off and the pace of growth slows, does the support for more and greater institutional changes increase, or is there a call for retreat and consolidation of existing institutional changes? As decentralization leads to budget deficits, inflation, unemployment, balance of payments deficits in the current account, and so forth, do the authorities push forward with more reforms and decentralization or try to strengthen the control of the central authorities over the economy? As the going gets tougher and the results less dramatic, will the Chinese keep pushing forward, or will the critics and popular opinion turn against the reforms?

4. Whatever the outcome of the economic reform program, China's economic problem must be solved by the Chinese themselves. They will be the ones who adapt and implement the institutional changes that will make up their new economic system. They will staff the bureaucracy and management positions that will determine how well that system will work. The level and allocation of investment will remain one of the most important determinants of growth, and the bulk of the resources devoted to investment will come from domestic savings.

5. Foreign supplies of technology and funds, of course, would greatly facilitate domestic Chinese efforts to develop their economy.

Foreign sources of funds, however, are likely to remain less than 10 percent of total investment due to one or both of two considerations—(a) very conservative Chinese attitudes toward both foreign loans and investment and an unwillingness to modify existing policies and regulations (or lack of regulations) to make these more favorable to foreign investors and (b) the slow growth or even decline in the availability of foreign public and private loans and investment for the developing countries in Asia.

6. Increased reliance on imports of technology and capital goods or growing foreign trade is important and is an obvious objective of the "open economy" policy. Thus, although foreign investment will be limited to key projects financed by the foreigner, a great many more investment projects will rely on imported technology and equipment paid for by the Chinese with domestic savings. This will lead to a foreign exchange problem in the process of converting domestic savings into domestic investment. In other words, a failure to resolve the problem of needing to earn foreign exchange to pay for the import needs of China's development program would force the Chinese to seek more foreign loans and direct investment, despite the surplus of domestic savings.

7. Faced with this dilemma, the Chinese could (a) increase the degree to which they are willing to open their economy to foreign investment and change their conservative attitude toward foreign loans; (b) reduce their development program to make it more consistent with the available foreign investment and import capacity; and (c) revert to past practices of greater self-sufficiency. Choice (c) is the least desirable. Choice (a) is probably politically impossible and would be difficult to achieve or sustain. Foreign loans and investment on the scale needed may not be available, and having spent 100 years of struggle to restore their national pride and independence, the Chinese are unlikely to follow the foreign dependency route of several other countries of the Third World. Thus, the foreign exchange constraint may become the major constraint on China's future economic development.

8. Especially in relation to U.S. policy, however, it is very important to note that more foreign loans and investment are not the only way to remove this constraint. In fact, most experts believe that it was export-promotion policies and not foreign loans and investments that explains the successful economic growth programs in the newly

developed countries and territories of Asia. Thus, in terms of China's successful economic development, the resolution of the trade problems between the United States and China—controls on the export to China of U.S. technology and quotas on imports from China—may be a much more important and difficult task than seeking to induce the Chinese to change their attitudes about and policies on foreign loans and investment.

REFERENCES

State Statistical Bureau, People's Republic of China. 1986. *Statistical Yearbook of China.* Hong Kong: Economic Information Agency.

Lin, Justin Yifu. 1985. The Household Responsibility System in China's Agricultural Reform: A Theoretical and Empirical Study of an Institutional Reform. Ph.D. diss., University of Chicago.

Dernberger, Robert F. Forthcoming. "Financing China's Development: Needs, Sources and Prospects." In Financing Asian Development: China and India in *Asian Agenda Report* no. 8. The Asia Society.

10 INDIA
New Policies and Potentials

Richard S. Eckaus

India is changing direction in its important economic policies as a new generation of political leaders and their advisers reshape major guiding premises. The reworking of guidelines began in the last months of the leadership of Indira Gandhi. After her assassination, the assumption of the prime ministership by Rajiv Gandhi, and his confirmation in the elections of 1985, it became clear that there would be new policy positions.

These new policies have not been set out in detail, and it is always difficult to distinguish intentions from effective commitments in Indian planning documents, simply because they are so comprehensive. However, by focusing on the changes in emphasis, the general directions of movement can be discerned. Although changes are being considered in many areas, attention will be concentrated here on innovations that are of particular interest and significance for the United States: (1) liberalization of the economy by reduction of quantitative government controls and increased reliance on price incentives; (2) stimulation of exports and increased receptivity to imports and foreign investment; (3) increased recourse to private international loans.

To provide a background for the appraisal of these initiatives, the next section will review briefly economic trends and policies since

The author is indebted to Ms. Lakshmi Kapoor and to Mr. Dan Kessler for invaluable assistance.

117

independence. After that, the apparent content and significance for India of the new policy proposals will be examined. The possible implications for the U.S. economy and U.S. policy will then be considered.

ECONOMIC TRENDS SINCE INDEPENDENCE

Indian economic policy has been made in a series of Five-Year Plans starting in 1951 and broken only in the late 1960s by three Annual Plans. The successive plans provide a convenient means of tracing the patterns of Indian development that are summarized in Table 10-1.

The partition of India in 1947, the associated trauma, and the creation of a national system were the first preoccupations of the government. That delayed only slightly the formulation of the First Five-Year Plan. The assumption by the government of the responsibility for stimulating and guiding the economy was, strikingly, not the subject of major debate.

The colonial economy inherited by the First Five-Year Plan was, in terms of output proportions, roughly 50 percent agricultural, 17 percent manufacturing, 19 percent transportation, communication, and commerce, and the rest various services. Over 70 percent of the active population was occupied in agriculture, and only 9 percent in manufacturing. Although relatively small, the manufacturing sector was vigorous; it had been constrained by the English colonial system until its output became necessary for support of World War II.

The First Five-Year Plan was a collection of projects that had been in the pipeline or prepared quickly after India's independence. The plan achieved a 3.6 percent average annual growth rate, implying roughly a 1.8 percent growth rate in per capita income. The Plan seemed to demonstrate the benefits of ending colonialism and the effectiveness of national initiative. It was easy to believe that this would be followed by further successes with more attention and effort being given to economic policy.

The strategies that came to dominate most of Indian development—relatively high rates of investment with emphasis on heavy industry and import substitution to be achieved largely by means of government enterprise or government regulation of the private sector—were first formulated in the Second Plan. A severe balance-of-payments crisis occurred during the Plan, however. It was overcome

Table 10-1. Major Features of the Indian Economy (billions of 1970 rupees).

	1950	Average Annual Rate of Growth (percent)	1960	Average Annual Rate of Growth (percent)	1970	Average Annual Rate of Growth (percent)	1980	Average Annual Rate of Growth (percent)	1983
Population (millions)	358.3	1.96%	434.9	2.33%	547.6	2.30%	687.3	2.19%	733.3
Real gross national products	174.7	3.82	254.2	3.67	364.5	2.57	506.0	4.72	581.1
Consumption	147.1	3.72	212.0	3.48	298.4	3.00	400.9	4.97	463.7
Investment	23.8	6.64	45.2	4.73	71.8	5.40	121.4	1.86	128.3
Government	8.9	8.03	19.2	7.05	38.0	6.86	73.8	9.98	98.1
Net exports	-5.1	15.94	-22.3	6.97	-43.6	11.29	-127.1	-5.04	-108.9
Domestic saving	23.3	4.63	36.7	6.34	67.8	5.26	113.3	2.28	121.2
Foreign saving	-0.5	25.89	8.5	-7.26	3.9	7.55	8.2	-4.81	7.0
Gross national product/capita, rupees	487.6	2.07	598.4	1.07	665.7	1.01	736.2	2.49	792.5
Consumption/capita, rupees	410.5	1.74	487.6	1.12	544.9	0.68	583.3	2.73	632.3
Domestic savings/gross national product	0.13		0.14		0.19		0.22		0.21
Investment/gross national product	0.14		0.18		0.20		0.24		0.22

Source: The World Bank.

with increased recourse to a system of quantitative import controls that had been put in place during the World War II period and by the start of a large foreign economic assistance program in which the United States played the major role. Yet the Plan was considered a major success. The average annual growth rate, at 4 percent, was even higher than during the First Plan, and the development strategies appeared to be vindicated.

The Third Five-Year Plan was, in some ways, a high-water mark in Indian economic policy. The "big plan" advocates won the support of Nehru, and the rationale of investment in heavy industry was developed further. An extensive system of controls over investment, imports, and prices had been developed by this time, and it was clear from the comprehensive detail of the Plan that the civil service had learned a great deal about programming the economy. All of this appeared to work well after a slow start due to the Sino-Indian border war in 1962. The average annual growth rate increased to 4.5 percent.

Preparations for the Fourth Plan indicated that it would continue the tactics of the Third Plan when it became apparent that, after the unusually favorable monsoons of the 1950s and 1960s, the system was, in fact, extremely vulnerable to bad weather. The monsoon failure in the last year of the Third Plan was one of the worst of the century, and the consequent drought affected manufacturing as well as agricultural output. Falling agricultural incomes reduced the demand for industrial goods, and the falling levels of the hydroelectric reservoirs reduced the supply of electric power for all production sectors as well as for consumers.

The disruption of the economy due to the drought was compounded by the conflict with Pakistan in 1965, and that, in turn, contributed indirectly to a reduction in foreign economic assistance. The sudden death in 1966 of prime minister Lal Bahadur Shastri, the successor to Nehru, inaugurated a period of political uncertainty as well. The Fourth Plan was postponed, and a series of three annual plans was started. These contained a new emphasis on agricultural development that was stimulated not only by the economic impact of the bad weather but also by the belief that India's foreign policy had been hostage to the country's need for food-grain imports. New high-yielding varieties of wheat and rice were introduced and spread rapidly in the Green Revolution. Although there have continued to be sometimes severe droughts, agricultural output was set on a clear upward trend.

There is an active controversy as to whether the growth of the Indian economy as a whole slowed down in the late 1960s and 1970s or whether that slowdown was confined to the industrial sector. In any case, it was not until the late 1970s that the Indian economy appears to have recovered its earlier impetus.

Nonetheless, there were important policy successes in the 1970s. There were two major oil price shocks in this decade to which many developing countries responded by undertaking large-scale international borrowing in order to maintain their investment programs. As a consequence of these and other internal policies, many developing countries experienced relatively high inflation rates. Although India also felt the oil shocks, it had sharply reduced its dependence on foreign finance after 1967 through its program for food self-sufficiency. In addition, after the first oil price shock in 1973-74, the rupee was devalued, an export campaign was mounted, and a more aggressive program of oil exploration and exploitation was started. As a result in 1976 and 1977, there were small current account surpluses, and the country was able to face the second oil price shock in a relatively strong position.

Oil production increased in the late 1970s, and oil imports fell, as was also true of food-grain imports. Remittances from emigrant workers to the Arab oil-producing countries also rose rapidly. There was an increase in foreign borrowing after the second oil shock, but not on the scale of many Latin American and African countries. As a result, India entered the 1980s in a relatively strong external position.

Growth during the Fifth Plan, from 1974-75 to 1979-80, averaged only 3.7 percent but accelerated in the Sixth Plan to 5.2 percent. Although the industrial sector continued to grow relatively slowly, there was a strong upward trend in agricultural production in spite of severe droughts. There were important economic reforms in the late 1970s and early 1980s with relaxation of some government regulatory and price controls. A loan of roughly $4 billion (U.S.) was obtained from the IMF in 1981, not because of an imminent balance of payments crisis but to assist in structural adjustment toward an internationally more open and viable economy.

THE BARRIERS TO GROWTH

At its independence, India was commonly considered to be the prototype of Malthusian poverty with a population that had grown to the limits that the land would support. It was, perhaps, a residue of colonialist attitudes that inspired the identification of other, supposedly almost insurmountable barriers to development: lack of entrepreneurial spirit and nonresponsiveness to economic incentives, the low status of technical, managerial, and manual activities, and the absence of political administrative ability.

It is striking that none of these original worries have been justified by the experience of the last forty years. Taking the last set of concerns first, studies of Indian businesspeople in the early 1950s and, more important, immediate experience demonstrated that there was no lack of entrepreneurship when opportunities existed. There are, of course, sociological differences among peoples in their attitudes and these may be regional as well. But the Bengali, Gujerati, Keralan, Maharashtrian, Punjabi, and so forth farmers and businesspeople have become almost legendary entrepreneurial types. One study after another has demonstrated peasant responsiveness to economic incentives, and the training of scientists, engineers, and technicians has been limited by capacities, not by the number of applicants for enrollment.

As for political administrative ability, perhaps there has been too much of a good thing. The frequent complaint, within and outside of India, that the government interferes too much in economic life, is, undoubtedly, due in part to the fact that the Indian civil service is very good at administration. As a result, it has been given responsibilities that might not have been attempted in other places.

It would be quite inaccurate to deny the existence of population pressures in India, but they have taken a form not originally envisaged. The Indian population has not eaten up all of the output that it has produced and approached some natural limit determined by its subsistence requirements. Indian development has not been held back by a "vicious circle of poverty" that has kept savings and therefore investment at low levels and prevented growth out of poverty.

In fact, a remarkable development that has emerged, one that has been relatively little appreciated abroad, is the dramatic increase in the Indian savings rate over the last thirty years, as shown in Table 10-1. In some years domestic saving reached almost 25 percent of GNP. The Indian savings rate is now one of the highest in the world, outside of the centrally planned economies. Moreover, Indian savings have not been forced by the central government. Although public savings have grown, so have private savings, and there is little, if any, trend, up or down, in their relative shares in total savings.

Given the high levels of saving that have been achieved, it is hard to believe that, if the population growth rate had been lower, the savings rate would have been quite substantially higher. But per capita consumption would have been greater!

The problem of Indian economic growth, that was not foreseen at the outset of its postindependence development process, is the decline and continuing low levels of productivity of the economy. It is difficult to separate the economic contributions and therefore the relative changes in productivity of land, labor, and capital, but the inclination is to believe that the problem is mainly in capital productivity. Land yields in agriculture have grown, unevenly to be sure in the various states but, on the average, considerably, and the productivity problem is particularly severe in industry, in any case. Indian labor has its share of stoppages and other troubles, but with the possible exception of some of the major public enterprises, there is no general feeling that lack of diligence and skills are major barriers to increased output. Labor productivity in the private sector has actually grown substantially. Nor is Indian management lacking in organizational expertise and willingness and ability to respond to incentives.

By the late 1970s the productivity associated with new investment had fallen to less than half the levels of the first three five-year plans. The incremental capital-output ratio (ICOR), which is the change in GNP divided by the previous investment, more than doubled from a ratio of about 2.5 in the 1950s, to almost 6.0 in the 1970s. Even the current Seventh Five-Year Plan, with an emphasis on stimulating productivity, does not foresee an improvement in the ICOR. It must be emphasized again, however, that the productivity problem is not exclusively in the use of capital but represents, to varying degrees, a decline in the productivity of all resources.

There is, however, not even general agreement on the facts about the problem. One line of rebuttal is that the Indian economy is really quite efficient, with a large and flourishing underground economy. According to this claim, although investment is measured reasonably well, national output in the denominator of the ICOR is underestimated because the output of the underground economy is not included, thus making the ICOR itself larger than warranted.

It is difficult to assess this argument because it is difficult to measure the size of the underground economy. It is clear that the hypothesis does not fully explain the problem. Government-sector enterprises, where the ICOR has been the highest and labor productivity lowest, do not participate in the underground economy to an important degree, and agricultural output is measured directly. This means that most of any measurement errors in output due to the existence of an underground economy must be in the remainder of the economy, which amounts to about a third of the total. The measurement error in this third would have to be quite large to have an important effect on the calculated ICOR.

Several other explanations have been offered for the high ICORs. The Rajiv Gandhi administration emphasizes the relatively low rate of technological change in Indian industry, which affects the productivity of both capital and labor. This still leaves unexplained the reasons for the low rate of technological change. Moreover, a low rate of technological change might explain why the ICOR has not fallen, but it does not account well for why it has risen.

Another approach, instead of explaining low growth by low productivity, inverts the relation and explains low productivity by low growth. The latter results in low levels of capacity utilization, and thus high ICOR's, as investment is added to the numerator but less than full capacity output appears in the denominator. The source of the problem, it is alleged, is inadequate government investment, resulting in both supply bottlenecks, especially in electric power production and rail transport, and inadequate effective demand.

The argument that effective demand is too low due to low rates of government investment is inconsistent with the unusually high overall levels of investment. On the other hand, it is true that there are persistent complaints about electric power and rail transport supply problems. But the supply constraint argument is also not consistent with the low levels of capacity utilization in electric power production and rail transport, unless inefficient practices in these sectors are accepted as inevitable and unchangeable. Moreover, there are clear differences among the states in the degree of capacity utilization in electric power production.

The explanation for relative inefficiency that has come to be most widely accepted is that there is excessive and obstructive government interference in the economy through detailed regulation of the private sector and extensive reserved areas for ineffective public enterprise. It was noted above that, by the Third Plan period, a pervasive system of government controls over investment and imports—and, in some sectors, prices, types, and quantities of production—had been put in place. Subsequently these controls became even more extensive and specific. It is argued that these regulations have prevented private enterprise from operating efficiently. Quoting the Seventh Five-Year Plan document, itself (Government of India Planning Commission 1985: 73):

> as the economy developed and the industrial structure became more diversified and complicated, the licensing mechanism and other physical controls became more difficult to operate. With the fast growth in the number and variety of products, determining proper capacities became increasingly unsatisfactory. At the same time, the manner of operation of industrial licensing created undue delays and led to wastage of opportunities. Often small and uneconomic sizes of plants were licensed leading to high costs. Similarly quantitative import controls led to a high wall of protection and the creation of high cost industries. Rigid price controls in many cases led to stagnation of output and perpetuation of shortages.

The elaborate system of controls also created opportunities for corruption in the civil service that have perverted the original intent of the controls and have become another source of inefficiency.

The evidence on productivity suggests that public enterprises have been particularly inefficient, being protected from competition and without strong incentives for cost saving on the part of labor or management. The recommendations of the Seventh Five-Year Plan (Government of India Planning Commission 1985: 71) are also an indictment:

> The reform of the public enterprises system with a view to making them efficient and capable of generating surpluses commensurate with the scale of capital invested in them must rank high in the agenda of fiscal reform. The aim should be to make the public enterprises financially viable and productive of surpluses. This financial autonomy must be matched by a corresponding managerial autonomy, with secretariat intervention being limited to policy guidelines and the direction of major investment programmes. An arm's-length relationship between the commercial enterprises in the public sector and the government will also require major changes in the mode of organisation of departmentally run activities.

In addition to the effects of import controls, noted above, an overvalued exchange rate has reduced incentives for export. Direct investment by foreign firms has been discouraged by another set of regulatory barriers. As a result the effects of international competition in stimulating domestic efficiency have, at best, been minor, and the contributions of foreign technology limited.

It really is not necessary to decide whether or not the regulatory and control mechanisms in India have been the most important source of relative inefficiency. There is enough evidence to warrant the reconsiderations and revisions that are in progress.

The efficiency issue has broad ramifications. India has received massive amounts of foreign capital on concessional terms, though not more than would be justified by its size and relative poverty. In 1960-61 it received 16.8 percent of all official development assistance. That is defined as having at least a 25 percent grant element and thus does not include World Bank and regional development bank lending. In 1970-71 and 1982-83, the shares were 14.0 and 6.3 percent, respectively. These flows constituted 2.1 percent, 1.6 percent, and 0.9 percent of India's GNP in 1960-61, 1970-71 and 1982-83, respectively. Many other countries had much larger concessional flows in relation to their GNPs, though receiving much smaller absolute amounts. Indeed, aid to India from all OECD countries is a smaller fraction of its GNP than for any other low-income country (Poats 1985: 121).

If, as expected, concessional flows decline further and borrowings on commercial terms increase, an increase in the productivity of new investment becomes even more critical. A number of other countries have found that low-productivity investments financed by private borrowing can lead to major loan and balance of payments crises. This is a road that India certainly wants to avoid.

INDIAN POLICY ISSUES

India is a continental country and poses all the issues of such an economy. The choice of policy issues on which to focus—liberalization, opening of the economy, and international borrowing—is somewhat arbitrary and is made here having in mind not only the limitations of space but also the questions of particular relevance to the United States.

Liberalization

There seems little doubt that the diagnosis—that current problems of inefficiency in the Indian economy stem in large part from excessive government regulation—lies behind the emphasis by the Rajiv Gandhi administration on liberalization. The sectors in which large companies and foreign enterprises will be allowed to operate have already been expanded, and the investment licensing requirements have been somewhat relaxed. Yet some of the steps taken have been so hedged and restricted in their scope that the full extent of the proposed liberalization is not yet clear.

Another feature of liberalization has been tax reform. Personal and corporate tax rates have been reduced, and some simplifications have been made. These changes have been accompanied by more vigorous enforcement, and tax collections have actually risen.

There are both economic and political reasons for liberalization by small stages rather than through sweeping, across-the-board changes, although it is impossible to know the arguments made inside the government. Sequential decisionmaking, that makes small changes and observes their impact before taking another step, is a prudent procedure when obviously catastrophic conditions do not require radical actions. Adjustment has an economic cost that has to be balanced against the costs of not moving more quickly.

If the Indian situation is like others in which major changes in economic policy are contemplated, there will be losers as well as gainers from the proposed reforms. The direct losers in the private sector, as well as those civil servants whose power has derived from their administration of a complex system of contols, constitute interest groups that can be expected to oppose change. Attempts to reorganize public-sector entities face similar opposition.

Those in the private sector and the civil service who would lose from liberalization have political allies whose opposition to change is based on their own diagnoses of India's problems as well as self-interest. The Congress-I party covers a wide political spectrum so that opposition to Rajiv Gandhi's economic policy initiatives exists within as well as outside his party.

It is difficult to know how quickly the Indian economy will respond to liberalization. Although that will reflect the intensity with which the policy is pushed, it depends also on structural characteristics of the economy. Advocates of liberalization programs within the World Bank and the IMF, as well as outside of official institutions, often argue as if it can be expected that the benefits will be achieved quickly. Why else, for example, would liberalization be required as part of stabilization programs that are intended to be completed in two or three years?

If adjustments on the output side are to be quick, then just the right kind of capital must already be in place, even if it is not currently being used efficiently. Alternatively, capital must be nonspecific to particular sectors so that it can be moved around easily—for example, like light and medium trucks. Or it must be easily adjusted for use in other sectors, like light machine tools. Thus, quick adjustments are likely to occur only where the capital is not highly specific to a sector, a feature that is not common for much of the capital stock.

Resources have been allocated and used in India for many years in a relatively controlled environment with constraints on domestic competition as well as the competition of foreign imports and investment. It would require a long leap of faith to believe that the productive facilities are just those that would have been created in a fully efficient environment but are only being used inefficiently now. It seems more likely that inefficiency has been built into the structure of production and that a substantial amount of time and resources will be necessary to convert to a more efficient system.

Industrial production does not yet seem to have responded strongly to the new policies. The growth rate has actually fallen slightly as compared to last year. This might reflect the adjustment problems mentioned or be a reaction to the slowing down of the world economy.

International Opening

Opening the economy more widely to imports, further stimulus to exports and encouragement of foreign investment are also ideas that appear to have been adopted by the Rajiv Gandhi administration. These too will generate economic and political losses as well as gains and therefore economic and political opposition as well as support. The gains from increased imports are potential ones—from improved technology, lower costs, and greater product variety. The losses from increased competition from imports and from foreign investment are both immediate and actual as well as potential. Thus, it can be expected that opposition will be generated more easily than support.

The risks in this type of policy are also large. The reduction in import barriers will allow previously unsatisfied demands for both consumer and producer goods to be expressed. The demands are unsatisfied, not necessarily in the sense that people have hoarded funds to be spent on imports when trade barriers are eliminated, but at least in the sense that consumption will expand quickly into the new range of goods available through imports. In the present relatively depressed conditions in the major industrial countries, the supply can also be forthcoming immediately.

On the other hand, there will be a lagged response to new export incentives. Indian products face vigorous competition in export markets. It will take time and effort to penetrate these markets, and new designs and capacities may have to be created. The easy supply conditions for imports also imply the existence of buyers' markets for Indian exports. Thus, export growth is likely to be preceded by an import surge, generating a balance of payments problem. If the exchange rate has been overvalued, that will only exacerbate the situation.

It is too early to determine whether this scenario is now being played out in India. It is true that imports rose by 16 percent in the first five months of 1985–86 as compared to the previous year. Exports, on the other hand, actually fell and the trade imbalance doubled, resulting in a fall in reserves, only somewhat ameliorated by an increase in emigrant remittances.

The Use of International Finance

As noted, Indian use of foreign resources started on a large scale during the Second Five-Year Plan. During the late 1950s and early 1960s foreign savings often supported 20 percent or more of total investment. In the late 1960s a reduction in foreign economic assistance as well as the determination to be more self-reliant resulted in a sharp reduction in net foreign financial inflows and their virtual elimination by the mid-1970s. Subsequently, the use of foreign finance has increased to become 5 to 7 percent of total investment, and there has been growing recourse to private international loans.

The Seventh Five-Year Plan contains the projection that 6.2 percent of total investment will be financed by foreign capital inflows. The source of these flows is not described, but there are indications that a substantial part would be private international loans.

This will be the result of several different influences. First, the total amount of official assistance available to all countries in the future is expected to grow only slightly, if at all. Second, the share that India will receive is expected to decline, in part because of diversion of finance to Africa and to China, a major new claimant. Finally, there is, as yet, no evidence of important increases in equity investment in India.

India is now a good credit risk by conventional standards with relatively low ratios of international debt to GDP and debt service to exports. If exports expand as planned, it will look even better.

Experience is a hard teacher, however, and a response to its warnings about international private debt require reflection on the questions raised above: the efficiency of the Indian economy and its ability to expand its export earnings. Debt service must be paid from the foreign exchange earnings of new investment because there is little, if any, cushion in the present Indian balance of payments. That means that the net productivity of the investment in foreign exchange must exceed the interest charges.

One might expect that the net productivity of capital in India is so much above the interest rate and the potential for exports is so substantial that this would not be a worry. However, as noted, the productivity of Indian investment has been relatively low for reasons not fully understood, and Indian exports have not been able to maintain sustained growth. Thus, there must be some concern about India incurring foreign private debt and the burdens of relatively high debt service that go along with it.

In fact, this concern has become a new argument for concessional economic assistance by the OECD and the World Bank: that such assistance will dilute the debt service burden and make it easier for India to meet the payments on private loans. The OECD and the World Bank seem to implicitly accept the low productivity of investment in India and its relative limitations in generating foreign exchange through exports. That is not an optimistic outlook.

U.S. POLICY ISSUES

The international relations of India and the United States have been the source of both mutual admiration and sometimes dismay. In a long hiatus in the late 1960s and the 1970s a mutual coolness affected official Indian-U.S. relations and spread to areas of private relationships as well. That hiatus now seems to be coming to an end, and an interest that never really disappeared is being renewed. This note will focus on three aspects of Indian policy that pose new issues for the U.S. economy: export promotion, opening of the economy to foreign investment, and private international borrowing.

India exports about 7 percent of its gross domestic production, and the export growth target in the Seventh Five-Year Plan is a 7 percent annual increase. The United States is India's largest single market, taking about 25 percent of its total exports, which are only 0.8 percent of total U.S. imports. Thus, the U.S. market is quite important for India, but imports from India are not now very important for the United States. It is reasonable to expect that success for India's export drive will be achieved more readily with increasing penetration of the U.S. market and, indeed, that may be a necessary condition. This combination of circumstances means that small accommodations by the United States may help India a lot.

That expectation is countered by the growing resistance within the United States to imports. Although a restrictive trade law has not yet passed Congress, there are threats of its imminence, and a number of quotas and "voluntary" import restraints have been negotiated by the executive branch.

All of this might change if the international economy becomes more buoyant and the United States and other markets expand more rapidly. If the present circumstances continue, it will not be easy to make room for more Indian exports in the U.S. market without generating some political heat somewhere. For example, Chinese textiles accounted for only 1.3 percent of U.S. woven textile imports in 1981, when imports of these goods from India were only 0.1 percent of total textile imports. By 1985 imports of woven textiles from China had more than tripled in absolute volume but were still only 1.6 percent of the total. Yet these imports created difficult domestic and international problems for the United States. It is easy to foresee that, if Indian textile exports to the United States were to grow to the same levels as the Chinese, the same kind of political problems could be generated.

Access to U.S. markets through quotas is an established tool of U.S. foreign policy. U.S. decisions on Indian exports will certainly be interpreted in India not only as a reflection of its support for the current government but also as an indication of U.S. attitudes toward the economic reforms being pursued.

Turning to the significance of a wider opening of the Indian economy to imports, that would certainly excite interest among U.S.

exporters due to the potential market size. Imports from the United States are already the largest single component of total imports into India. Even if U.S. consumer goods exports could be marketed to only the top 1 percent of Indian consumers, that would still be a market of more than 70 million people. Given the considerable income inequality that exists in India, this top 1 percent is relatively affluent compared, say, to the corresponding market in China. Capital and intermediate goods are also important market areas. However, Indians will point out, with justice, that their ability to import depends on the reception accorded to their exports.

The particular concern in India over access to new technologies will raise with new force questions regarding the conditions under which these will be transferred abroad. The issues are related to foreign investment, and an increased receptiveness to such investment by India could lead to the even more intensive interactions. There are many potential advantages to direct investment in India: well-established legal and administrative procedures, a large pool of skilled professionals and craftsmen with relatively low labor costs and English as a common working language, and a diverse supply network. It is not difficult to imagine that, with some important but feasible changes, India could become a preferred location for U.S. direct foreign investment.

Although such a development could be advantageous for both India and the United States, it also would generate more points for potential friction. There are in India active and articulate groups with a high level of sensitivity to foreign interference. That can clash with the U.S. business style of participation in all types of local activities, including politics. The Bhopal incident involving Union Carbide also comes to mind. The same problems with direct investment can arise in any country, and other countries have vigorous journalists and ambitious politicians. It might be too much to ask for detailed mutual planning to deal with future Bhopal-like incidents. It is not too much, however, to suggest that a clear Indian policy would reduce uncertainty for all foreign investors.

An expansion of U.S. private lending to India would provide another area for increased interaction that would provide mutual benefits as well as potential for more points of irritation. On the assumption that India and the lending banks avoid future debt crises of the Argentinian-Brazilian-Mexican type, both sides can benefit. If the existing international debt problems blow up into open defaults that lead to reductions in international lending, then India might well feel unrewarded for past good behavior.

More immediately, it would be plausible for India to be somewhat innovative in its international finance to avoid the concentration of its privately held debt in short-term and fixed-interest commercial bank loans. That, in turn, would require new flexibility in the capital markets. If India were to float bonded debt in U.S. capital markets, there could well be a surge of interest in India in the U.S. public mind. That would have some benefits as well as impose some constraints.

Economic assistance issues may be raised by India if the relations between the two countries become sufficiently cordial. As noted, India's problems are receiving less notice from the multilateral and bilateral economic assistance sources, including the United States, than its relative poverty and size warrant. India receives virtually the same amount of aid from the United States as does Costa Rica, with a population of less than 2.5 million and GNP per capita that is almost eight times larger.

Rather narrowly focused political calculations are more important now in the distribution of U.S. aid than in the 1960s when India received 10 percent or more of total U.S. aid. That is a reality that all aid recipients have to live with, but there is a case for political calculation that concludes that relations between India and the United States could be improved somewhat with a relatively small amount of additional assistance.

CONCLUSIONS

This brief survey indicates that changes in Indian economic policy that are underway can be expected to lead to more intensive interaction with the United States, not just at the level of formal, intergovernmental relations but involving more of the economy and the public of both countries. This can enrich relationships. It also can generate more irritation when, as will certainly happen, everything does not go smoothly.

There are some, but not many, things that official U.S. policy can do about many of the problems that can be expected to arise. Attention to the implications of import quotas for the success of economic policy changes in India would be desirable, as would clarification of the rules for recourse to U.S. courts in Bhopal-like situations. Most of all, it would be desirable for U.S. policymakers to update their perceptions of India. Political and economic issues and policies in India appear to be changing rapidly now, and perceptions based on the 1960s and 1970s are outdated.

REFERENCES

Government of India Planning Commission. 1985. *Seventh Five-Year Plan, 1985-90, Vol. I.* Delhi: Government of India.
Poats, R.M. 1985. *Twenty-five Years of Development Coopration: A Review.* Paris: OECD.

11 THE NICs
Profiles of Economic Growth

Rose Carcaterra and Judy Farrell

The newly emerging industrial countries of East Asia and Latin America are attracting widespread international attention as their roles in the world economy expand. The NICs as individual nations may have only a marginal influence on the global economy, but their combined impact is significant.

Although the NICs are in different stages of development and need to be examined individually, they share some important characteristics. The NICs have made economic growth a priority. In doing so, they have emphasized manufactured exports and have been assisted through extensive government intervention. The NICs are extremely reliant on U.S. markets to absorb their exports, and highly indebted NICs rely extensively on their export earnings to finance debt payments. Many NICs impose import restrictions on U.S. goods and services, which add to their trade imbalance with the United States and fuel protectionist sentiments. At the same time, however, the U.S. and global economies are becoming increasingly intertwined, giving the United States a considerable stake in the economic success of the NICs.

The NICs are also marked by some important differences. The East Asian NICs have more outward-oriented policies and have

The authors would like to acknowledge the invaluable assistance of Kyong-Su Im in the preparation of these country profiles.

135

tended to emphasize export-led growth and internal liberalization. Latin American NICs, on the other hand, have tended to be more inward oriented to enhance the growth of their domestic economies through import substitution and restrictions on foreign investment. In recent years, however, severe debt-service requirements have driven many Latin American NICs to drastically reduce imports and push exports. China and India have also begun to liberalize their domestic economies and adopt more outward-looking, export-oriented policies.

The newly industrializing countries cannot be classified as either developing or industrial nations, nor can they be neatly described as export-led or import-substituting countries. The following country profiles offer glimpses of some individual NICs and the factors affecting their economic growth.

BRAZIL

Brazil is the NIC most often cited as a potential leading economic power. Of the large Latin debtors, only Brazil has been favored by the fall in the price of crude oil, the fall in interest rates, and the fall in the dollar. In 1986 Brazil's GDP of $256 billion and its trade surplus of $9.6 billion were among the world's highest (U.S. Department of Commerce 1986). Manufactured goods account for 60 percent of its exports, and it has been identified as the leading agricultural export rival to the United States (Gall 1986: 47).

In 1985 Brazil installed its first civilian government after twenty-one years of military rule. After the untimely death of President-elect Tancredo Neves, Jose Sarney took office and introduced the cruzado plan, ending the indexation of inflation and instituting price and wage freezes in an attempt to get the domestic economy under control. Preliminary indicators estimate that inflation, which reached 235 percent in 1985, was 65 percent in 1986, but is on the rise again in 1987. It became apparent in late 1986 that Brazil's anti-inflation plan, which created a new currency (the cruzado), was headed for failure. The plan resulted in a repressed inflation and caused increased demand, rising black market prices, and shortages throughout the country. The collapse of the cruzado plan has had a severe impact on the Brazilian economy. It has been projected that Brazil's growth rate, which was 8 percent in 1986, will be only 2 percent in

1987. Another problem that remains for Brazil is income maldistri-
bution, because the top 10 percent of the country's population of
135 million holds half the national income (Gall 1986: 47).

With a foreign debt of $10 billion in 1986, Brazil is the world's
largest developing country debtor. In February 1987 Brazil dramatically changed its strategy for dealing with its debt problem and
suspended interest payments on the country's $68 billion commer-
cial debt. As a result of Brazil's actions, many regional banks in the
United States are concerned about the rescheduling process, and
some have even indicated that they will not grant any further loans
to Latin American debtors. Several of the largest U.S. banks have
already put Brazilian loans on a nonaccrual basis, and there is considerable concern about the direction of Brazil's economy and the
implications for the debt crisis.

Brazil has opposed many economic reforms proposed by the IMF
and is working to get its future funding from governments and commercial banks. In its April 1987 negotiations with American banks,
Brazil insisted that its debt service payments not be more than 2½
percent of GDP per year, and it also requested $4 billion in new
loans.

The United States is Brazil's largest trading partner. Trade relations between the two countries have been strained by U.S. concern
over Brazil's restrictive import policies, particularly its *informatica*
law. The United States is also concerned about Brazil's opposition to
liberalizing trade in services in the GATT talks. U.S.-Brazilian trade
tensions are complicated by Brazil's foreign debt, much of which is
owed to U.S. banks.

U.S. government officials reject the argument that Brazil's debt
and development must be taken into account in trade negotiations
because Brazil has a diversified economy and enjoyed a $3.5 billion
trade surplus with the United States in 1986. The United States also
firmly believes that Brazil should begin to accept the responsibilities
that go along with becoming a leading player in the world economy
(see Table 11-1).

Leading U.S. exports to Brazil include aircraft equipment, wheat,
coal, organic chemicals, office machines, and parts and telecommunications equipment. Leading U.S. imports from Brazil include footwear, coffee, petroleum products, motor vehicles and auto parts,
orange juice, and iron and steel.

Table 11-1.   Brazilian Debt and Trade with the United States (billions of U.S. dollars).

	1981	1983	1985	1986
External debt	$75.6	$91.6	$101.9	$102.0
Percentage held by U.S. banks	23%	22%	23%	N/A
U.S. exports	$ 3.8	$ 2.5	$ 3.1	$ 3.9
U.S. imports	$ 4.8	$ 5.4	$ 8.1	$ 7.3
Trade balance with United States	$+1.0	$+2.8	$ +5.0	$ +3.5
Trade balance with world	1.2	6.5	12.4	9.6

Source: U.S. Department of Commerce (1986, 1987).

Brazil's industrial strategy is to protect those industries that will enable it to be competitive in upscale manufacturing. In October 1984 Brazil introduced the *informatica* law, which bans imported robotics, minicomputers, and microcomputers and which prohibits foreign manufacturers from owning more than 30 percent of a company that makes computer equipment, computer-aided design, and robotics. This law has become a central part of Brazil's industrial policy. It is estimated that it could cost U.S. industry $15 billion by 1992 (Cohen 1986: 30).

Two of Brazil's leading industries, footwear and autos, have also received extensive assistance from the government. Brazil began to promote the export of shoes in the 1960s when Cuba was prohibited from supplying the United States. Because footwear is a labor-intensive industry, U.S. importers realize significant cost advantages by importing Brazilian shoes. Workers in Brazil earn seventy cents an hour (or about $700 annually), whereas workers in the United States earn $6 per hour (about $14,000 annually). In the 1970s the Brazilian government helped its shoe industry modernize, but because of U.S. pressure government assistance ended in 1984. Over the past five years Brazil's exports of footwear have increased by 500 percent, and it has emerged as the largest exporter of shoes to the United States. In 1985 it exported more than $935 million worth of shoes to the United States. It is estimated that Brazil's footwear exports have cost the United States 26,000 jobs in a one-year period (U.S. Department of Commerce 1986).

Brazil's auto industry has also grown rapidly. Over the past decade its auto exports have tripled. In 1974 autos accounted for 4.7 percent of the country's total exports of $7.9 billion; by 1985 they had risen to 12.5 percent. The demand for new cars in Brazil is likely to grow at an annual rate of 5 percent, much faster than in the United States, Europe, or Japan.

In early 1987 it became evident that although the price freeze embodied in the cruzado plan did spark increased consumption and rapid economic growth, it also disrupted industrial production. By October 1986 Brazil's trade surplus was only $200 million, $1 billion less than projected. Brazil's role in the world economy is expected to continue to expand, but in 1987 its growth rate is expected to decline significantly. Low petroleum prices will continue to free up foreign exchange for non-oil imports, which is important because Brazil will still face pressure to import capital goods and foodstuffs.

Brazil is planning to modernize its agricultural industry and obtained a $500 million loan from the World Bank for this purpose. This move heightened trade tensions with the United States because U.S. farmers objected to concessionary loans to Brazil that subsidize agricultural exports. The U.S. government also opposed a $500 million World Bank loan that would help Brazil expand and modernize electric power facilities. Questions remain, however, about Brazil's ability to recover from its current economic crisis and resume servicing its considerable external debt.

Although Brazil has refused to open its markets to more imports, it might consider some changes if an accord is reached to lighten its debt burden. Brazil's opposition to IMF-imposed adjustment, however, makes a significant new debt accord unlikely in the near future. As a result, Brazil will probably continue to protect domestic industries. It is unlikely that Brazil will make any major concessions on its computer restrictions, although it may agree to some adjustments in such areas as copyright on software. The biggest obstacles Brazil's economy faces in the near-term future are a resurgence of inflation, servicing of foreign debt, and the growing public-sector deficit.

MEXICO

Mexico is of special concern to the United States because of the 2,000-mile border shared by the two countries and their extensive economic ties. Mexico's rapid economic growth during the 1970s and early 1980s was led by the expansion of its oil industry and heavy external borrowing, but overreliance on these sources of revenue led to economic reversals in the early 1980s. After a deep recession in 1983 Mexico's GDP rose in 1984 and 1985, but declined by 3.5 percent in 1986.

By 1986 Mexico's foreign debt totaled $100 billion, and interest payments alone were $9 billion. The collapse of world oil prices hurt Mexico's economy and compounded concern about Mexico's ability to generate the economic growth necessary to service its foreign debt. The country's inflation reached 100 percent in 1986, and it is estimated that Mexico's economy will contract by at least 4 percent between 1986–87 (Stockton 1986: D1).

In order to cope with slow economic growth and to make the interest payments on its $97 billion debt, Mexico sought new loans from the international banking community in 1986 and will receive about $13.7 billion in new money (Berg 1986: D1). The new loans are contingent on Mexican economic reforms, such as stemming capital flight, allowing increased foreign investment, reducing the budget deficit, controlling inflation, and selling off government-owned businesses.

Commercial banks hold some $70 billion of Mexico's foreign debt. U.S. banks hold $24 billion of the total, followed by Japan with $13 billion, and Britain with $9 billion. Many bankers have been reluctant to make new loans to Mexico because of concern about extensive capital flight, but as a result of Mexico's loan agreement with the IMF, the commercial banks have agreed to continue to provide new loans.

Mexico is the world's fourth-largest oil producer following the USSR, Saudi Arabia, and the United States. Mexico relies on oil for 70 percent of its export revenue, and the collapse of oil prices has had a serious impact on Mexico's economy. Oil prices dropped 50 percent in 1985, and Mexico's petroleum sales declined by 11 percent. As a result, petroleum export revenues fell by $2 billion, and the country's trade balance fell by 34 percent.

Despite Mexico's difficulties, it remains the third-largest trading partner of the United States (see Table 11–2). U.S. exports to Mexico, which include auto parts, electronic tubes, soybeans, electrical switches, and parts of office machines, increased by 14 percent in 1985. U.S. imports from Mexico, encouraged by the continuing

Table 11-2. Mexican Trade Flows (*billions of U.S. dollars*).

	1981	1983	1985	1986[a]
Total exports	20.9	23.1	21.8	15.8
to United States	13.8	16.9	19.4	17.6
Total imports	24.0	8.6	13.4	11.4
from United States	17.8	8.8	13.6	12.4
Trade balance				
With world	-3.1	+14.5	+8.4	+4.4
With United States	-4.0	+ 8.1	+5.8	+5.2

a. 1986 figures are estimates.
Source: U.S. Department of Commerce (1986, 1987).

weakness of the peso, rose in 1985 by 6 percent. Oil sales were again chief among U.S. imports. Auto parts shipped to Mexico and re-exported to the United States also showed strong increases.

In November 1985 Mexico announced that it intended to apply for membership to the GATT, and it completed the accession by August 1986. It remains uncertain, however, whether Mexico will conform to GATT rules on customs valuation, local content requirements, import licensing, and restrictions on agricultural imports.

In 1985 the United States and Mexico reached a bilateral trade and investment agreement (the U.S.-Mexico Understanding on Subsidies and Countervailing Duties), which will complement Mexico's GATT agreement. Foreign direct investment, inadequate protection of foreign intellectual property rights, and treatment of transfer of technology are of particular concern to the United States. Mexico's system of import licenses has traditionally represented the biggest barrier to U.S. exports, and the Mexican government took action in July 1985 to eliminate license requirements on all but approximately 900 tariff schedule categories. Licenses are still required on 35 percent of Mexican imports, but this move was seen as an important step in liberalizing Mexico's import regime.

One major source of tension in U.S.-Mexico relations has been illegal immigration (see EPC 1981). The U.S. Immigration and Naturalization Service estimated that 1.8 million illegal aliens were caught at the border in 1986. Although new immigration legislation has been approved by Congress, it is unlikely that the United States will act soon to stem the flow of illegal aliens. The President's Council of Economic Advisers suggested that penalizing employers for hiring illegal aliens could be damaging to the U.S. economy; others fear that such action would hurt the Mexican economy and U.S.-Mexican diplomatic relations. The immigration of workers is seen as a vital safety valve for Mexico, with Mexican workers sending home almost $1 billion from their earnings in the United States ("Mexico Slips" 1986: 34-36).

Another concern is the *maquiladora* program, in which foreign goods, mostly U.S., are assembled in low-wage Mexican manufacturing plants and reexported to the United States. The *maquiladora* industry has become the second-largest industry in Mexico and is seen by some U.S. labor and congressional leaders as a growing threat to U.S. jobs.

Another great concern to U.S. authorities is the unprecedented flow of drugs crossing the border. According to the State Department, Mexico is one of the largest suppliers to the United States of marijuana and has recently emerged as a major supplier of heroin. It is estimated that Mexico is also a conduit for about one-third of the United States' cocaine traffic.

The Mexican government is aiming for economic growth of 3 to 4 percent over the next year. In order to meet the IMF's requirements, Mexico plans to reduce its budget deficit from 13 percent to 10 percent of GDP by increasing revenue, reducing government subsidies on various commodities and services, and continuing to sell off government-owned businesses to the private sector.

Although the proposed $13.7 billion loan package agreed on in 1986 will help Mexico through its immediate economic crisis, the nation may face debt-servicing difficulties again in 1988. As was the case during the 1970s, Mexico's economic performance in the future will be significantly influenced by the international petroleum market and international interest rates.

SINGAPORE

With a population of 2.6 million and an area of 224.3 square miles, Singapore is one of the most densely populated countries in the world. Singapore has capitalized on its strategically located trade routes and its energetic and skilled work force to achieve high economic growth over the past two decades. In 1982 per capita GNP was nine times greater than it was in 1960. Although Singapore's economic growth has been uneven during the 1980s, its 1984 GNP per capita of $6,922 was the highest in Southeast Asia.

Although its economic strategies have changed, Singapore has maintained its traditional role as a free port with industries unprotected by tariffs and quotas. When Singapore won its independence from Malaysia in 1965, it had a small domestic market and high unemployment. As a result, the government changed its strategy from import-substitution to labor-intensive manufacturing for export. By the mid-1970s Singapore faced domestic labor shortages, declining competitiveness in export manufacturing, and a narrow manufacturing base. In 1979 the Singapore government formally announced a new strategy of accelerated industrial restructuring that focused on upgrading technology, labor productivity, and skills in order to export more capital-intensive, high-valued manufactured products. The policies behind this strategy were threefold (see International Labor Organization 1986: 18–20).

1. *Wage correction policy.* Wages were raised 20 percent to promote the efficient use of scarce labor, and as a result Singapore soon had the highest wage level in Southeast Asia. By 1985 average hourly manufacturing wages were $2.44 as compared to $1.46 in Taiwan and $1.44 in South Korea. Although this program sparked foreign investment, wage increases surpassed productivity gains. This policy was phased out in 1985.

2. *Industrial investment incentives.* To make Singapore attractive to foreign investors, several investment incentives were initiated. From 1978 to 1981 net investment commitments grew at an average annual rate of 58 percent. The proportion of foreign-owned manufacturing industries in Singapore is higher than in Taiwan, China, or Hong Kong.

3. *Expansion of training and education facilities.* Formal post-secondary technical and professional training was given high priority, and training opportunities for those already in the workforce were expanded. Policies such as flexible work hours and part-time work were also instituted to encourage women to enter the labor market. The offer of a quality education also encouraged foreigners to enter the Singapore workforce, and in 1986

Table 11-3. Singapore World Trade (*billions of U.S. dollars*).

	1981	1983	1985	1986
Total exports	$21.0	$21.8	$22.8	$22.5
to United States	2.8 (12.9)	4.0 (18.3)	4.8 (21.0)	5.3 (24%)
to Japan	2.1 (10.0)	2.0 (9.1)	2.1 (9.2)	1.9 (8%)
to EEC	2.3 (11.0)	2.0 (9.2)	2.4 (10.5)	2.5 (11%)
Total imports	27.6	28.2	26.3	25.5
From United States	3.5 (12.7)	4.3 (15.3)	4.0 (15.2)	3.8 (15%)
From Japan	5.2 (18.8)	5.1 (18.1)	4.5 (17.1)	5.1 (2%)
From EEC	2.7 (9.7)	3.0 (10.7)	3.0 (11.4)	3.0 (12%)
Trade balance with world	-6.6	-6.4	-3.5	-3.0
Trade balance with United States	- .7	- .3	- .8	-1.5

Source: IMF (1986: 351, 352); (1987: 354-55).

one-tenth of Singapore's 1.1 million labor force was comprised of foreigners. Although the government continues to encourage skilled foreign professionals to enter the workforce, it plans to phase out all unskilled foreign labor by 1992.

The United States is Singapore's major investor and largest trading partner (see Table 11-3). By the end of 1984 the United States had total assets in Singapore worth approximately $5.2 billion. In 1986 Singapore's trade with the United States represented 23 percent of its total trade.

The bulk of U.S. imports from Singapore are made up of electrical and electronic equipment, computer and other office machine components, telecommunication aparatus, and petroleum products. The principle U.S. exports to Singapore are aircraft and avionics, electronic components, computers, electrical machinery, and refined petroleum products. In 1984 Singapore ran a trade surplus with the United States for the first time in fifteen years, as exports to the United States rose by approximately 22 percent and imports fell by 1.8 percent, resulting in a trade surplus of $642 million. By the end of 1986, this figure reached $1.5 billion.

For the past two decades Singapore's economic progress has been spurred not only by favorable market forces but also by the government's tight political control. Singapore never really lost its pre–World War II role as a marketing and service center for Southeast Asia, but it now faces significant external and internal economic constraints. Singapore's closest neighbors, Malaysia and Indonesia, are striving to become more efficient, to conduct more trade with the rest of the world, and to rely less on Singapore. Economic problems and weaknesses in developing countries are further limiting Singapore's options as a trading center, and rising protectionist sentiment in the United States is another source of concern.

Internally, Singapore is confronting fundamental structural problems. Overcapacity and competition from low-cost countries are putting pressure on Singapore's more mature industries, such as shipbuilding and oil refining. The government hopes to encourage the growth of high-tech industries but faces shortfalls in investment, skilled manpower, and relatively high wage levels. Singapore's future growth will depend to a large extent on the government's ability to attract foreign investment and increase the skills and productivity of its workforce.

Between 1962 and 1974 the manufacturing sector grew an average of 20 percent per year and from 1975–82 by 10 percent a year. In 1980 the manufacturing share of GDP was 23 percent, and by 1990 it is expected to reach 31 percent (International Labor Organization 1986: 107–08). The Singapore government's Economic Committee recently reported (Kirkpatrick 1986) that "The government must promote services actively, the same way it successfully promoted manufacturing." The areas of growth recommended by the report were (1) banking and finance, (2) transport and communications, and (3) international services. The service sector's share of GDP is currently 60 percent. It is expected to rise to 69 percent by 1995 (*Far Eastern Economic Review* 1986a: 78).

In the past, Singapore's industrial strategies have emphasized tight government control. In the future the government will loosen some of its controls on foreign investment, stress greater privatization, and encourage employer-employee relations more along the lines of Japanese companies. Barring any general shocks to the world economy, Singapore should be able to maintain an average growth rate of 5 to 7 percent for the remainder of the decade. This represents a notable decline from the 9.4 percent annual average that prevailed during the 1970s but a rate that most governments would be pleased to achieve.

TAIWAN

Taiwan, an island about one-third the size of Ohio with a population of 19 million people, had the third-largest bilateral trade surplus with the United States in 1985. Taiwan's GNP was only $71 billion in 1986, but its foreign exchange reserves of approximately $40 billion rank among the largest national reserves in the world.

Because of Taiwan's limited domestic market, the government began to promote export-led growth in the early 1960s. Initially Taiwan exported mainly agricultural products and textiles. By 1980, however, its exports had shifted overwhelmingly to manufactured products. As shown in Table 11–4, since 1984 Taiwan's exports of electrical machinery and appliances have surpassed the combined volume of its textile, clothing, and footwear exports.

U.S. protectionism and competition from low-wage nations, such as China, India, and Malaysia, have forced Taiwan to alter its industrial strategy. Five years ago, the government introduced the Strategic Industrial Program, which shifted the emphasis of Taiwan's economy to high-tech industries. Under this program, the information, telecommunications, automobile, and electrical machinery industries receive tax breaks and low-interest loans from government banks. The program has significantly changed the structure of Taiwan's economy and, over the past five years, the information industry has emerged from virtually nothing to a $12 billion export industry.

The government is also encouraging the establishment of technical cooperation projects with foreign firms. It has lifted some restric-

Table 11–4. Major Export Commodities as Percentage of Total Exports.

	1965	1975	1978	1984	1985
Rice and paddy	9.1%	—	.3%	0.1%	—
Sugar	13.1	5.0%	1.2	0.2	0.1%
Textile	10.3	11.5	8.2	6.3	7.1
Clothing and footwear	4.9	16.4	14.4	13.7	12.6
Plastic products	2.6	6.5	7.4	7.9	8.6
Electrical machinery and appliances	2.7	14.7	18.2	21.6	21.0

Sources: Republic of China Inspectorate General of Customs (various years); Liang and Liang (19: 5).

tions on investment and ownership to attract foreign companies, and in 1984 foreign investment increased 38 percent. Of Taiwan's four top electronics exporters, three are subsidiaries of U.S. corporations.

To help implement its high-tech program, the Taiwanese government opened the Hsinchu science park in 1980. The park has attracted many Taiwanese who received their Ph.D.s in the United States, and eleven of its forty-nine companies are from the United States. In 1981, the park generated only $3 million worth of exports, but in 1985 it accounted for approximately $350 million of Taiwan's exports. It is projected that by 1995 the park will export $10 billion worth of high-tech products (Stokes 1985: 2699). In addition, the government has launched an ambitious program, known as fourteen projects, to improve Taiwan's infrastructure, help develop the domestic economy, and relieve unemployment. A new subway system, a new long-distance highway, and a new nuclear power plant are all part of this program.

To succeed, the government's new industrial strategy must overcome three fundamental problems. First, Taiwan is composed mainly of family-operated, small and medium-sized companies that employ less than 100 people each. In 1985 they generated 85 to 90 percent of Taiwan's GNP (Stokes 1985: 2702). These firms are generally labor-intensive, are often undercapitalized, have little R&D ability, and lack modern management skills.

Second, Taiwan's investment in R&D in 1985 was only 0.7 percent of GNP. (The United States invested 2 percent of its GNP in R&D in 1985.) Although the government is pushing to increase R&D investment to 2 percent of GNP within seven years, small businesses are expected to resist this push.

Third, Taiwan's capital investment has declined in both absolute terms and as a percentage of GNP over the past five years. Widespread business uncertainty exists about where to invest in the rapidly changing economy. There is a lack of faith in the banking system (which has been subject to several recent scandals) and political uncertainty about ailing President Chiang.

U.S. firms have invested well over $1 billion in Taiwan, but the scope of Taiwan's trade with the United States often goes unrecognized by the American public because many of Taiwan's products enter the country under U.S. brand names. Taiwan was the United States' sixth-largest trading partner in 1985, and the United States was Taiwan's largest trading partner. Japan, however, is the leading exporter to Taiwan. In 1985 Taiwan imported $5.5 billion from Japan and $4.7 billion from the United States. In 1985 Taiwan had a $2.1 billion trade deficit with Japan (Republic of China Board of Foreign Trade 1986: 26).

U.S. imports from Taiwan have more than doubled since 1980, but U.S. exports to Taiwan have increased only slightly. As a result, Taiwan's trade surplus with the United States has more than quadrupled. The U.S. trade deficit with Taiwan was $3.2 billion in 1980; by 1986 it had increased to $15.7 billion. Of Taiwan's total exports of $37.5 billion in 1986, $18.2 billion went to the United States. The United States absorbed nearly 50 percent of Taiwan's exports, but it had only a 22 percent share in Taiwan's imports.

Under tremendous pressure from the United States, Taiwan has agreed to respect U.S. intellectual property, widen the scope of foreign bank operations, and substantially ease trade restrictions on 192 items, including beer and cigarettes. In order to have a meaningful impact on the trade imbalance, however, the United States insists that Taiwan must implement these actions quickly, lift more restrictions on imports (especially in the insurance and banking fields), and lower tariffs on consumer goods, which average around 40 to 50 percent.

As Taiwan's competitiveness in high-tech industries increases, trade conflicts with the United States are also likely to increase. The recent appreciation of the New Taiwan dollar (NT) against the U.S. dollar should help slow export growth; however, to alleviate the trade imbalance Taiwan will need to import more U.S. products.

Since Taiwan is conservative in the management of its economy, it is positioned to do well over the next decade. While Taiwan will probably be better able to adapt to a harsh international economic climate than Korea, it probably will not be as well positioned to take advantage of favorable economic trends.

REPUBLIC OF KOREA

Acute political unrest in South Korea and the export of the highly visible Hyundai car caught the attention of Americans in 1986. Korea's rapidly increasing trade surplus with the United States, which hit $7 billion last year, has further heightened Korea's visibility. With a population of 42 million, a literacy rate of 95 percent, and a

GNP of $93 billion in 1986, Korea is one of the most prominent NICs.

In 1962 Korea launched a highly successful export-oriented economic policy. In the 1960s and early 1970s, in order to reduce unemployment and encourage economic growth, Korea borrowed heavily, gave low-interest loans to large export-oriented companies, and encouraged companies to borrow in international markets. In the mid-1970s the government shifted its emphasis from labor-intensive light industries to heavy industries, such as shipbuilding, automobiles, steel, and chemicals. This strategy resulted in a growing industrial base and annual GNP growth rates that averaged between 9 and 10 percent during the 1960s and 1970s. Although this policy was successful, it has led to an increasing economic concentration. In 1985 ten product lines made up 70 percent of Korea's total exports, and 40 percent of its exports went to the United States. By 1986 the top ten companies accounted for 50 percent of Korea's exports. A resulting buildup in foreign debt totaled $47 billion in 1986.

Like many other NICs, Korea's economic growth has slowed dramatically in the 1980s. Real GNP declined by 6 percent in 1980 because of worldwide recession and soaring oil import costs. In recent years GNP growth has averaged about 5 percent and, in response to slower growth, rising protectionism, and increasing international competition, Korea is attempting to diversify its exports, establish joint ventures, expand medium- and small-scale enterprises, and increase domestic demand.

The United States is Korea's largest foreign market, accepting about one-third of all Korean exports. Until 1981 the United States ran a trade surplus with Korea, but since then it has accumulated a rapidly growing trade deficit. U.S. imports from Korea nearly doubled between 1981 and 1985 (from $5.5 billion to $10.7 billion), whereas U.S. exports to Korea did not even keep up with inflation (increasing from $5 billion to only $5.7 billion). By 1986 Korea's trade surplus reached $7.1 billion.

Korea is the third-largest supplier of apparel and the fifth-largest textile exporter to the United States. As indicated by Table 11–5, Korea's exports of electronics to the United States have more than doubled since 1981. Korean-U.S. joint ventures, especially those in the automobile industry are expected to cause an increase in Korean-manufactured exports to the United States over the next few years.

Table 11-5. U.S. Imports of Korean Manufactured Products (*billions of U.S. dollars*).

	1981	1983	1985
Textile and apparel	$1.6	$2.0	$2.8
Electronics and telecommunication equipment	1.0	1.8	2.7
Footwear	.6	.9	1.2
Total U.S. trade deficit	-.5	-1.9	-5.0

Sources: *National Journal* (1986: 814); IMF (1982).

Agricultural products and raw materials still account for the majority of U.S. exports to Korea. In 1986 Korea was the seventh-largest U.S. export market and the fifth-largest importer of U.S. agricultural products.

The United States views Korea primarily as an exporting country, pointing out that Korean exports to the United States have steadily increased in recent years, while U.S. exports to Korea have remained stagnant. But Korea sees itself primarily as an importing country, stressing that in 1986 it had an overall trade surplus for the first time, amounting to $4.5 billion. Consequently, trade tension between the two countries is high.

In 1985 the Reagan administration filed two unfair trade cases against Korea for restrictions on U.S. insurance companies and for infringement of U.S. intellectual property rights. As a result, Korea agreed to enact legislation to protect U.S. intellectual property and to permit U.S. insurance companies to sell life insurance policies in Korea. These two areas (services and intellectual property) are at the heart of many of the trade disputes between the two countries.

Korea has also agreed to restrain textile exports to the United States to 0.8 percent a year for four years, a sharp reduction from the 8.6 percent average growth between 1981 and 1985. The United States has also pressured Korea to implement a five-year program (1984-88) to remove import licensing restrictions and reduce tariffs. Korea has responded by reducing tariffs and liberalizing its law in investment and imports. In October 1985 the Ministry of Trade and Industry of Korea announced a plan to liberalize 603 import items by 1988. The United States, however, would like Korea to move more quickly towards liberalizing its markets.

Korea, on the other hand, thinks that it is being singled out unfairly. It argues that its trade surplus with the United States is small compared to Japan's; that even though Hong Kong and Taiwan are smaller than Korea, their trade surpluses with the United States are much larger; that its economy must grow by 6 to 7 percent a year to generate enough jobs for new entrants; that, unlike Japan, it spends about 6 percent of its GNP for defense; and that its $46.7 billion foreign debt, which is the third-largest in the world, means that it must run a trade surplus to generate needed foreign exchange.

Moreover, Korea argues that it is facing a crucial period. The Chun Doo-hwan government fears that harsh U.S. trade policy will weaken the Korean economy and increase antigovernment and anti-U.S. forces. These in turn, could create a backlash against the United States.

The Olympics will take place in Seoul in 1988. Korea hopes that, if its economy remains strong, the Olympics will be its rite of passage into the industrialized world just as the Tokyo Olympics were for Japan. Korea's GNP expanded by 5.1 percent in 1985, but it grew 11 percent in 1986 as a result of low oil prices, reduced interest rates, and the lower value of the dollar. Lower oil prices alone saved the Korean economy about $1.8 billion, and reduced interest rates significantly reduced the interest payments on the nation's foreign debt. The Korean won is closely tied to the U.S. dollar, and the rapid appreciation of the Japanese yen against the dollar in 1985 has made Korean products more competitive against Japanese goods in world markets.

Korea has become the world's fifteenth-largest trading nation and 80 percent of Korea's economy is dependent on trade. Because the United States is its largest market, some trade tension between the two countries is inevitable. As Korean exports continue to increase and the country moves into more technologically advanced fields, trade tensions with the United States are likely to increase as well. These tensions, however, may be counterbalanced by the increasing numbers of joint ventures that Korean companies are forming with U.S. firms, the progressive opening of Korea's markets to U.S. exports, and the growth of small and midsize Korean industries that respond more readily to the internal Korean economy. As is the case with Taiwan, the liberalization of Japanese markets would help reduce U.S.-Korean trade tensions because it would allow both countries to redirect some of their exports to Japan.

HONG KONG

Hong Kong, with a population of only 5.4 million, has emerged as one of the most prosperous economies in Asia through international trade. In 1986 it had a slight overall trade surplus of $.074 billion, and its per capita income was $6,763. Hong Kong's future economic direction is uncertain, however, because of increasing U.S. protectionism and its reversion to China in 1997.

A high population density (13,000 people per square mile), little arable land, virtually no natural resources, and excellent harbors led Hong Kong to concentrate on light manufacturing and reexport industry for economic growth. Unlike Korea and Taiwan, which have strict restrictions on imports, Hong Kong, with its small domestic market and heavy reliance on international trade, has a genuinely laissez-faire economy.

Hong Kong did not follow the example of other Asian NICs and shift its economy into high-tech industries in the late 1970s. In 1985 garments and textiles still accounted for approximately 40 percent of total exports, about the same level as 1980. Although the export of electronics and electrical goods increased in 1985, it amounted to only 14.5 percent of total exports ("Hong Kong's Money Sector" 1986: 43).

Between 1984 and 1985 Hong Kong's dependence on reexports over domestic exports increased sharply. Because of the increase in reexports, Hong Kong registered an overall trade surplus for the first time in 1985 (see Table 11-6).

Hong Kong is becoming more dependent on China for economic growth. China is Hong Kong's largest supplier and second largest export market. In 1985 reexports to China from Hong Kong grew 64 percent to $5.9 billion; in 1986 they declined by 11 percent to $5.2 billion (Bowring 1986: 77).

Trade with China has helped Hong Kong's service sector to grow much faster than its manufacturing sector. In 1979 only 18.6 percent of Hong Kong's workforce was in the service sector; by 1984 the service sector employed 23 percent of the workforce and accounted for almost $2 billion of the trade surplus.

Table 11-6. Trade Trends in Hong Kong (*billions of U.S. dollars*).

	Imports	Exports	Reexports	Merchandise Trade Balance
1980	$14.3	$ 8.7	$ 3.9	$-1.7
1982	18.3	10.6	5.7	-2.0
1983	22.5	13.4	7.2	-1.9
1984	28.6	17.7	10.7	-0.2
1985	29.7	16.6	13.5	+0.5
1986	35.4	19.7	15.7	+0.07

Sources: *Far Eastern Economic Review* (1986b: 78); and the Hong Kong Census and Statistic Department.

In recent years, Hong Kong's economic dependence on the United States has significantly increased. In 1981 the United States bought 26 percent of Hong Kong's exports; by 1985 the U.S. share had increased to 44 percent ("Hong Kong's Money Sector" 1986: 43). And in 1986 the $6.4 billion U.S. trade deficit with Hong Kong represented an increase of $4.4 billion from the 1980 level.

Most of the U.S. trade deficit with Hong Kong is in textiles and apparel. In 1985 Hong Kong exported $3.3 billion worth of textiles to the United States (Farnsworth 1986: D5). In response to U.S. pressure, Hong Kong has agreed to reduce the rapid growth of textile exports. Under the new agreement, imports will be permitted to grow 1/2 percent in 1986, 3/4 percent in 1987, 1 percent in 1988, 1¼ percent in 1989, 2½ percent in 1990, and 2½ percent in 1991 from the 1985 level (Farnsworth 1986: D5).

The June 1986 Textile Pact seems to have settled the U.S.-Hong Kong trade problem for the next five years and should help keep the lid on the U.S. trade deficit with Hong Kong. In order to reduce its trade deficit with Hong Kong, however, the United States should do everything it can to help Hong Kong penetrate Japanese markets. Japan exports to Hong Kong more than ten times the amount it imports.

Over the next decade Hong Kong will watch China closely for indications of how it will be treated once it becomes Chinese territory in 1997. If China maintains its liberal economic policy, most experts agree that Hong Kong will remain a major economic force. With closer ties to China, Hong Kong is expected to increase reexport and service industries. Because Hong Kong has not encouraged high-tech industries, however, its manufacturing competitiveness is expected to decline due to low-wage competition from other newly industrializing countries. Tokyo's emergence as the financial center of Asia is expected to further lessen the importance of Hong Kong.

Although Hong Kong is losing its competitive edge against Taiwan and South Korea, it will remain an important Asian commercial center because it is the only deep-water port off the southern coast of China. It also has an infrastructure, developed during the British colonial era, that will keep it decades ahead of other Chinese cities.

PEOPLE'S REPUBLIC OF CHINA

China is paradoxically both a newly industrializing country and a less developed country. Its per-capita income was only $340 in 1986, but under Deng Xiaoping its economy has been growing rapidly. Deng, who came into power in 1978, has successfully introduced individualism and private ownership into Chinese communism. Although his reforms have already had a significant impact, his long-term influence remains uncertain. If his reforms take hold, China could emerge as a powerful force in the world economy over the next few decades.

China's economy has improved dramatically as a result of Deng's economic reforms. Food production has increased 8 percent per year since 1978, about two and one-half times the rate in the proceeding twenty-six years (Reefs 1986: 57). Industrial output grew by approximately 9 percent from 1980–84, 14 percent in 1984, and 18 percent in 1985 (United Nations 1986: 63). Trade rose from $12 billion in 1978 to over $50 billion in 1985, and China's GDP increased 18.0 percent in 1984–85.

Deng's reforms have especially benefited small-scale private and collective sectors. Rural collective industrial output increased an average of 45 percent between 1983 and 1985. More than 64,000 small state-owned commercial enterprises were leased or sold to collective or private businesses in 1985 ("Business International" 1986: 90), and by the end of the year 10 percent of China's total retail business was privately owned and 40 percent was collectively owned. China has also set up Special Economic Zones (SEZ) to attract foreign business and to selectively test its economic reforms. In the SEZ, people are free to sign contracts and set prices without state approval.

Unfortunately, fast economic growth has also increased corruption and inflation and decreased the percentage of food production in the agriculture sector. From 1984 to 1985 the grain harvest dropped by 7 percent, and cotton production fell 33.7 percent ("Business International" 1986: 90) as farmers opted for cash crops at the expense of grain and cotton. The overall growth of agriculture was only 3.5 percent in 1986, a 1 percent drop from the average growth rate between 1965 and 1984 (IMF 1986). These developments have pressured Deng to tighten control over the economy.

The $1.5 billion smuggling racket involving top party officials revealed that China's "who do you know" system is as entrenched as ever. In 1985 overall inflation was a record 9 percent, compared to 2.7 percent in 1984, but has since declined to 6 percent.

The problems with agriculture, inflation, and corruption were the main reasons for the downfall of the Kuomintang government in 1949. Some Communist Party leaders believe that Deng's economic policy is reintroducing decadent capitalist idealogy back into China. These sentiments are shared by many urban workers who have not benefited as much as farmers from the current reforms and by mid-level and local bureaucrats who came to power under Mao.

The record $15.2 billion trade deficit in 1985 alarmed many Chinese. In 1984 the trade deficit was only $1.1 billion, but during 1985 imports jumped 39 percent to $42.5 billion, and exports increased only 9 percent to $27.3 billion. As a result, the government lowered the value of the Rwb by about 14 percent against major currencies in 1986 (Delf 1986: 50). This currency misalignment will discourage imports, which are expected to decline by 20 percent. At the same time, China will encourage exports by awarding tax, loan, and supply benefits to companies that generate foreign exchange. This plan is expected to reduce the trade deficit and increase China's foreign exchange reserves, which fell from $17.4 billion in 1975 to $11 billion in 1985 (Delf 1986: 50). In order to deal with these problems, China has opted to slow its economic growth rate. By the end of 1986, China's overall trade deficit declined to $12 billion, imports were $43.5 billion, and exports reached $31.4 billion.

Table 11-7. China's Trade with the United States, Japan, and Hong Kong[a]
(*billions of U.S. dollars*).

	Exports				Imports			
	1977	1982	1985	1986	1977	1982	1985	1986
U.S.	.2	1.8	2.3	2.6	.2	4.3	5.2	4.7
Japan	1.4	4.8	6.1	4.7	2.2	3.9	15.2	12.5
Hong Kong	1.6	5.2	7.1	9.8	.04	1.3	4.8	5.6

a. Exports, F.O.B.; imports, C.I.F.
Source: IMF (1981; 1987).

There will be considerable tightening in investment and domestic lending, and China's annual GDP growth is expected to increase by only about 7 percent from 1986-90.

In 1977 the U.S.-China trade balance totaled $391 million. By 1985 it had increased to $7.5 billion. China had a $2.0 billion trade deficit with the United States in 1986. The primary U.S. imports from China are petroleum and textiles, with the latter amounting to over $1 billion in 1985. China's primary imports from the United States are machinery and transportation equipment.

Japan is far and away China's most important trading partner (see Table 11-7). In 1986 Japan accounted for 29 percent of China's imports whereas Hong Kong and the United States—China's second- and third-largest trading partners, respectively—together accounted for only 24 percent of China's imports.

In mid-1985 Hong Kong and Macau accounted for 60.7 percent of China's total foreign investment, whereas Japan and the United States accounted for 10.5 percent and 8.7 percent respectively. Although U.S. investment has been increasing rapidly in China (Boeing, IBM, and Occidental Petroleum have recently invested nearly $6 billion) (Lord 1986: 31), few U.S. firms are enjoying profits. The U.S. embassy in China has reported that "China's door is being allowed to swing mostly in one direction: out" (Lord 1986: 31).

China's modern history is one of extreme swings. Many fear that Deng's economic reforms may not last long after his death because radical leftists still hold power at middle and lower levels of the gov-

Table 11-7. continued

	Total				Balance		
1977	*1982*	*1985*	*1986*	*1977*	*1982*	*1985*	*1986*
.4	6.1	7.5	7.3	—	-2.5	-2.9	-2.0
3.6	8.7	21.3	17.2	-.8	.9	-9.1	-7.7
1.6	6.5	11.9	15.3	1.5	3.9	2.3	4.2

Note: IMF figures do not include re-exports.

ernment. On the other hand, the Chinese people will not give up their new benefits easily, and a sudden shift in economic policy is unlikely.

China's economic future will depend on whether Deng's reforms continue to broaden and succeed. The key to Deng's success lies in effectively managing economic growth and keeping corruption in check. To accomplish these objectives, he is expected to pursue only a moderate economic growth rate over the next five years.

China's economic emergence will bring profound changes to the international economy. It is potentially both a huge market and a huge manufacturer of consumer goods. China is already a growing threat to the Asian NICs in textiles and other labor-intensive industries because of its low labor costs.

Although U.S. companies are not presently doing as well in China as could be hoped, it remains a very important market. Japan already has sizable investments in China, and if China does emerge as a major new economic force, the United States may find itself hard pressed to compete with Japan.

INDIA

Like China, India is both a newly industrializing country and a Third World nation. It has the potential to emerge as an important international economic power, but it remains a very poor country. India's population of 750 million comprises one-sixth of the world's total.

Although its GNP of $182 billion is double that of South Korea, its GNP per capita of $270 is among the lowest in the world. Less than 10 percent of Indians account for 40 to 50 percent of the country's GNP, and half of its population lives in extreme poverty. India's annual economic growth rate has averaged 3.5 percent for decades. During 1980–85, growth rose to an average 5.2 percent. Even though there are speculations on the effect of the liberal economic reforms introduced by Prime Minister Rajiv Gandhi on the economy, growth averaged 5.3 percent in 1986 and is expected to average between 5 and 6 percent throughout the near term.

India's government is interventionist insofar as it defines trade policy, decides on foreign investment and licensing agreements, regulates industrial production and expansion, and directs the economy through development plans. India has had seven Five-Year Plans and for some thirty years has pursued import-substitution. The Seventh Plan (1985–90) represents India's most liberal economic development strategy to date. It stresses consolidation, public-sector investment expenditures, and the increased privatization of industry. In order to foster domestic production, the prime minister lowered export requirements, simplified the application procedures for industrial licenses, and encouraged exports and technology through a variety of tax incentives.

Agriculture remains the most important sector in the Indian economy. Seventy percent of the population works in the agricultural sector, which accounts for one-third of India's exports and 38 percent of India's GNP. As a result of modernization, food grain output increased 24 percent between 1950 and 1986. Seventy-two percent of India's cropland is not irrigated, however, and total output in this area is low. But due to improved fertilizers, hybrid seeds, and better storage and preservation methods, India is approaching agricultural self-sufficiency.

Although there is wide disagreement over Indian trade statistics, the trend is clear: Imports are consistently outstripping exports. India's total exports in 1985–86 were approximately $9.5 billion, and its total imports were approximately $17.0 billion. India's trade deficit rose from $4.2 billion in 1984–85 to $7.5 billion in 1985–86 (calendar year is April 1 through March 31).

The United States is India's largest trading partner and second-largest foreign investor. From 1980–85 bilateral trade between India and the United States grew by $1.3 billion to $4.1 billion. In

Table 11-8. India-U.S. Trade by Total Value, 1980-86 (*millions of U.S. dollars*).

	U.S. Imports (c.i.f. value)	U.S. Exports (f.a.s. value)	Total Bilateral Trade	Trade Balance
1980	1,209	1,689	2,899	+ 480
1981	1,325	1,747	3,072	+ 423
1982	1,522	1,596	3,119	+ 74
1983	2,334	1,827	4,161	- 507
1984	2,737	1,565	4,302	-1,172
1985	2,479	1,642	4,121	- 837
1986	2,464	1,536	4,001	- 928

Sources: U.S. Bureau of the Census (1985); U.S. Department of Commerce (1986).

1986 U.S. exports to India totaled $1.5 billion, and U.S. imports were $2.5 billion (see Table 11-8). The United States currently accounts for 22 percent of India's exports and 9 percent of its imports. The Soviet Union, Japan, South Korea, Hong Kong, and several other ASEAN countries, however, are all trying to increase their share of India's capital-goods market.

The bulk of U.S. exports to India are fertilizers, semiprocessed materials, machinery and components, oil and gasfield equipment, aircraft spares and parts, industrial machinery, steel scrap, and chemicals. Principle U.S. imports are crude petroleum, gemstones, textiles, seafood, leather goods, and nuts.

India is a member of GATT and is covered by GSP nonreciprocal preferences until mid-1993. In 1986 it ranked eleventh out of 140 countries in the GSP program's beneficiary listing, and GSP exports to the U.S. totaled $219 million. Because of India's low income and low penetration of the U.S. market, it is not threatened by graduation from GSP.

Like other NICs, India has posted a trade surplus with the United States in recent years. The primary source of U.S.-Indian trade tension, however, stems not from the bilateral trade balance but from India's approach to the new GATT round. Along with Brazil, India has resisted inclusion of services in the upcoming GATT negotiations. India's service sector currently accounts for 38 percent of its GDP.

The success of India's Seventh Plan is uncertain. Antipoverty measures are conflicting with business interests; balance-of-payments imbalances remain a problem; relations with the Sikhs in the Punjab are tense; and pressure to use military force in Sri Lanka is rising.

The major emphasis of the Seventh Plan is to increase productivity and efficiency in the Indian economy. By opening itself to international foreign investment and export promotion, and by increasing recourse to private international loans, the Indian government hopes to develop its resources for future growth. The plan is based on a fifteen-year perspective and has a target of 5 percent annual growth through 1990. But the Seventh Plan will have to overcome industrial bottlenecks to reach its targets. Furthermore, the plan is expected to result in increasing government budget deficits and a rise in inflation (U.S. Department of Commerce 1986). Rajiv Gandhi's push to break India's relative isolation from world trade will result in efficiency increases but may exacerbate balance of payments problems. India's debt-service ratio is projected to rise to approximately 20 percent by 1990 (*Far Eastern Economic Review* 1986c), and any improvements in the near-term balance of payments will be heavily dependent on international crude oil prices and declines in imports of major commodities.

REFERENCES

Berg, Eric. N. 1986. "Mexico Debt Link Seen as Precedent." *The New York Times*, Oct. 2, p. D1.

Bowring, Philip. 1986. "A Plaid Surface Hides Opposing External Currents." *Far Eastern Economic Review*, May 29, p. 77.

"Business International." 1986. *Business Asia*, Nov. 24, p. 90.

Cohen, Roger. 1986. "Brazil Toughs Out U.S. Trade Complaints." *The Wall Street Journal*, June 5, p. 30.

Delf, Robert. 1986. "Peking Cuts Its Losses." *Far Eastern Economic Review*, July 17, p. 50.

EPC. 1981. *Illegal Immigration: Challenge to the United States.* New York: UNA–USA.

Far Eastern Economic Review. 1986a. March 27, p. 78.

_____. 1986b. May 29, p. 78.

_____. 1986c. June 26, p. 84.

Farnsworth, Clyde H. 1986. "U.S. and Hong Kong in Textile Pact." *The New York Times*, July 1, p. D5.

Gall, Norman. 1986. "Don't Push Us Too Far." *Forbes*, Feb. 10, p. 47.

"Hong Kong's Money Sector." 1986. *Asian Business* (April): 43.

International Labor Organization. 1986. *Trade, Employment and Industriali-zation in Singapore.* Geneva: ILO.

International Monetary Fund. Various years. *Direction of Trade Statistics.* Washington, D.C.: IMF.

Kirkpatrick, Melanie. 1986. "Singapore Looks to the Supply Side." *The Asian Wall Street Journal,* Feb. 24.

Liang, Kuo-shu, and Ching-ing Liang. 1986. Trade policy and industrial policy in Taiwan. Paper presented to Economic Policy Council NICs Panel.

Lord, Mary. 1986. "Each Chinese Bought Just One—." *U.S. News & World Report,* July 14, p. 31.

"Mexico Slips into Reverse." 1986. *Newsweek,* March 17, pp. 34–36.

National Journal. 1986. April 5, p. 814.

Reefs, Robert. 1986. "China Off the Boil." *Far Eastern Economic Review,* June 5, p. 57.

Republic of China Inspectorate General of Customs. Various years. *The Trade of China.* Taipei.

Stockton, William. 1986. "Rescue Plan for Mexico Viewed as No Cure-All." *The New York Times,* Oct. 2, p. D1.

Stokes, Bruce. 1985. "Rising Trade Deficit, High-Tech Growth Are Threats to U.S.-Taiwan Relations." *National Journal,* Nov. 30, p. 2699.

United Nations Conference on Trade and Development. 1986. *Trade and Development Report, 1986.* Geneva: United Nations.

United States Bureau of the Census. 1985. *Overseas Business Reports.* Washington, D.C.: U.S. Government Printing Office.

United States Department of Commerce. 1986, 1987. *Statistical Abstracts.* Washington, D.C.: U.S. Government Printing Office.

THE POLICY
FRAMEWORK

12 THE USTR VIEW OF THE NICs

Michael Smith

As is the case with developing countries as a whole, U.S. policies toward the NICs reflect their diversity. This group includes Korea, Taiwan, Brazil, Mexico, the ASEANS, Argentina, and Chile. Each of these countries has its own unique concerns and relationship with the United States.

Although the Asia and Pacific NICs have received the most attention, it is perhaps Brazil that poses the greatest challenge to U.S. policy. Brazil is the fourth-largest user of GSP. Unlike many of the other NICs, it is a country that has abundant natural resources. By applying the right economic policies Brazil could be in ten to twenty years self-sufficient in a great number of products, a major resource exporter, and a major manufactured goods exporter. Brazil has already made progress. Thirty years ago goods represented 1 percent of Brazil's exports. Last year they represented 70 percent of Brazil's exports—not merely radios and cassette players but also highly sophisticated manufactures, such as aircraft armaments. Last year Brazil had the third-highest trade surplus in the world, after Japan and West Germany, and the highest growth rate in the world.

How did Brazil do this? In trade they cut back significantly on imports and embarked on a major campaign to reduce its dependence on oil. If oil is excluded from the trade equation, Brazil's import ratio is only 3 percent. Brazil defends its closed trading system as necessary to generate the large trade surplus that it needs to service its $100 billion foreign debt.

Brazil preoccupies government circles as much, if not more than, any other developing country in the world not only because of what it is doing now but also because of the implications for the future. As a very powerful NIC, and maybe someday as a developed industrial country, Brazil is setting, or has the power to set, patterns that will influence the trade of other developing and newly industrializing countries. Specifically, Brazil has embarked on a major market reserve policy, one that cuts across all sectors. Automobiles and products relating to national security—as well as computers—have to be produced in Brazil. It has taken the informatics reserve policy and extended it across the entire semiconductor field. Anything with a digital component is reserved for companies in Brazil—including everything from measuring devices and computers to teddy bears. Anything with a semiconductor in it is off limits to foreign producers. Brazil is going to expand this policy because the international community is not challenging it; only the United States is. Brazil is going to expand this reserve policy into what it calls fine chemicals and eventually into more and more areas.

This policy raises some fundamental trade problems. We cannot get Brazil to join with us in pressing for liberal trade in services. All sorts of smoke screens are used to cover up the fact that they simply do not want to liberalize because they do not think that they have to. Brazil itself is a major exporter of services, but it does not want to cooperate in discussions on trade in services. The Brazilian government is providing no direction on the trade side of the equation. The people overseeing the trade situation in Brazil would rather pursue a policy of confrontation—not cooperation—with the advanced industrial countries. Many other countries are thinking about this type of confrontation. Argentina, Malaysia, and even Korea are wondering whether the Brazilians are not doing the right thing. The Brazilians, in turn, are saying that Brazil is merely imitating the Japanese. This trend could have serious implications for the future of the GATT trade system.

It is the unanimous view of the U.S. government that the situation in Brazil is delicate. Brazil's economic situation, its outlook, and its philosophy as a newly industrializing country fail to acknowledge that Brazil has certain international obligations and responsibilities in the world trading system.

Brazil's policies and attitudes contrast strikingly with those of most of the other NICs. The NICs in general, for example, have been supportive of a new round of trade negotiations. The more responsible NICs have even said that they would be delighted to eliminate GSP on one condition—that we revert to Article 19 of the GATT as the traditional escape clause, rather than structure voluntary trade arrangements. In other words, if the United States would resort to classic GATT responses to trade problems, the NICs would relinquish GSP. Some of the NICs, in this case including Brazil, India, and Thailand, also share a common interest with us in the question of agriculture. Furthermore, although dispute settlement is a major issue between the United States and other countries within the GATT, a number of NICs agree with us on this issue. They have been hurt by some of the European Community restrictions, and they would like to see stronger discipline established. The NICs also agree with us that the developed countries have done their duty in reducing their tariffs and that it is now up to the developing countries to do so. This would indicate that tariffs should not be a major problem in the new trade round.

One area in which we have serious disagreement with the NICs is on issue of intellectual property. The NICs simply do not agree with us. Whether they want continued permission to pirate, or whether they think that they cannot enforce copyright and patent laws, we are having a difficult time resolving this issue. My own view is that the likelihood of developing a GATT code with equal participation from the developed countries and the NICs is unlikely. The Reagan administration has also singled out investment as an important issue in the new round. The NICs agree that investment is important but are not willing to grant some of the major fundamental principals that we seek, such as national treatment, transparency, and arbitration.

I might also say a few words about South Korea. Some people talk about Korea as a new Japan, but it is not a new Japan—at least not yet. It does not have the size or muscle to do the things that the Japanese do. The Japanese are nervous about Korea. They are concerned, for example, about Korea's ability to produce personal computers and its success in the United States market. Although the Koreans are not liberalizing their market as much as they could, they were the first to break with the G-77 and support the new trade round. They want to make the right economic decisions if they can.

Unfortunately, it is a long and laborious process to get them out of their semiclosed market attitude.

The ASEANS' pattern is similar to that of other NICs. Singapore would sign almost any trade liberalizing measure with anybody. But as an ASEAN, they are somewhat inhibited to do so because there are mixed views within ASEAN about trade liberalization. Indonesia is perhaps the least able to liberalize its trade patterns. The Philippines, as we all know, is a special case. After Singapore, Thailand is most enthusiastic about trade liberalization, with Malaysia falling in the middle.

What does all this mean for U.S. policy with the NICs? We do not want to have a new trade round if it is limited to discussions among the developed countries, with some of the developing countries tagging along at the end as they did in the Tokyo Round. At the same time, however, we are not naive. Out of the ninety-two members in the GATT, there are really only about thirty-five important players. And if you discount the twenty-four from the OECD that are members of the GATT, then you have roughly twelve or thirteen important NICs. We would like to get them to think that this new round is important to them. We would like them to assume more obligations because by and large they are enjoying the full benefits, but they are not contributing their appropriate share. Indeed, there seems to be some sign today in countries such as Brazil and India that the NICs are going to resist doing anything more or assuming any increased obligations, no matter how well they are developing. The United States is willing to take the position that if we cannot mobilize support for the new issues in terms of GATT discipline, we will put them into codes. And for codes on such issues as intellectual property or services, the benefits will only extend to the signatories.

The U.S. position on graduation from the generalized system of preferences is clear. Eventually, countries must be graduated. It is not credible for Singapore to continue to have GSP. Many people disagree on this issue, and the administration's position has been that we will graduate only by product. But in the end, that is not going to work. You can try to graduate a country by graduating enough products, but what about a country like Taiwan, which had a $13.1 billion trade surplus with the United States in 1985? Rather than just take Taiwan off of GSP, we would like to negotiate. If it means giving them some continued modified GSP in exchange for some other concession, we may be able to benefit from this. If you remember, the GSP was established as a unilateral action. Recipient countries were not expected to make any contributions. We are gradually changing that system. The recipients of GSP should be required to negotiate some concession to the United States.

It has been questioned whether any of these countries should join the OECD. Several years ago Singapore notified the United States that it expected to have a per capita income of $9,236.00 by 1988, and at that time they would formally apply for OECD membership. That timetable is no longer realistic because it had a down-turn last year, but it will reach that income level by 1990. Singapore will apply, and Korea also would like to apply after 1988. They may be afraid of the Japanese and Europeans blocking their application to the OECD. The European community still tends to think of the OECD as an European entity.

The United States would like to see the LDCs, particularly the NICs, playing an active role in the new trade round. Some of the more advanced NICs, like some of the ASEANS, have asked in an informal way about a free trade arrangement with the United States, which will not happen in the foreseeable future. The United States has recently established a free trade arrangement with Israel and may do one with Canada. We should not push things too fast. To return to my original point, U.S. policy takes into account the range of issues and interests relating to the NICs. The Brazilian situation is disconcerting right now. Unless it can be turned around, it could jeopardize trade issues in the future. Argentina, on the other hand, seems to be interested in multilateral negotiations. It is not as enthusiastic as Korea and Singapore but seems to be retreating from the hard-line position that it took as recently as six months ago. Chile may be sliding the other way. I've avoided Mexico in this discussion because trade issues there have been overtaken by other events. The trade element is a relatively minor aspect of their overall economic picture at the current time. They are applying for membership in the GATT, but trade is a relatively minor portion of the economic problem that they face and that we face with them. As with all of the NICs—who after all are the success stories of the developing world—we hope and trust that Mexico will play an increasingly prominent and responsible role in fostering world trade.

13 THE UNITED STATES AND THE NICs

Bruce Smart

There is no single, authoritative document in Washington entitled "U.S. Policy toward the Newly Emerging Industrial Countries." Instead, U.S. policy toward this group of countries consists of a collection of actions, attitudes, and laws that respond to a constantly changing economic scene. This policy has evolved rapidly during the past year as the Reagan administration has taken an activist approach in the trade area.

U.S. trade policy is closely interrelated with all other aspects of foreign policy. The idea that a country's trade ministry operates independently of its finance ministry, its foreign affairs ministry, or its defense establishment is an oversimplification. Similarly, when considering trade policy options, it is nearly impossible to look at events in one country in isolation from those occurring in other countries. In the trade area, therefore, it is important to think of U.S. government policy in the aggregate.

The formulation and implementation of U.S. trade policy are complicated by the fact that many developments and trends are beyond the control of either the U.S. people or the U.S. government. One such trend is the rapid growth of human knowledge and our ability to transmit that knowledge to others. What is discovered in a U.S. laboratory today will be known in countries around the world much more quickly than ever before. Developing countries, and the newly industrializing countries (NICs) in particular, are participating in this accelerating process as both creators and users of new technologies.

171

A second and partially related trend—the growing integration of the world economy—also has a huge impact on U.S. trade policy while being far beyond our control. In a recent *Foreign Affairs* article, Peter Drucker (1986) suggests that neither the United States nor any other major country can set economic policy in isolation or control the course of the world economy through independent action. Thus, U.S. policy must anticipate and respond to shifting world economic trends without expecting to dictate them.

A basic fact of life that many Americans find hard to accept is that the economic conditions prevailing in the 1940s and 1950s, when the United States sat astride the world as the only major industrial power, no longer hold true. In that era, the United States was preeminent in almost anything it set out to do. It had the world's biggest market, best economic infrastructure, broadest educational system, and most advanced scientific establishment. The unique set of conditions that made this possible no longer prevails. The United States is much closer to being first among equals than to being the dominant player.

The consequences of this loss of dominance are perhaps most visible in the trade area. U.S. trade relations with all countries have become more difficult to manage as bipartisan support for traditional free-trade principles has eroded. In response to this disturbing trend, the present administration is working to strike a new balance in U.S. trade policy. This effort combines a reassertion of the United States' firm belief in open international competition based on comparative advantage, with an increased determination to eliminate unfair trade and investment practices.

The NICs, along with our developed-country trading partners, have been most directly affected by this more activist trade policy because (1) they are most significant as markets for U.S. goods and services and (2) the United States must have their support to maintain an open trading system. The United States believes that the NICs should be strongly encouraged to provide greater support for multilateral liberalization of trade and investment. Without the fuller participation of the advanced developing countries in this effort, the prospects for future growth in world trade and global economic progress will be considerably less.

There are clear precedents in post–World War II history that support this view. If one returns to the 1950s, the emerging industrializing countries were Japan, Germany, and the rest of Europe. Following a destructive period of protectionism that preceded World War II, these countries joined the United States in building an international framework to promote major trade liberalization. This framework, embodied in the General Agreement on Tariffs and Trade (GATT), has contributed significantly to world trade and economic growth since 1948.

Today, another group of newly industrializing countries is coming under pressure to play a greater role in maintaining and strengthening this trade framework. This group includes Korea, Taiwan, Brazil, Mexico, Hong Kong, and Singapore and possibly a few other advanced developing countries. By the early twenty-first century, additional Latin American and Asian nations may join this small but important group of NICs.

Until recently, the United States has tolerated a high degree of market intervention by the NICs. This policy has shifted, however, as the U.S. trade deficit has grown and pressures have increased within all industrialized countries to encourage some form of "graduation" by advanced developing nations.

Many of the present-day NICs are internationally competitive in the production of a broad range of industrial products. They therefore have less of a need than in the past to limit foreign access to their own rapidly growing markets. Given their significant and expanding impact on world trade, they are now being asked to reduce historic import barriers and accept greater responsibility for maintaining the open international trading system on which they depend.

It is important to recognize both the similarities and differences among the individual members and regional clusters within the NIC group that shape U.S. trade policies. For example, both the Latin American (Brazil and Mexico) and the Asian (Hong Kong, South Korea, Singapore, and Taiwan) NICs experienced rapid economic growth during the 1960s and 1970s and have recorded large surpluses in their merchandise trade with the United States within the last three to five years. The Asian NICs, however, do not depend as heavily as Brazil and Mexico on exports of agricultural commodities and other raw materials. The Asian NICs also are far less indebted relative to their net export earning capabilities than the Latin American NICs and have more favorable short-term growth outlooks.

The United States has tailored its policy approach toward the NICs to fit individual national circumstances, while uniformly pushing for removal of unfair and highly restrictive trade and investment practices in all of these countries. Since the announcement of the president's Trade Policy Action Plan in September 1985, the United States has held intensive consultations with most of the NICs to eliminate unfair and unjustifiable practices that adversely affect U.S. commercial interests.

Recent U.S. trade consultations with the NICs have covered issues ranging from the lack of intellectual property protection in Korea, to market access problems for U.S. computers, telecommunications equipment, and related services in Brazil, to tight restrictions by Mexico and Taiwan on consumer goods and other imports. These and other issues have been discussed in a variety of contexts, including consultations under Section 301 of the Trade Act of 1974, talks regarding Mexico's request for GATT membership (recently approved by the GATT), and bilateral meetings related to the general review of the U.S. Generalized System of Preferences (GSP) program. The NICs as a group (Taiwan, Korea, Brazil, Mexico, Hong Kong, and Singapore) are the largest beneficiaries of GSP, accounting for nearly 70 percent of total duty-free imports under the U.S. program in 1985.

Although pushing hard through bilateral channels for liberalization of trade and investment policies in the NICs, the U.S. government has strongly resisted protectionist efforts to close the U.S. market. This policy is based in part on a recognition of the importance of U.S. market access for the NICs, whose manufacturing sectors are steadily evolving. Access to the large textile and apparel markets of the United States and Europe continues to be the single most important form of access required, particularly for the Asian NICs, but is now only one of several market access issues.

Given major concerns about the domestic effects of rising textile and apparel imports from developing nations, the United States and other industrialized nations have not been able to provide unlimited access to their markets in this sector. Through the recently renewed Multi-Fiber Arrangement (MFA) and other mechanisms, a special international framework has been established that permits "orderly" growth in textile and apparel imports from developing countries. This approach balances the need of lesser developed countries and the NICs for secure access to U.S. textile and apparel markets with the need of U.S. industry for adequate time to make essential competitive adjustments.

The problems of international structural adjustment are not confined to the textile and apparel sector. An increasing number of advanced developing countries have developed their own steelmaking capacity and seek access to world markets, now severely strained by problems of excess production capacity. Some of these countries also are moving up the developmental ladder into production of motor vehicles and components, where international trade pressures also are increasing. A select few have become important producers of sophisticated consumer electronics and semiconductors by making effective use of foreign-developed technology. This is the same economic transition that Japan followed only a few decades ago.

Reciprocal U.S. concerns over the lack of access to NIC markets can be grouped into four broad categories: (1) the increasingly heavy reliance of the NICs on trade restrictions of all kinds to protect infant industries; (2) inadequate protection of U.S. intellectual property rights; (3) barriers to trade in services; and (4) restrictions on foreign investment. The specific nature of these problems and the degree of success achieved in resolving them vary greatly across countries, but some generalizations are possible.

Like the Japanese before them, the present-day NICs are prone to erect barriers that protect a large number of infant industries, often well beyond their early stages of development. In addition to imposing high tariffs and limiting imports through strict licensing procedures, many of these countries insist that foreign investors meet stringent local content requirements. They also directly or indirectly subsidize import substituting manufacturing enterprises—even when their production costs are higher than the equivalent import price. As a result, many have created inefficient industries while failing to develop other sectors that might give them a significant export capability. Following the Japanese prototype, many of the NICs also are using subsidies and other mechanisms to develop targeted industries that they hope will take them forward into the future.

Another common pattern among the NICs is their relatively weak protection of intellectual property rights, a problem that increasingly hurts both domestic and foreign innovators. Although this problem is not limited to the NICs, their comparatively advanced technological and manufacturing capabilities have positioned them to become the leading producers and exporters of counterfeit and pirated goods. In some cases, NIC government officials continue to view weak protection of intellectual property as necessary to promote low-cost development. Contrary to this view, the cost of failing to protect intellectual property can be quite high, as the infringing country's access to new technologies and desired products is reduced.

Protecting U.S. trademarks, patents on pharmaceuticals and other products, and copyrights on books, software, and videotapes has become a very big problem. U.S. industry losses are currently estimated to total about $20 billion annually. Accordingly, the United States has made increased international protection of intellectual property a top negotiating priority. It is responding through bilateral discussions with major infringing countries and by pushing for negotiations on this issue in the new multilateral trade round.

Foreign barriers to international trade in services also are a growing concern that affect U.S. policy toward the NICs. Through bilateral channels, the United States is making major efforts to remove foreign government restrictions affecting international shipping, insurance, banking and other financial services, and motion picture distribution. The U.S. government also is working to have the broad issue of services trade addressed in the next round of multilateral trade negotiations, which is expected to begin in late 1986 or early 1987.

U.S. commercial relations with the NICs also are complicated by major differences in investment policy. In contrast to most industrialized nations, many NICs believe that they need to tightly regulate investment in support of development objectives. They often fail to recognize that to meet these objectives they must attract large amounts of foreign equity capital. Over the longer term, most cannot afford to discriminate between domestic and foreign capital because they must compete with other countries for critical foreign investment funds. Some of the NICs, through a combination of poor macroeconomic policies and restrictive investment requirements, have actually encouraged domestic capital to flow abroad in search of more adequate or secure returns. The United States and other industrial countries have then been forced to loan these countries additional funds to replace what should have been available from domestic sources.

To mediate the rising trade frictions associated with expanded and more complex economic relations, the world needs a broader trading arrangement than the GATT now provides. This new trading arrangement must go beyond liberalized trade in manufactured goods to promote improved protection of intellectual property rights, freer trade in services, less restrictive investment policies, and strengthened rules for agricultural trade. This arrangement also must be structured to permit more effective enforcement than is possible under the present system.

This suggested broadening of the GATT should help put world trade relations on a sounder course. However, the United States cannot rely exclusively on multilateral agreements to resolve its trade difficulties. It also must address serious domestic economic and industrial competitiveness problems. Efforts are underway to reduce massive U.S. budget deficits, enact tax reform, and provide a strong climate for increased domestic investment and growth. Further trade liberalization must complement these broad economic reforms; protectionist policies would undermine or delay private sector adjustments that must be made to enhance long-term U.S. competitiveness.

To facilitate necessary competitive adjustments and rebuild support for an open trading system at home, the United States must learn to deal more effectively with the difficult problem of shifting people from one industry to another as the economy changes. This challenge is becoming more urgent as advances in technology shorten the average length of specific vocations and careers.

In conclusion, four points should be highlighted. First, the United States faces an unsustainable situation in the developing world today. In 1984 and 1985 this country absorbed more than 60 percent of all manufactured goods produced in developing countries. Although the strength of the U.S. dollar was a factor, it is not the only source of our trade difficulties. In fact, the currencies of many developing countries are pegged in some way to the U.S. dollar, so that U.S. trade with these nations responds primarily to other competitive factors.

A second problem is that the developing world, including many of the NICs, remains extremely dependent on the United States as an export market. This complicates trade relations with developing countries and contributes to rising protectionist sentiment in the United States. Protectionist sentiment gains further fuel from the fact that the United States cannot expect automatic improvements in its trade balance with several key NICs in response to the weakening dollar.

A third problem is one of timing as it relates to the upcoming multilateral trade negotiations. Assuming that the new round begins in late 1986 or early 1987, major changes in existing trade rules probably will not be implemented until the late 1980s or early 1990s. As a result, the trade round will do little to resolve immediate U.S. trade difficulties. Both focused and comprehensive (such as with Canada) bilateral discussions will be necessary to fill this gap.

Finally, there is the question of how to improve the worldwide economic adjustment process. The United States, in addition to working toward more effective adjustment at home, needs to take a hard look at the NICs and their adjustment problems. The Baker plan calls for industrial countries to provide debtor nations with additional funds so that they can expand investment and buy needed goods from the rest of the world. To attract necessary external support, however, debtor nations must be prepared to reform domestic economic policies that block faster growth. This kind of adjustment tradeoff, which is a key element in the Baker plan, must be made in tandem with hoped-for improvements in the international trading system.

REFERENCES

Peter F. Drucker. 1986. "The Changed World Economy." *Foreign Affairs* 64 (4) (Spring): 768–91.

14 SWAMPED BY DEBT
U.S. Trade with the NICs

John W. Sewell and Stuart K. Tucker

U.S. relations with the newly industrializing countries (NICs) hinge on trade and debt policy. The NICs will continue their rise in importance in the international system. However, the United States has not crafted a strategy toward the NICs that reflects growing U.S. economic and political interests in their prosperity. U.S. relations with these countries no longer are dominated by foreign aid because they are too advanced to receive official development assistance, and military security relations have little relevance because most of these countries are not of security interest to the United States. The key issue involving the United States and the newly industrializing countries revolve around economic issues—particularly trade and the financing of trade.

Due to their rapid economic progress, the NICs have become substantial export competitors in world markets in general and in the United States in particular. This competition has caused growing concern in government, business, and labor circles in the United States.

Most policy attention and debate has focused on U.S. imports from the NICs, and what is often overlooked by Americans is how important the NICs have become as markets for U.S. exports. Over the last twenty years, these advanced developing countries have grown rapidly. With internal demand outstripping production of

The views expressed in this paper are those of the authors.

179

indigenous industry, the NICs became important markets for the United States and other industrial countries. In fact, the NICs have been the most dynamic market for U.S. exports—growing an average of 7 percent per annum in the 1970s.

Unfortunately, the dual economic crises of recession and debt in the 1980s have had a drastic impact on U.S. exports to the developing world, and the NICs have become convenient scapegoats for U.S. concerns that unfair trade practices abroad have blocked exports of U.S. products. The critical constraint on U.S. exports to most developing countries has been the lack of finance, however, not barriers to trade. With recession retarding other industrial markets and debt constraining imports by the Third World, the NICs (many of which have substantial debt problems) have sent a growing share of their products to the fast-growing U.S. market.

The United States has responded to these balance of payments problems in the Third World in two contradictory ways. Debtor countries have been told to cut imports and expand exports. But the United States also has focused on import management—contributing to the worldwide trend of increasingly restrictive trade practices.

A continuation of this import protection trend—especially when aimed at the NICs—threatens to depress the economic prospects of our formerly most dynamic markets and directly affect the U.S. trade balance and key sectors of U.S. industry.

WHO ARE THE NICs?

When trying to develop policies appropriate to one set of countries, it is useful to set out a definition of the common denominator that makes these countries a discrete group. Defining the newly industrializing countries (NICs) is both easy and exceedingly difficult. On the one hand, policymakers and analysts generally agree that certain developing countries are advancing rapidly along the path toward industrialization and fall into this category. For instance, few question that Brazil, Korea, and Singapore are now in a much different economic class than Bangladesh, Peru, and Sudan. Yet it is difficult to define what the NICs have in common. In fact, the similarities of countries classified as NICs, both among themselves and with the industrialized world, is easily exaggerated.

Table 14-1 shows that the per capita income of those classified as NICs by even the most narrow definition is quite varied. An income definition overstates the development of the rich, oil-exporting countries. A definition based on the share of the labor force in certain sectors of the economy is also inadequate because countries differ widely in their resource endowments. The level of exports may indicate the importance of these countries in the world economy, but exports are also a function of economic size (which in itself is unrelated to industrial advancement).

In short, various classifications of NICs often reflect the policy priorities of the classifier. The inherent danger of this ad hoc approach is that policy thinking is often based on sets of economic facts and perceptions that have not been updated as quickly as reality changes. Thus, the perceptions lag behind the changing conditions of economic relations with these developing countries. In fact, the last fifteen years have been marked by a tendency to underrate the importance of the NICs to the international economic and foreign policy decisions of the United States, despite a great deal of discussion and analysis of the emergence of the NICs.

The effort to find a clear way to define countries is also fraught with pitfalls. Economic measures, even if they are accurate, may not adequately capture the social, political, and economic realities. South Africa is one example. Often classified as industrialized, its economic profile is perplexing. By income per capita measures it is only slightly better off than Mexico. Of course, in reality South Africa has a dual economy in which a minority of the population is in an advanced industrial country and the majority is impoverished and living in conditions comparable to the poorest developing countries. South African manufactures are similar to some industrial countries, but its consumption patterns are typical of the Third World. Dualism is present in a variety of forms throughout the NICs and semi-NICs, although not as strikingly as in South Africa.

Much of the current concern with the NICs that pervades the U.S. government and the private sector often is based on the notion that the NICs are an economic threat—if not on a national level then certainly within specific industries. This fear reflects the very real gains that the NICs have made in developing productive industrial sectors with low wages, but it also mirrors concerns about the future as much as about the present. The policymaking process, because it is generally a crisis-response process, lends itself to overestimation of the negative aspects of interdependence with the NICs and underestimation of the positive. This is sometimes due to misperceptions about the rate of change taking place. Although the NICs have made

Table 14-1. Economic Data on Selected Developing Countries.

Country	GNP Per Capita 1984 (U.S. $)	Manufacturers' Share of Exports 1980 (percentage)	Export Diversi-fication Index[a] 1982	Merchandise Exports 1983 (U.S. $ billions)	Labor Force Share: Ag. 1980 (percentage)	Mfrs. 1980	Serv.	PQLI[b] 1981
NICs								
Singapore	$ 7,260	54.0%	0.529	$20.3	2%	39%	59%	89
Hong Kong	6,330	96.5	0.744	22.0	3	57	40	95
Taiwan	2,540[c]	N/A	N/A	22.2	N/A	N/A	N/A	92
Argentina	2,230	23.2	0.661	7.8	13	28	59	89
Korea	2,110	89.9	0.647	23.2	34	29	37	86
Mexico	2,040	39.6	0.529	22.2	36	26	39	80
Brazil	1,720	38.6	0.502	21.9	30	24	46	74
Sometimes considered NICs								
South Africa	$ 2,340	53.6%	0.779	$18.2	30%	29%	41%	68
Yugoslavia	2,120	73.2	0.456	9.9	29	35	36	87
Portugal	1,970	71.7	0.564	5.2	28	35	37	86
Turkey	1,160	26.9	0.662	5.9	54	13	34	67
People's Republic of China	310	N/A	N/A	22.1	69	19	12	75
India	260	58.6	0.671	9.2	69	13	18	46

Selected semi-NICs and non-NICs

Saudi Arabia	$10,530	0.6%	0.801	$45.4	61%	12%	27%	45
Malaysia	1,980	19.1	0.658	13.7	50	16	34	73
Chile	1,700	20.2	0.855	3.8	19	19	61	85
Colombia	1,390	20.3	0.728	3.0	26	21	53	77
Peru	1,000	17.0	0.644	3.0	39	18	43	69
Thailand	860	28.1	0.753	6.3	76	9	15	79
Philippines	660	36.9	0.772	5.0	46	17	37	75
Indonesia	540	2.4	0.734	18.7	55	15	30	58
Pakistan	380	48.5	0.774	2.9	57	20	23	39

a. Diversification index is the absolute deviation of the country commodity shares from the world's structure. Expressed on a scale of 0 to 1, with smaller numbers indicating less deviation (less concentration). Calculated by UNCTAD (1986).

b. 1982.

c. Physical quality of life index. For an explanation of the derivation of this index see Morris (1977).

N/A = Not Available.

Sources: GNP per capita from World Bank (1986). Export data from IMF (1986) and UNCTAD (1986). Labor force data from World Bank (1985).

tremendous advances, successful countries like Taiwan or Korea remain relatively poor in comparison to the rest of the industrialized world.

There is substance to the perception that the 1980s are very different from the 1960s. These differences will require updated thinking on U.S. policy toward the NICs. Most important, the mere classification of countries as NICs may be irrelevant. As these countries advance, they have greatly differentiated themselves not only from the rest of the Third World but also among themselves. Just as each country within the industrial world is in a somewhat different position, so too the NICs will increasingly demand individualized policy attention. These countries insist that their economic circumstances warrant special treatment. Whether the issue is intellectual property rights or informatics trade, each NIC brings a different perspective on issues of fundamental importance not only to U.S. trade but also to the international trade regime as a whole. The rest of the century will reinforce such trends.

CHANGING WORLD

The world is a very different place in the mid-1980s than it was two decades ago.[1] In the current uncertain economic situation, the remarkable aggregate economic progress achieved by the Third World is often forgotten. The share of developing countries in world GNP has grown from about 15 percent in 1960 to 19.2 percent in 1979. The Third World's share of the *increase* of world GNP over the last decades has grown as well. In 1973–79 it was over 30 percent. However, this progress was spread unevenly.

Extraordinary growth of output by forty middle-income developing countries in the 1970s raised their share of global growth above the increment contributed by the United States and above that by West Germany and Japan combined. Coincidentally, the gap between the output of the NICs and that of low-income developing countries has increased because Third World development has proceeded unevenly. Consequently, the NICs were the fastest-growing markets for U.S. goods during the 1970s, but since 1980 the highly indebted middle-income developing countries, including the NICs, have become a significant drag on the world economy.

Developing countries became important participants in the international commercial financial system. The recycling of petrodollars, the decline in the relative importance of concessional aid flows, and the steady growth of direct foreign investment and debt in the Third World have left North-South commercial relations in a pivotal position in the global financial system. Developing-country debt grew at a rate of 23 percent per year during the 1970s. The debtor countries now have the potential of bringing down the pillars of the international financial system around their heads.

The U.S. economy has become internationalized over the last two decades. Today the United States is a debtor country, with ramifications for U.S. foreign policy that cannot yet be fully foreseen. The U.S. merchandise trade deficit is over $150 billion per year. The health of the U.S. banking system is integrally tied to the international debt crisis. Earnings on U.S. direct foreign investment overseas dropped dramatically during the global recession and remain low while the global economy experiences one of its most lackluster recoveries.

The 1970s and 1980s have shown the U.S. economy to be less independent from external shocks than it was in the 1960s. Far from being an exception, the oil crisis of 1973-74 proved to be the first of several external shocks that the U.S. economy would suffer in the 1970s and 1980s. In the area of trade policy, the standard responses to the U.S. trade imbalance have failed to produce the desired results. The dollar depreciation has been no panacea. Import restrictions, "voluntary" and otherwise, have failed to stop the ballooning of imports during the strong recovery. U.S. monetary policy is less autonomous than it has ever been in the postwar years. There is no fiscal policy flexibility anymore because structural budget deficits have built up over the years.

TRADE BETWEEN THE UNITED STATES AND THE NICs

The pattern of U.S. trade with the NICs has undergone a number of important shifts since the mid-1960s:

The 1980s witnessed U.S. trade with Asia surpass trade with Latin America in value. This growth was particularly concentrated in Southeast Asia.

Trade with the People's Republic of China has grown rapidly from virtual nonexistence to the point that China now numbers among the top twenty trading partners of the United States. Among developing country trading partners, it is ranked seventh.

The rise of oil prices in the 1970s has elevated the importance of a number of Latin American trading partners for the United States, particularly Mexico.

Despite the relative slip in the importance of Latin America as a whole, Mexico is still the most important Third World trading partner of the United States, and Brazil has undergone a rapid industrialization process, making it a major competitor to industrial country goods in a number of manufactured lines.

THE LINKAGE BETWEEN DEBT AND TRADE

The interdependence between the Western financial system, growth in the debtor countries, and industrial-country export industries is the most significant change in U.S. relations with the NICs in the 1980s. Although considerable attention is being paid by policymakers to the value of the dollar and the need to speed up growth in Japan and West Germany, the debt crisis remains the most critical factor in industrial country relations with the NICs. Although unfair trade barriers have received a large amount of discussion in recent months, the debt crisis remains the critical bottleneck to renewed growth of trade. The continuing difficulties faced by debtor nations have been a major drag on the global economy, despite rapid recovery in the United States.

U.S. exports and the trade balance have been damaged significantly by the events of the first half of the 1980s. Since 1982 the U.S. trade deficit with the Third World has ballooned rapidly (see Table 14-2). The 1984 U.S. trade deficit with the Third World was a record-high $53 billion—an amount equal to 1.4 percent of U.S. gross national product. Furthermore, the surplus in U.S. trade in services narrowed as a result of the decline of income from U.S. overseas investment, loans, and other services. Data on 1985 trade indicates that the deficit with developing countries did not significantly change. The 1986 U.S. trade deficit with the Third World is likely to be in the $50 billion range also. If so, the U.S. economy will have sustained three years of unparalleled trade deficits with developing countries.

The U.S. trade deficit with developing countries is largely due to the burden of the debt and the weakness of world growth, especially

Table 14-2. U.S. Trade with Developing Countries ($ billions).

	U.S. Exports	U.S. Imports	Trade Balance
1980	$88.2	$124.5	$-36.5
1981	97.0	127.3	-30.4
1982	88.4	109.1	-20.7
1983	77.1	113.0	-35.8
1984	80.0	133.3	-53.3
1985	77.2	130.0	-52.8

Source: U.S. Department of Commerce (various issues).

Table 14-3. U.S. Merchandise Trade Balances by Region, 1980-85 ($ billions).

	1980	1981	1982	1983	1984	1985
World	$-32.1	$-39.7	$-42.6	$-69.4	$-123.3	$-148.5
Developing countries	-36.5	-30.4	-20.7	-35.9	- 53.3	- 52.8
Latin America	0.0	1.3	- 6.0	-17.9	- 20.4	- 18.1
Asia	-11.9	-15.9	- 6.7	-11.8	- 26.7	- 29.6
Africa	-24.5	-17.0	- 8.3	- 6.4	- 6.2	- 5.2
Europe	0.4	0.3	0.3	0.3	0.0	0.0

Note: Imports are c.i.f. values and exports are f.a.s. values.
Source: U.S. Department of Commerce (various issues).

in developing countries (Tucker 1985: 1). These causes are particularly evident in U.S. trade with the NICs (see Table 14-3).

Of course, some of the NICs have indeed constricted imports and promoted exports using barriers and subsidies. But for the most part, these offenders are the countries that also are suffering from debt crisis. This trade policy action, therefore, should be seen in part to be a result of the pressures to service the debt. Indeed, the United States, particularly through its role in the international financial institutions, has urged debtor countries to expand exports and restrict imports as a means of resolving debt problems. Most of the U.S. trade deficit with the NICs is a result of debt, not unfair trading practices.

One major cause of the U.S. trade deficit is the pattern of the global recovery. The U.S. economy has expanded much faster than most other countries in the world. This has had a very predictable effect on the U.S. trade balance. With the U.S. market growing rapidly, the recovery of other countries' exports have been centered on selling to the U.S. customer. Because the European industrial countries have been experiencing a slow recovery, they have not bought as many of the Third World's goods as has the United States.

The effect of this difference in growth rates can be seen in world trade statistics. The U.S. share of world imports rose from 13.3 percent in 1980 to 19.2 percent in 1985. Also, the U.S. share of industrial-country imports has risen from 18.8 percent in 1980 to 26.6 percent in 1985. These trends also hold true for imports by industrial countries from developing countries. The U.S. share of industrial-country imports of all commodities from the Third World has risen from 32 percent in 1980 to 40 percent in 1984. The U.S. share of industrial-country imports of Third World manufactures has risen from 39 percent to 53 percent for the same period. Despite these increases in the U.S. share of world imports, however, the share of imports as a percentage of U.S. GNP has not risen since 1980, due to the parallel rise of U.S. GNP. In fact, U.S. merchandise imports as a percentage of GNP in 1985 were still slightly below the level reached in 1980.

Thus, it is incorrect to say that the United States has been experiencing an extraordinary import surge. The level of imports has been nothing more than should have been expected during a recovery.

Differences in growth rates around the world have had a more significant effect on U.S. *exports.* In 1980, U.S. merchandise exports accounted for 8.4 percent of GNP. By 1985 that figure had fallen to 5.3 percent. Even if one adds in the export of services, U.S. exports fell from 12.9 percent of GNP in 1980 to 9.3 percent of GNP in 1985. The growth of U.S. GNP only explains a small portion of this drop.

Thus, one of the important causes of the deterioration of the U.S. trade balance has been the economic problems in the Third World, which have damaged U.S. export opportunities. On the import side of the equation, the slow growth in other industrial countries has made the United States the major market for developing country exports. Of these two effects, the decrease in U.S. export opportunities has been more significant than the change of imports into the United States.

Table 14-4. Trade and Debt of Top Ten Third World U.S. Trading Partners[a] (*billions of dollars*).

	U.S. Imports	U.S. Exports	Debt
Mexico	19.4	13.6	23.9
Taiwan	17.8	4.7	1.8
Korea	10.7	6.0	8.7
Hong Kong	9.0	2.8	2.8
Brazil	8.2	3.1	23.3
Venezuela	6.8	3.4	9.5
China, People's Republic of	4.2	3.9	0.9
Singapore	4.4	3.5	1.5
Saudi Arabia	2.0	4.5	1.5
Indonesia	4.9	0.8	2.5

a. Total amounts owed to U.S. banks after adjustments for guarantees and external borrowing as of June 1986. Trade data for 1985.

Source: Federal Financial Institutions Examination Council (1986). U.S. Department of Commerce (various issues).

Differential growth rates in the industrial world, however, do not fully explain the fall of U.S. exports. The Third World debt has been the other major factor (see Table 14-4). Because Third World growth rates on average rebounded to a higher rate in 1984-85 than did growth rates in European industrial countries, one should have expected that U.S. exports to the Third World would have increased at a faster rate than exports to Europe in 1984-85. However, this was not the case. In 1984-85, U.S. exports to developing countries did not recover as fast as U.S. exports to other countries. In 1984, U.S. exports to developing countries rose 3.7 percent from the 1983 level. Exports to the rest of the world rose 11.7 percent in the same period. In 1985, U.S. exports to developing countries fell 3.5 percent, while exports to the rest of the world fell only 1.4 percent.

U.S. exports to the developing countries also declined more than other exports during the five-year period 1980 to 1985. In that period, U.S. exports to the Third World fell 24.4 percent in real terms, while exports to the rest of the world fell by 11.7 percent. Even more to the point, real U.S. exports to debt-strapped Latin America have fallen 30.9 percent. Further, U.S. exports to twenty-one developing countries heavily burdened with debt fell by 31.3 percent in real terms between 1980 and 1984.

These figures confirm that the Third World debt has had a major impact on U.S. exports. This is not surprising, since six major Latin American debtor countries reduced total imports from the world by 33.5 percent during the 1980–84 period. In the same period, imports from the world by developing countries with debt-service problems fell by 43 percent in real terms. Yet these facts have not yet been taken into account by policymakers.

U.S. JOB LOSSES

The decline of U.S. exports to developing countries in the period 1980 to 1985 also has had a significant impact on employment in the United States (see Table 14–5).[2] The first thing to be sacrificed by a country when it is forced to take austerity measures is spending on expensive consumer goods. The second is spending on heavy capital goods—especially the big ticket items such as aircraft, railroads, cars, trucks, construction machinery, and machine-tools. These are the sectors of the U.S. economy that have suffered the most due to Third World recession and debt.

More than 1.7 million U.S. jobs have been lost due to the recent recession and debt crisis in the Third World. This represents nearly 21 percent of official U.S. unemployment in 1985. In 1985 the United States had 650,000 fewer jobs due to the decline of exports to the Third World since 1980. Additionally, about another 1.1 million jobs have been lost that would have been created if the growth trend of the 1970s had continued after 1990.

Analysis of the job losses through 1985 show that of the 650,000 jobs that did not exist in 1985 that existed in 1980, 460,000 were due to the fall of nonagricultural exports. About 225,000 of those were due to the machine and transport equipment export decline alone.

The second major sector to suffer has been manufactured goods classified by materials. About 140,000 jobs were lost from this sector due to the lost exports to developing countries in 1980–85.

Although U.S. exports to almost every developing country have suffered during the 1980s, U.S. job losses have been particularly acute due to the fall of exports to the NICs because these countries

Table 14–5. U.S. Exports and Job Losses by Country and Region, 1980–85.

	U.S. Exports 1980	U.S. Exports 1985	Direct Job Decline	Lost Potential Job Increase	Total Job Loss	Share of Loss in Region
	($ billions)		(thousands of jobs)			(percentage)
Developing countries	$88.0	$77.2	650	1074	1724	
Latin America LDCs	38.7	31.0	363	472	835	
Mexico	15.1	13.6	103	185	287	34.4%
Venezuela	4.6	3.4	50	56	106	12.6
Brazil	4.3	3.1	50	53	103	12.3
Argentina	2.6	0.7	61	32	93	11.1
Asia LDCs	39.4	38.1	198	480	678	
Saudi Arabia	5.8	4.5	58	70	128	18.9
Taiwan	4.3	4.7	9	53	62	9.1
People's Republic of China	3.8	3.9	13	46	59	8.7
Singapore	3.0	3.5	1	37	38	5.6
Republic of Korea	4.7	6.0	-14	57	44	6.4
Hong Kong	2.7	2.8	9	33	41	6.1
Africa LDCs	9.1	7.4	82	111	192	
Republic of South Africa	2.5	1.2	43	30	73	38.1
Europe LDCs	0.9	0.7	8	10	19	

Source: Authors' calculations.

represent a large proportion of U.S. trade with the Third World and have been bearing the brunt of the debt crisis. The decline of exports to Mexico, the United States' most important developing country trading partner (and third most important overall), cost the United States nearly 300,000 jobs between 1980 and 1985. U.S. exports to Argentina suffered one of the most severe contractions, wiping out a large proportion of the jobs associated with those exports. The Big Four (Argentina, Brazil, Mexico, and Venezuela) cost nearly 600,000 jobs, 70 percent of the losses associated with Latin America and more than one-third of all job losses due to the Third World.

Even though the United States posted small nominal export increases with its major Asian trading partners, this growth was nowhere near the level to be expected in a healthy economic climate. About 372,000 jobs were lost or not created due to slower trade with six major Asian countries—China, Hong Kong, Korea, Saudi Arabia, Singapore, and Taiwan. Even without counting Saudi Arabia, where the export decline is due to the fall of oil prices, the impact has been substantial.

ELEMENTS OF CURRENT U.S. TRADE POLICIES

The U.S. government adheres to free trade principles, but U.S. trade policy is nonetheless marked by preferences and interventions in support of bilateral or industry goals. The record of U.S. intervention has been largely inconsequential or negative toward the NICs, with the exception of a couple of promising initiatives in the multilateral arena. Preferential schemes, bilateral negotiations on import restraints, quantitative restrictions, trade and international financial institutions, multilateral trade negotiations, and export promotion are discussed below.

Preferential Schemes

The generalized system of preferences was first passed in 1974 amid hopes that this trade-not-aid assistance to developing countries would bring about faster development. The implementation of similar programs by other industrial countries augured well for the program. The results have been positive, though moderate in magnitude.

Although critics have derided the concentration of benefits among a few NICs, the top fifteen beneficiaries represent more than 60 percent of the people in the.Asian and Latin American developing countries. Although not of major significance, the GSP does provide benefits to those industrializing countries that can produce the goods facing the highest U.S. tariff barriers. Furthermore, most studies indicate that the lower-income countries (which receive few benefits currently) would not be able to take up the slack left by removing eligibility of the NICs. Such removal would generally raise the price of the supplied good, but in most cases the dominant supplying country would remain the same. Thus, the trend during recent years for the U.S. president to "graduate" certain products of the major beneficiaries out of the program will not benefit the poorer developing countries and is likely to unnecessarily aggravate tensions with the NICs, without appreciably altering trade patterns (Tucker 1984: 6ff).

The U.S. government has been willing to pursue limited preferential trade schemes to support particular economic and strategic interests. The Caribbean Basin Initiative is one program that offers the hope that a triangle of cooperation can be achieved that will help the United States, the low-income countries of the Caribbean and Central America, and the NICs. By the United States' giving preference to imports from the Caribbean basin, there is an incentive for NIC producers to shift operations to the Caribbean basin for final assembly of labor-intensive goods, such as apparel. The trade diversion may be miniscule in comparison to total U.S. trade or to U.S.-NIC trade imbalances, but the benefits for the region would help speed development. Unfortunately, product exclusions and the lack of investment incentives have curtailed the potential of the CBI (Tucker 1986c,).

Toward Mexico, the most important NIC for U.S. policy, the administration has pursued a well-coordinated bilateral trade strategy, but the effort has yielded great conflict in U.S.-Mexican relations because of the interconnection of trade policy with other bilateral issues, particularly debt management.

Bilateral Negotiations on Import Restraints

Although the Reagan administration resisted the use of import relief laws during its first term, it has pursued an active policy of bilateral negotiation and threatened import restraint to achieve greater market access for U.S. exports to specific countries.[3] The NICs have borne the brunt of the countervailing duty and antidumping investigations and Section 301 actions against perceived unfair trade practices abroad. Much of this maneuvering was aimed at pacifying rising protectionist pressures in Congress, but the negotiations with Brazil and Korea over market access are being pursued vigorously. This drive to open up developing-country markets has very little chance of success due to sovereignty and infant industry considerations. By and large, unfair trade practices are in the form of nontariff barriers (NTBs) that are only loosely regulated by GATT. These obstacles are growing in importance in the 1980s because of the balance of payment difficulties that most NICs are facing. Furthermore, with the economic recovery of 1984 and 1985, many NICs have reduced their use of NTBs. If the United States is to successfully negotiate reductions in NTBs, multilateral talks are necessary. In this regard, the United States will have to be willing to put its own NTBs on the negotiating table. The variety and complexity of NTBs make bilateral discussions unmanageable without globally applicable rules. It is here that the Uruguay Round can be most useful (Tucker 1986b).

Quantitative Restrictions

Of course, the NICs are not the only countries using a variety of NTBs these days. Industrial country NTBs against Third World textiles, iron and steel, and agricultural products are particularly high. The United States is as much guilty as other industrial countries in these areas. About 64 percent of U.S. textile imports are covered by NTBs. The figure is 49 percent for iron and steel and 25 percent for agricultural products. In the cases of textiles and iron and steel, the NICs are the major suppliers (Nogues, Olechowski, and Winters 1986). Some NICs, especially Argentina, are also major suppliers of agricultural products—which face substantially subsidized competition from industrial-country producers. The announcement this year of "voluntary" restraint measures against machine-tools continues this U.S. trend to restrict market access in the goods in which the NICs are becoming most competitive. Despite all of these measures, the little industrial restructuring that has taken place is not attributable to the NTBs, and U.S. industries remain uncompetitive in most of these protected sectors. The farm sector is experiencing its most significant crisis since the 1920s, despite generous benefits from the 1985 farm bill. Although no clear solution to these problems is readily apparent, quantitative restrictions have proven to be costly for the limited "breathing space" they provide.

Trade and International Financial Institutions

A promising initiative that emerged in 1985 is the possibility that the trade liberalization measures advocated by the World Bank and the IMF will be rewarded with greater debt relief. Even though the formal link of debt relief to GATT round liberalization has not been officially endorsed, internal World Bank/IMF discussions have been viewed positively by U.S. officials. To date, trade liberalization has been one of the least successfully implemented "conditions" of World Bank structural adjustment lending. When push comes to shove, borrowing countries have been able to scrap liberalization goals while maintaining some commitment to the other conditions to ensure continued financial help. Perhaps the GATT discussions will be more fruitful in getting solid commitments to liberalization in exchange for debt relief. In any case, there can be little hope of Third World trade liberalization without debt relief, regardless of any explicit connection. In the future, the financial assistance may have to precede considerably the timing of the liberalization if the debtor is to accept the tradeoff.

Multilateral Trade Negotiations

Another promising initiative is the start of the new round of trade negotiations (the Uruguay Round). Unfortunately, these talks will not be finished and the deals implemented for another decade or so. The round is of vital importance to the United States and the NICs, but it will have no immediate impact on the protectionist landscape that is currently causing conflict.

The new trade round provides an opportunity for fundamental change in U.S.-NIC relations in the trade area. The Punta del Este meeting in Uruguay produced a shift in negotiating stances among the major developing countries. Although the preliminary negotiations in Geneva during January–July 1986 seemed to indicate some Third World unity behind the "hardliners" (Brazil, India, and so forth), September negotiations produced shifting alliances in which the United States found itself joined by developing countries as well as industrial countries in its maneuvers against other industrial countries. The South became a greatly disaggregated grouping of countries taking widely differing positions. Moreover, the industrial countries did not ignore those differing interests but instead cooperated to find a ground for consensus. As a result, the United States now has closer allies among the developing countries than among the industrial countries on a wide number of issues to be discussed in the Uruguay Round.[4]

Export Promotion

One of the least well-developed forms of current U.S. trade policy is export promotion. Most of the trade bureaucracy is oriented toward import management. By and large, U.S. industrial policies are uncoordinated. Export promotion in the form of subsidized access to credit from the Eximbank has been plagued by the lack of budgetary resources. If anything, the Treasury Department is reluctant to engage in what it considers to be market distorting practices (Feinberg and Tucker 1986). Up until 1985, mixed credits were an issue of industrial-country competition over Third World markets. However, in 1985 the Eximbank used subsidized credit to deny sales to developing country firms. The first use, against Brazil, might only be a "shot across the bow." However, the NICs are the most likely targets of a greater use of this policy because Eximbank must marshal its limited resources in largely symbolic actions, and actions against the NICs will get the most press. This export policy will yield fewer exports, not more exports, for U.S. firms in the short-run, while having uncertain ramifications for the long-run. The United States could go much further toward crafting an export promotion policy that benefitted U.S.-NIC trade. With the commercial banks retrenching, the U.S. government is the only source of finance that can re-ignite trade with the NICs, yet Eximbank programs are small and shrinking. At a minimum, the direct lending levels of Eximbank need to be restored (being one-third of their peak at the beginning of the decade). Commerce Department marketing assistance is useless to big businesses (which have their own capacity) and underused by small business. Foreign market demand reports need to be deeper—analyzing more of the societal and political variables that affect economic decisions. Twin planting and offshore assembly receive little U.S. governmental attention, although these modes of production require the most intergovernmental attention if they are to prove satisfactory to both countries.

NEED FOR A NEW POLICY FRAMEWORK

The public adherence of the Reagan administration to free trade principles is largely being complemented by a policy of damage limitation—restrictions aimed at appeasing domestic interests without destroying the fabric of the liberal trade order. Unfortunately, this procedure is resulting in very little appeasement of domestic interests, largely because the structural causes of U.S. trade problems are not being addressed. Action against the overvalued dollar came several years later than necessary to head off imbalances with Japan and Europe. Now, action on debt relief is coming too late to halt complaints about barriers to access to NIC markets.

A policy that combined debt relief with export promotion, instead of the current policy of import management, would be far more effective for exports, and potentially for domestic political pressures, as well as global economic prosperity. Once debt relief measures reignite growth, the United States will need to pursue active export promotion policies to remain competitive.

The dynamic NIC markets of the 1990s will be nothing like the NIC markets of the 1970s or the low-income developing-country markets of today. NIC import needs have changed over time. Just as U.S. business will have to reorient its thinking, the U.S. government would be well advised to alter its conceptions of the economic world to fit these realities. NICs cannot be lumped together with other Third World countries. Nor can they be handled as if they were all alike.

Furthermore, the North-South dichotomies of the 1970s may no longer apply. The small but strategic Office of the U.S. Trade Representative must take the lead in reorganizing institutional thinking on trade policies toward the NICs. As long as there are more officials working on import restriction mechanisms than on all of Latin American trade bilateral issues, there is no hope that U.S. policy toward the NICs will be forward-thinking.

POLICY ALTERNATIVES

The debt crisis is having an adverse effect on the U.S. economy as a whole, not just on the banking sector. It is imperative that the U.S. government begin to move toward a policy of cutting the costs of the debt crisis. Through wise debt management policies, it may be possible to limit the extent of the damage to the global economy as well as to our own economy.

Baker Plan

The Baker initiative shows a significant shift in attitude on the part of the U.S. government toward the gravity of the crisis. The plan calls for renewed lending to the major debtor countries in an effort to reduce the net capital outflow from debtors that presently marks the debt crisis. This will certainly forestall a major collapse of the system for the time being, but this strategy does not offer a light at the end of the tunnel. Although nominally calling for growth in the Third World to alleviate the debt crisis, in fact the main emphasis is still on austerity and policy reform in the Third World. The amount of money that the World Bank can currently commit to the problem is insignificant compared to the net capital outflows. Furthermore, the plan proposes only a small increase in new commercial lending, which in any event shows little sign of materializing. Prudent bank practices are wary about creating new exposure in such risky financial circumstances. Thus, Third World policy reform seems to be the only instrument of the Baker plan that is being implemented. The likely medium-term outcome of this policy is minimal changes in net capital flows, continued growth in the absolute size of the debt burden, and continuing austerity in developing countries.

Broader Debt Relief

The reduction of current and future debt service burdens is an option that implies losses for the banking community. In fact, the U.S. economy as a whole is already losing because of the debt crisis. The choice facing the U.S. government is one of how to reduce the over-all loss to the U.S. economy and how to distribute the impact of these losses fairly. Until the shift in attitude signified by the Baker plan, the U.S. government showed every sign of letting the banks and the developing countries decide these effects. Unfortunately, the Baker plan does not go far enough toward finding a way of burden-sharing that is both fair and likely to reduce the impact of the losses.

Effective debt relief can be carried out only by active intervention by the United States and other industrial-country governments. A wide variety of debt relief measures has been suggested in recent years.[5] The issue is one of the political will to act. The precise recipe for debt relief always will be controversial. However, once the over-arching necessity to act is agreed on, the mechanical obstacles to debt relief will be seen as minor compared to the costs of not acting.

DEBT RELIEF AND INTERNATIONAL TRADE POLICY

A more activist governmental approach to resolving the debt crisis should encompass the issue of appropriate, complementary trade policies in the United States, in other industrial countries, and in debtor countries. The tremendous, recent shift in the U.S. trade bal-ance has been beneficial to debtor countries, in that our deficit is the mirror image of their trade surpluses, which in turn are necessary if the debt is to be serviced. However, the size of the U.S. trade deficit is unsustainable politically, if not economically. Just as the Third World economies cannot sustain the large drain of their export earn-ings to service their debts, the U.S. export sector should not continue to suffer from contracting markets.

Of course, the United States has to run trade deficits with debtor countries if debt repayment is expected. Otherwise, there would be no way for the debtors to transfer real value to creditors. Thus, the United States would be amiss to expect a rapid return to balanced trade with debtor countries. Yet current U.S. trade prospects promise not only deficits in the immediate future but also no expansion of U.S. exports. If the U.S. export sector is to revive, then total trade with debtor countries will have to increase. This is possible only in an expanding economic climate. Despite the mild recovery undergone in some parts of the Third World in the last two years, growth prospects remain dampened by the austerity measures required by current debt strategies.

More than simply a matter of austerity, current debt policies have advocated trade liberalization in debtor countries. Trade liberalization policies in debtor countries seek to establish more efficient, export-oriented growth, but the short-run impact of such policies is usually the reverse—a rapid rise in imports. This is temporarily good for U.S. exports but potentially disruptive to debt service. For most developing countries, liberalization can succeed only if undertaken gradually. Even then, these countries will continue to experience difficulty importing due to debt service problems and slow growth. Further, liberalization may be politically discredited if it is tied to austerity measures. Moreover, political pressures within the debtor countries feeds on the structural dislocations caused by these liberalization measures.

Thus, rapid trade liberalization measures within debtor countries, at this point in time, will politically and economically endanger debt management policies. Attempting to use World Bank lending to rapidly alter the trade policies of debtor countries may lead to ruin for debt management policy.

A more appropriate global trade strategy that complements a solution to the debt crisis should seek the opposite—an expansion of the economies of the creditor nations. The U.S. market has been the major recipient of the Third World's exports in recent years. If this cannot be continued, then the burden of change should rest on other industrial countries. Europe and Japan need to pursue expansionary policies that lead to stronger import demand. Further, European and Japanese trade practises need to accommodate such a rise in import demand. If all three major industrial areas—the United States, Europe, and Japan—pursue open trade policies and sustained rapid growth, then the Third World will be able to significantly increase both its exports *and* its imports. Although the effect on the U.S. trade balance with developing countries may be only gradual, at least the expanding export markets abroad will help revive U.S. export industries and jobs.

CONCLUSION

Concern about the link between trade and debt issues in today's global economic environment is rising. However, the cart must not be put in front of the horse. Financial constraints are the major barrier to U.S. trade with the Third World. Any attempt to rectify the U.S. trade deficit by restricting imports from the developing countries will only exacerbate the debt crisis. Yet providing debt relief will help U.S. export industries and reduce the U.S. trade deficit. Debt management should be placed ahead of trade deficit reduction on the U.S. policy agenda with the Third World.

Furthermore, debt relief must come soon. U.S. export-related jobs are being lost. Import-competing industries are being pressed. With each passing day, Third World leaders and populations become less willing to follow the current approach to the debt crisis.

NOTES

1. See Sewell and Contee (1984) for a further description of the changed international economic environment.
2. See Tucker (1986d) for an explanation of the methodology used to produce these job loss estimates.
3. See Lande and Van Grasstek (1985) for an analysis of Reagan administration use of import relief measures.
4. See Preeg (1985) for a comprehensive review of the issues and opportunities presented by the new round to U.S. relations with the Third World.
5. See Feinberg (1984) for a more detailed analysis of these measures.

REFERENCES

Federal Financial Institutions Examination Council. 1986. *Country Exposure Lending Survey, June 1986.* Washington, D.C.: Board of Governors of the Federal Reserve System.

Feinberg, Richard E. 1984. "Restoring Confidence in International Credit Markets." In *Uncertain Future: Commercial Banks and the Third World,* edited by Richard E. Feinberg. ODC Policy Perspectives No. 2. New Brunswick, N.J. Transaction Books.

Feinberg, Richard E., and Stuart K. Tucker. 1987. "Export Credits in U.S. Trade, Development and Industrial Policy." In *The Export-Import Bank at Fifty,* edited by Rita M. Rodriguez. Lexington, Mass.: Lexington Books.

International Monetary Fund. 1986. *Direction of Trade Statistics.* Washington, D.C.: IMF.

Lande, Steve, and Craig Van Grasstek. 1985. "Trade with the Developing Countries: The Reagan Record and Prospects." In *U.S. Foreign Policy and the Third World: Agenda 1985–1986*, edited by John W. Sewell, Richard E. Feinberg, and Valeriana Kallab. ODC Policy Perspectives No. 3. New Brunswick, N.J.: Transaction Books.

Morris, Morris David. 1977. *Measuring the Condition of the World's Poor: The PQLI.* New York: Pergamon Press.

Nogues, Julio J., Andrzej Olechowski, and L. Alan Winters. 1986. *The Extent of Non-tariff Barriers to Imports of Industrial Countries.* Working Paper No. 789. Washington, D.C.: World Bank.

Preeg, Ernest H., ed. 1985. *Hard Bargaining Ahead: U.S. Trade Policy and Developing Countries.* ODC Policy Perspectives No. 4. New Brunswick, N.J.: Transaction Books.

Sewell, John W., and Christine Contee. 1984. "U.S. 'Costs' of Third World Recession: They Lose, We Lose." *ODC Policy Focus* 2 (July): Washington, D.C.: Overseas Development Council.

Tucker, Stuart K. 1984. "The U.S. GSP Program: Trade Preferences and Development." *ODC Policy Focus* 6 (September).

_____. 1985. "U.S.-Third World Trade Deficit: Going after the Causes." *ODC Policy Focus* 7 (November).

_____. 1986a. "The Caribbean Basin Initiative: Elevated Expectations and Limited Means." Paper prepared for the Conference on Selective Preferential Arrangements between Developed and Developing Countries (Mini-NIEO), Helsinki, Finland, November 28–30.

_____. 1986b. "Non-Tariff Barriers: Growing Obstacles to U.S.-Third World Trade." *ODC Policy Focus* 4 (July).

_____. 1986c. "Statement before the Subcommittee on Trade of the House Committee on Ways and Means, February 25, 1986, on the Impact of the Caribbean Basin Initiative." 99th Cong., 2d Sess.

_____. 1986d. "Update: Costs to the United States of the Recession in Developing Countries." Working Paper No. 10. Washington, D.C.: ODC.

UNCTAD. 1985. *Handbook of International Trade and Development Statistics, 1985 Supplement.* Paris: UNCTAD.

U.S. Department of Commerce. Various years. *Highlights of U.S. Export and Import Trade.* Washington, D.C.: U.S. Government Printing Office.

World Bank. 1985. *World Tables, 3d ed.* Washington, D.C.: World Bank.

_____. 1986. *World Development Report.* New York: Oxford University Press.

15 A LABOR PERSPECTIVE ON U.S. POLICY TOWARD THE NICs

Jay Mazur

The U.S. economy is in serious trouble. Its rebound from the disastrous recessions of the early 1980s was built on a shaky foundation. The recovery and expansion in the last three years has been lopsided and fueled by debt to a greater extent than is usually the case.[1]

Economic growth in the 1980s has been characterized by a weaker industrial sector, higher unemployment and underemployment, and concentration of job growth in the service sector. Manufacturing production worker employment has regained only half of the job decline that occurred during the 1981–82 recession and is still nearly 2 million below the peak level reached in 1979.

The extraordinary increase in debt by households, corporations, and the federal government provided an illusion of prosperity that masked the sharp deterioration in our industrial base. By borrowing heavily from abroad the United States was able to induce an expansion that added millions of jobs. Yet the outlook remains fragile, and the damage to the industrial base is on the verge of becoming permanent.

The decline in the U.S. industrial base is primarily a result of the deteriorating trade balance, particularly the surge in imports. U.S. exports of manufactured goods declined by 6 percent between 1981 and 1985, while imports of manufactured goods increased by 73 percent. The manufacturing trade balance went from a $5 billion surplus in 1981 to an astounding $113 billion deficit in 1985. The dramatic oil price decline kept our total merchandise trade deficit from soaring over $150 billion last year (U.S. Bureau of the Census 1981a, 1985).

It should be noted that to the extent that U.S. imports originate in low-wage countries (over a quarter of the dollar volume of U.S. manufactured imports comes from low-wage countries), a dollar of imports displaces more than a dollar of domestic production.

U.S. industrial production has remained basically flat for the last year-and-a-half as business and consumer spending has increasingly gone to the purchase of imports. Imports account for a significant share of a growing number of consumer and capital goods sectors. In 1985 import penetration as a share of the domestic market was 23 percent in steel, 26 percent in autos, 43 percent in machine tools, 30 percent in all capital goods, 53 percent in apparel, and 77 percent in footwear ("President's Steel Program" 1986: 11; *U.A.W.* 1986: 21; U.S. Department of Commerce 1987: 21-3; "U.S. International Transactions" 1986: 291; ILGWU 1986; U.S. Department of Commerce 1986b: 44-9).

Unchecked imports have prevented a sustained rebound in business investment in the United States and have focused the efforts of U.S. manufacturing firms on foreign sourcing of parts and final products for the U.S. market. In 1977 intrafirm transactions between foreign subsidiaries and the U.S. parent companies of multinational corporations accounted for 58 percent of U.S. imports. The current share of imports accounted for by the captive trade of multinationals is undoubtedly much higher ("World's In-House Traders" 1986: 61).

Following the assessment of a Japanese corporate leader, *Business Week* labeled this trend the "hollowing" of U.S. manufacturing:

> In industry after industry, manufacturers are closing up shop or curtailing their operations and becoming marketing organizations for other producers, mostly foreign.
>
> Unchecked, this trend will ultimately hurt the U.S. economy. The traditional industrial sector has long been the leader in U.S. growth in productivity, the wellspring of innovation, and the generator of a rising standard of living (The Hollow Corporation 1986: 57).

Moreover, many U.S. firms increasingly turn to foreign production to supply overseas markets. Whether to supply the domestic or foreign markets, U.S. corporations increased their direct foreign investment by 25 percent between 1979 and 1984. When U.S. parent borrowings from their overseas affiliates are excluded, the equity position of U.S. firms in foreign production grew by 39 percent between 1979 and 1983 (Little 1986: 43, 51). This rate of foreign investment was more than double the growth in domestic business fixed investment over that period.

Certainly the combination of tight monetary policy and loose fiscal policy that pushed the foreign exchange value of the dollar higher has been responsible for some of the trade imbalance and resulting deterioration of the industrial base. However, although the dollar has declined in the last year, particularly against the yen, the needed readjustment of currency rates will not significantly reduce the manufacturing trade deficit.

U.S. exports to the debt-burdened Latin American countries will not improve appreciably, and Japan simply will not increase its purchase of U.S. produced goods by much. Having allowed imports to capture a large share of a number of important domestic product markets, we will be hard pressed to reestablish the position of domestic production in the U.S. market through a more appropriately valued dollar alone. Foreign producers have already demonstrated a willingness to accept lower profits as the price of holding their place in the U.S. market. And in many cases, foreign industrial capacity was expanded specifically with the U.S. market in mind.

Having closed plants here and established foreign sourcing supply lines, U.S. firms will not readily reverse the process in response to a lower dollar. In addition, the currencies of some of our major trading partners, such as Mexico and Canada, have not risen against the U.S. dollar in the last year. Other countries, such as South Korea and Taiwan, have their currencies tied to the U.S. dollar—the dollar's decline will not relieve the trade pressures existing with those countries.

More important than the dollar's appreciation as a factor in the burgeoning trade deficit have been two longer-term factors: (1) the general U.S. approach to world trade and (2) the rise of export-oriented development in Japan and the newly industrialized countries.

The recent U.S. trade experience is a function of the untenable approach toward international trade prevailing in this country. To a great extent, this attitude is a holdover from policies developed in the early post–World War II period when the trading framework better served U.S. interests. At that time, our main objective was to rebuild the war-torn economies of Western Europe and Japan in order to establish a strong Western alliance. In the 1950s our attention broadened to encompass a concern for the economic development of the less developed countries that were just emerging from the shackles of colonialism.

During the first two decades of the postwar period, the U.S. economy was preeminently strong, and our trade policy was fairly consistent with developing our own economy and furthering our strategic political goals.

Assisted by U.S. aid and technology and protected by our military shield, Western Europe and Japan were able to reestablish and expand their industrial production systems and domestic markets. The industrial democracies became relatively less reliant on U.S. exports and developed strong export capabilities of their own. Through a policy of directed industrial stewardship, Japan pursued a model of export-oriented development in a number of key industries. Some of the less developed countries followed the Japanese model of export-led growth and eventually emerged as newly industrialized countries.

Today, the international trading environment is much different than it was in the early postwar period. The most important consideration is that other countries approach trade with a view toward enhancing the development of their own economies, while the United States subordinates domestic economic considerations to the ideal of "free" trade.

The postwar growth of world trade did not reflect open trading as much as it represented growth-induced trading in support of national development goals, or the trade of multinational corporations that either located low-skill, labor-intensive production in low-wage countries or that were drawn into direct foreign investment in order to sell in foreign markets.

A widely shared perspective among our trading partners has been, in effect, "buy from the U.S. what you need in order to acquire the technology and essentials to develop your own economy and treat the large U.S. market as a stepping stone to economies of scale and international competitiveness." There is a good deal of trade, but it is, with the exception of the United States, guided and regulated by national objectives.

It is unrealistic to assume that all imports that enter the U.S. market reflect the inherent comparative advantage of foreign economies. As the Japanese experience has so effectively demonstrated, comparative advantage can be created through the coordinated development and deployment of capital, labor, and technological resources along with insulation from international competition. In a global system with mobile capital and relatively transferrable technology, the only basis for comparative advantage soon becomes low wages. Whereas twenty years ago this was generally true only in the most labor-intensive industries, such as apparel, today it is clear that it is also the case with steel, autos, and a wide range of electronics goods.

The export-led growth of the newly industrialized countries illustrates the extent to which this has taken place. The NICs have progressed from the manufacture of apparel and textiles to the point where they are also able to produce a broad range of intermediate goods and machinery and even, in some cases, advanced electronics equipment.

The flip side of the record of export-oriented "successes," however, has been the availability of a market in which to sell. And to an inordinate extent, the United States has served as the major outlet for the products of export-oriented economies.

Although slow growth in the other industrial countries has kept total global trade from increasing as rapidly in the 1980s as in the prior decade, the attention of major exporting countries, both industrial and the NICs, has been focused mainly on the large and open U.S. market.

The United States cannot continue to function as the principal market for the growth in world imports. The U.S. share of world imports rose to 17.1 percent in 1984, up from 11.6 percent in 1973. Meanwhile, Japan's import share was only fractionally higher in 1984 than in 1973, and only about a third as large as the U.S. share. For every other industrial country the share of world imports was less in 1984 than in 1973 (General Agreement on Tariffs and Trade 1985: Table A6). Data for 1985 will almost certainly show yet a further worsening in the imbalanced industrial country shares of world imports. The United States takes three-fifths of the total manufactured exports of the LDCs.

Our trade with noncommunist developing countries in Asia and Latin America, including the NICs, accounted for only one-third of the deterioration in the balance of trade over the last four years. Yet the magnitude of the shifts in U.S. trade with these countries is ominous in its own right and portends greater problems unless we seriously reassess the nature of our economic relations with these countries.

U.S. manufactured exports to Latin America declined by a third in the last four years, while manufactured imports from those countries increased by 77 percent. Although our manufactured exports to the developing countries and NICs of the Far East grew slightly from 1981 to 1985, imports of manufactured goods from those countries increased by 84 percent. In 1985, manufactured imports into the U.S. from Far Eastern developing countries and NICs were over three times the volume of U.S. manufactured exports to those countries (U.S. Bureau of the Census 1985).

Direct foreign investment by multinational corporations has played a significant role in the growth of manufactured exports from many Asian developing countries and NICs. For example, in 1980 over 90 percent of Singapore's and Malaysia's manufactured exports were produced by enterprises wholly or partly foreign owned. The share of South Korea's manufactured exports accounted for by multinationals was about one-third in 1977 (Maex 1985: 14).

Much of the foreign investment in the Asian developing countries and NICs occurs in export processing zones. In addition to a host of financial and tax incentives for firms locating in the export processing zones, internationally recognized labor standards are less frequently observed in the zones than in developing countries generally. To ensure their "international competitiveness," many Third World countries suppress efforts to unionize and do not regulate health and safety conditions in their export zones (Debt Crisis Network 1985: 11).

The overriding problem is that neither the United States nor the NICs are on course for sustainable growth that provides for equitably distributed, rising living standards. There are obvious limits to the capacity of the U.S. market to absorb ever increasing imports. In addition, the extreme export-oriented nature of the Asian NICs economies raises questions that need to be addressed. Among these are the following:

1. Has the near-singular focus of the Asian NICs on the U.S. market made their economies excessively dependent on U.S. macroeconomic conditions?

2. Have the export "successes" of the Asian NICs limited the development potential of less developed countries? (South Korea, Taiwan, Hong Kong and Singapore account for 60 percent of all LDC manufactured exports (Linder 1985: 279).)

3. To the extent that low labor costs become the basis for competitive advantage in export markets, does this hinder balanced economic development within the NICs?

4. What are the consequences for labor and human rights of a low-wage based export orientation?

5. What is the effect on economic development of multinational corporate involvement in the NICs?

6. How can NIC and LDC growth be promoted without undermining the U.S. economy?

The enormous debt burdens in Latin American countries, exacerbated by high U.S. interest rates and rampant capital flight, also have created severe trade problems for the United States. In accordance with debt restructuring programs, imports have been slashed, and exports boosted at any cost. This has severely undermined one of the most important markets for U.S. exports. During the late 1970s, when petrodollars were being recycled in the form of ambitious loans to Third World countries, Latin America was a major growth market for U.S. exports. An estimated 800,000 U.S. jobs have been lost as a result of displacements related to the Latin American debt crisis (Adams 1985: 13).

The austerity programs implemented under pressure from the International Monetary Fund and the banking system have sharply reduced living standards and worsened income distribution in Latin America. To meet their interest payments, debtor countries have been pressured to reduce their domestic spending, end food subsidies, reduce real wages, and devalue their currencies. Social disorder has frequently resulted from such policies.

The precipitous devaluation of the Mexican peso since 1982 has contributed to a dramatic increase in border industrialization oriented to the U.S. market. The number of maquiladore plants, mainly U.S.-owned companies producing on the Mexican side of the border for shipment to the U.S. market, has increased by a third to 800 since then. Wages in the maquiladores are the equivalent of sixty to seventy cents an hour—lower than in most of the Asian NICs ("U.S. Businesses near Mexican Border" 1986: 29; "Mexico's Grand 'Maquiladora' Plan" 1986: 14).

The spread of export-oriented approaches has been disruptive for the U.S. economy and may ultimately be destructive of beneficial international economic relations. There is a growing recognition that the unwillingness of the Reagan administration to utilize the trade regulation mechanisms already at its disposal has been misguided and counterproductive. The administration has belatedly responded with promises of limited trade actions in terms of a few unfair trading practice cases and efforts to open foreign markets to U.S. exports, but these measures have largely been symbolic.

The administration operates on the assumption that whatever dislocations are created by disruptive trade can be addressed through the normal operations of the economy. However, our experience in the 1980s has been that very little positive adjustment has occurred. The economy's overall job mix has deteriorated, growth has been exceptionally dependent on debt, and income inequality and poverty have increased.

Officially, there were 8.3 million persons unemployed in April 1986. Less than 40 percent of the unemployed received unemployment insurance benefits. If the hidden unemployed and the underemployed are taken into account, the unemployment rate would have been 10.5 percent instead of 7.1 percent. The official unemployment rate for blacks was 14.7 percent and for Hispanics, 10.3 percent.

The bulk of job growth has occurred in the service sector, where wages for nonsupervisory workers are well below the average for industrial workers. Part-time jobs and self-employment, which have low pay and few fringe benefits, have both increased much faster than full-time wage and salary employment.

The deteriorating job mix has lowered living standards for millions of Americans and their families. The broad-based consumer purchasing power that underpins our economy, and the world economy to an extent, has suffered as a result.

The degree of inequality in family and household incomes has steadily increased in the 1980s. All the progress toward greater equity in the distribution of income achieved in the postwar period has been wiped out. Since the start of government data collection in 1947, the income share of the poorest 40 percent has never been lower, and the share held by the richest 20 percent has never been higher (U.S. Department of Commerce various years).

Our nation's willingness to tolerate widespread poverty and hunger should be a national embarrassment. Thirty-four million Americans, 40 percent of them children, live in poverty. The deteriorating job structure and growing income disparities mean that many in the younger generation, for the first time in over half a century, will be unable to attain the living standards achieved by their parents.

The Commerce Department (1986a: 31) estimates that in 1984 our trade deficit resulted in the displacement of 2.3 million domestic manufacturing jobs, with a net loss of 1.1 million jobs for the economy as a whole. Studies show that workers losing their jobs due to imports have fewer employment alternatives because they tend to be older, less educated, female, and minorities (Aho and Orr 1981: 34).

The U.S. Bureau of Labor Statistics study of workers displaced between 1979 and 1984 found that one-fourth of the 11.5 million displaced workers were still without work and another 15 percent had left the labor force. Moreover, almost one-half of the displaced manufacturing workers who found alternative employment were forced to accept lower pay and probably fewer fringe benefits. Because a large proportion were displaced from relatively good jobs in terms of pay and benefits, many of the displaced lost their health insurance coverage, including one-fourth of those who subsequently found work (Flaim and Sehgal 1985: 3–16).

Recognizing the magnitude of the adjustment problem facing workers and firms stemming from trade-related developments, some observers advocate an activist adjustment policy rather than reliance solely on market forces. These measures include expanded trade adjustment assistance encompassing retraining, relocation, and early retirement for workers and assistance to firms to encourage the shift of resources out of trade-impacted industries (Hufbauer and Rosen 1986: ch. 5).

In the not-too-distant past, many of those arguing for the need to more effectively adjust to imports looked to an expanding high-tech sector as a source of economic growth and employment opportunities to substitute for displaced workers and firms.

But many parts of high-tech electronics are similarly affected by the forces responsible for the deterioration in the U.S. trade balance. Technology flows relatively easily across borders. Many countries, including all of the NICs, are intent on developing their own high-tech industries. Almost all these countries insist on technology-sharing and local production as a condition for selling in their markets, and U.S.-based high-tech firms seem willing to comply.

Many major U.S. high-tech electronics firms now conduct one-third to one-half of their production outside the United States. Our imports of electronics goods have increased nearly three times as fast as exports in the 1980s (U.S. Bureau of the Census 1981b, 1981c, 1984a, 1984b).

Although the U.S. economy continued to expand in 1985, non-military electronics production and employment declined sharply. From the fourth quarter of 1984 to the fourth quarter of 1985, electronics production worker employment dropped by 120,000, nearly 14 percent of the total. In computer manufacturing, the employment contraction was 18 percent (U.S. Bureau of Labor Statistics monthly).

Even if one believes the U.S. Bureau of Labor Statistics employment projections for 1995, high-tech electronics manufacturing will still represent only 2.3 percent of total employment, compared to 2.0 percent now (Personick 1985: 26–41). It is highly unlikely that the production of high-tech equipment will generate nearly enough jobs to significantly offset the magnitude of import-related job loss, not to mention the job displacement related to the introduction of electronics equipment in offices and factories. As long as unemployment remains high, and it has never stayed this high for this long in the postwar period, adjustment will be extremely difficult and there will be stiff resistance to imports.

The economic and human costs of unemployment are tremendous. The nation loses billions of dollars in output, and the federal deficit grows by about $30 billion for every 1 million increase in unemployment. Unemployed workers lose not only their source of livelihood, but their skills deteriorate and they lose their self-esteem. High and persistent unemployment produces social disintegration.

In the 1980s, as the pressure for import restrictions has grown while the administration has followed a laissez-faire adjustment approach, a new view of the role of adjustment policy has emerged among those who acknowledge the need for active intervention in the economy. Rather than seeing adjustment assistance as a payoff for trade liberalization, this view emphasizes the need for adjustment policy to complement trade controls, but only temporary controls.

But the question remains of what industries will provide employment opportunities for trade-displaced workers and new labor force entrants. The unfortunate answer is that nearly all U.S. manufacturing industries are facing similar pressures from import competition and the bulk of jobs outside of manufacturing do not provide comparable earnings or job opportunities.

Average weekly earnings for manufacturing workers in 1985 were $386, while workers in the financial sector received $289, workers in retail trade $177, and employees in other service industries $261 (U.S. Bureau of Labor Statistics 1986, January: 219). Consumer buying power in this country, which accounts for two-thirds of our gross national product, will only erode further if we allow our manufacturing industries to whither away.

Labor-intensive manufacturing provides needed employment opportunities to older and less skilled workers and to recent immigrants
with limited English language communication skills. Labor-intensive
industries serve an important function in our economy by broadening the range of employment opportunities.

The administration's trade negotiating agenda—extending the
GATT to establish international trading rules for agriculture and services, protect intellectual property rights, and promote direct foreign
investment—offers little prospect of significantly improving our
trade balance. Given other countries' views on trade, it is unrealistic
to expect that foreign markets can be appreciably opened to U.S.
exports. Rather than further encouraging direct foreign investment
by U.S. firms, we should reduce the tax and tariff incentives to the
export of U.S. jobs.

The effort formalized at the 1986 Tokyo summit to improve the
coordination of economic policies among the industrial democracies
was long overdue. However, it remains to be seen the extent to which
such coordination can actually be carried out and what effects it will
have on reducing the present severe trade imbalances. The risk of too
sharp a dollar devaluation is a major concern.

There is still a need for a broad reassessment of U.S. trade policy.
Strong measures, and the political consensus to follow through, are
needed to

1. Provide effective relief from injury due to imports and protection
    from unfair trade;
2. Reduce excessive country trade surpluses with the United States;
    and
3. Condition access to the U.S. market on the basis of observance of
    internationally recognized labor rights, including the right to
    freedom of association, a safe work environment, and restrictions
    on the use of child labor.

In addition to reform of the general trading framework, we need
to develop and implement realistic approaches for coordinating
global trading in sectors characterized by global overcapacity. A coalition of domestic textile and apparel firms and labor unions has developed the following approach to reform. (This paper was presented in
May 1986 and refers to legislation then being considered.)

Although it is often alleged that the textile and apparel industries
are the most protected in the United States, imports have more than
doubled since 1980. When the Multi-Fiber Arrangement (MFA) was

negotiated in 1973, the import share of the domestic apparel market was 21 percent. Today, after twelve years of MFA, the import share is 53 percent and climbing.

The garment industry shares many problems with other industries, but its simple technology, small capital requirements, and dependence on relatively low-skilled labor make it particularly vulnerable to imports from low-wage countries. Hourly compensation for garment workers in the developing and newly industrialized countries ranges from 2 to 25 percent of U.S. levels. Since 1973 over 300,000 production worker jobs—a quarter of the total—have been lost in the garment industry, and imports have eliminated another potential 600,000 job opportunities.

Successive administrations have failed to implement and enforce the MFA quota system to avert serious market disruption. In particular, the current administration has allowed apparel imports to increase far beyond the growth of the domestic market.

By way of contrast, using the same MFA framework, the European community countries have reduced their apparel imports from developing countries in the 1980s. In 1984 the United States accounted for 60 percent of the apparel exports from developing countries to industrial countries, up from 45 percent in 1981. Meanwhile, the EC countries reduced their share from 38 percent in 1981 to only 26 percent in 1984. Japan reduced its share from 8 to 6 percent (General Agreement on Tariffs and Trade 1985: Table A17).

Although the Reagan administration has indicated that it will seek to modify the MFA in the 1986 MFA renewal talks, it already has at its disposal sufficient tools to more tightly regulate apparel imports. Legislation is needed to bring stability and predictability to the apparel import situation.

The Textile and Apparel Trade Enforcement Act was introduced in 1985 to serve the twin objectives of MFA: protection against market disruption in the importing countries and orderly growth for the exports of truly developing countries. In late 1985 this legislation passed both houses of Congress by sizable margins but short of the two-thirds needed to override the president's veto. The Textile and Apparel Trade Enforcement Act establishes realistic import levels and growth rates for shipments from the major exporting countries. The bill would slightly reduce the present level of import penetration and would provide for subsequent growth considerably closer to the rate of domestic market growth.

Since the four major shippers—Hong Kong, Taiwan, China, and South Korea— account for 60 percent of all apparel imports into the United States, the ability of truly developing countries to industrialize is severely restricted.

Consumers would not suffer; imports would still capture over half of the U.S. market. Moreover, it is generally the case that the use of low-wage labor abroad in garment production does not translate into lower prices paid by consumers. Retailers acknowledge that they prefer to sell imported garments because the markup taken on imports is higher than the markup on domestically produced goods.

The 20,000 firms comprising the domestic apparel industry operate on a fiercely competitive basis and have demonstrated that they can provide the quality, styling, and variety needed to provide consumers with freedom of choice in purchasing clothing.

Garment production in this country has traditionally provided jobs for workers facing limited employment opportunities whether due to lack of education or skill, language barriers, place of residence, labor market occupational segregation, or less subtle forms of discrimination.

Eighty-five percent of the apparel production workforce is female and well over a third is black, Hispanic, or Asian. In the major metropolitan centers of apparel production—New York, Los Angeles, San Francisco, Miami, and Chicago—thousands of recent immigrants are employed in the garment industry, including many who are undocumented. The domestic garment industry serves as an important source of employment for our own Third World population.

In conclusion, if the United States can move toward effective methods of regulating international trade, we will then be able to realize the true economic, social, and strategic benefits that an interdependent global system can offer. Our present policies of indifference toward the domestic repercussions of trade, unrealistic encouragement of export-oriented development in the NICs and developing countries, and self-delusion regarding the possibility of getting other countries to open their markets have placed us on an untenable and unsustainable course.

Our domestic industrial base is being undermined, and there is no attractive alternative foundation on the horizon capable of generating sustained, balanced economic growth that provides a fair distribution of economic rewards to a broad spectrum of our society. The economic growth we have experienced in the last three and a half years, as uneven as it has been, has been premised to a great extent on excessive borrowing, much of it from abroad. When the expansion falters, we will be hard pressed to turn further to debt to stimulate our way out of recession.

The U.S. simply cannot be expected to accept everyone else's exports. Nor should we think that export-led development can be generalizable to very many countries at the same time. The NICs should be encouraged to focus more on the development of their own internal markets and expand trade with less developed countries. The extension of international labor and human rights is essential to foster democratic institutions and to raise the living standards of workers in the less developed countries.

Although trade is not the only source of structural adjustment problems, trade-related disruptions in the 1980s have been occurring at a pace and on a scale that far outdistances our ability to adapt and still maintain a strong economy capable of providing benefits to our large and diverse population. Certainly American labor and industry needs to and can be more productive. But until we formulate sound macroeconomic policies and as long as imports flow unrestricted into the United States, there will be little incentive to commit substantial resources to the task of expanding our productive capacity and improving our productivity. A genuine national commitment to full employment would largely mitigate concerns over technology or import-related displacement and would benefit not only millions of Americans but the people of the developing countries and NICs as well.

We live in an interdependent global economy. To avoid the disruptions and convulsions that global economic forces can create, we need global views—not only of the economic relationships among countries but of the political and human considerations as well.

NOTES

1. Total domestic nonfinancial debt, both public and private, grew over 50 percent faster than GNP in the last four years. In contrast, total debt and GNP grew at about the same pace in the 1960s and 1970s (Federal Reserve Board of Governors 1986). Federal Reserve Chairman Volcker recently warned that the "vulnerability of the economy to unanticipated increases in interest rates or a shortfall in income appears to be increasing" as a result of the "extraordinary" debt buildup ("Volcker Warns" 1986: 2).

REFERENCES

Adams, Gerard. 1985. "Testimony before the Joint Economic Committee." Cited in *From Debt to Development*, edited by The Debt Crisis Network. Washington, D.C.: Institute for Policy Studies.

Aho, Michael C., and James Orr. 1981. "Trade-Sensitive Employment: Who Are the Affected Workers?" *Monthly Labor Review* 104 (February): 29–35.

The Debt Crisis Network, ed. 1985. *From Debt to Development*. Washington, D.C.: Institute for Policy Studies.

Federal Reserve Board of Governors. 1986. *Flow of Funds*. Washington, D.C.: Federal Reserve Board of Governors.

Flaim, Paul O., and Ellen Sehgal. 1985. "Displaced Workers of 1979–83: How Well Have They Fared?" *Monthly Labor Review* 108 (June): 3–16.

General Agreement on Tariffs and Trade. 1985. *International Trade 1984/85*. Geneva: GATT.

"The Hollow Corporation." 1986. *Business Week*, March 3, pp. 57–85.

Hufbauer, Gary Clyde, and Howard F. Rosen. 1986. *Trade Policy for Troubled Industries*. Washington, D.C.: Institute for International Economics.

International Ladies Garment Workers Union, Research Department, 1986.

Linder, Staffan Burenstam. 1985. "Pacific Protagonist—Implications of the Rising Role of the Pacific." *American Economic Review* 75 (May): 279–84.

Little, Jane Sneddon. 1986. "Intra-Firm Trade and U.S. Protectionism: Thoughts Based on a Small Survey." *New England Economic Review* (January/February): 42–51.

Maex, Rudy. 1985. "Employment and Multinationals in Asian Export Processing Zones." Working Paper No. 26. Geneva: International Labour Office, Multinational Enterprises Programme.

"Mexico's Grand 'Maquiladora' Plan." 1986. *New York Times*, Jan. 19, p. F4.

Personick, Valerie A. 1985. "A Second Look at Industry Output and Employment Trends through 1995." *Monthly Labor Review* 108 (November): 26–41.

"The President's Steel Program Is Working." 1986. *Business America* 9 (March 31): 11–12.

United Automobile Workers Research Bulletin. 1986. (February/March): 21.

United States Bureau of Labor Statistics. Monthly. *Employment and Earnings*.

United States Bureau of the Census. 1981a. *Highlights of U.S. Export and Import Trade*. Washington, D.C.: U.S. Government Printing Office.

_____. 1981b. *U.S. Exports* (FT 410). Washington, D.C.: U.S. Government Printing Office.

_____. 1981c. *U.S. General Imports and Imports for Consumption* (FT 135). Washington, D.C.: U.S. Government Printing Office.

_____. 1984a. *U.S. Exports* (FT 410). Washington, D.C.: U.S. Government Printing Office.

_____. 1984b. *U.S. General Imports and Imports for Consumption* (FT 135). Washington, D.C.: U.S. Government Printing Office.

_____. 1985. *Highlights of U.S. Export and Import Trade.* Washington, D.C.: U.S. Government Printing Office.

"U.S. Businesses near Mexican Border Move Fast to Cope with Changing Peso." 1986. *Wall Street Journal,* Jan. 27, p. 29.

United States Department of Commerce. 1986a. *Trade Ripples across U.S. Industries: Effects of International Trade on Industry Output and Employment.* Washington, D.C.: U.S. Government Printing Office.

_____. 1986b. *U.S. Industrial Outlook, 1986.* Washington, D.C.: U.S. Government Printing Office.

_____. 1987. *U.S. Industrial Outlook, 1987.* Washington, D.C.: U.S. Government Printing Office.

_____. Various years. *Statistical Abstract.* Washington, D.C.: U.S. Government Printing Office.

"U.S. International Transactions in 1985." 1986. *Federal Reserve Bulletin* (May): 291.

"Volcker Warns the Rapid Rise in Debt Is Serious Threat to Economy's Health." 1986. *Wall Street Journal,* Apr. 24, p. 2.

"The World's In-House Traders." 1986. *The Economist* (March 1): 61.

16 FOREIGN INVESTMENT AND THE NICs

Peter Hansen

There are many definitions of what constitutes a newly industrializing country (NIC), but any definition must recognize that the NICs have become major recipients of foreign direct investment. The NICs, along with petroleum-exporting nations, receive between 80 and 90 percent of the total flow of foreign investment to developing countries. This fact has led many observers to generalize from the experience of the NICs and argue that foreign direct investment and the expansion of private enterprise can solve many of the problems of development.

The reality, however, is far more complex. Although the proportion of foreign investment going to the NICs has been high relative to developing countries as a whole, the amount of such investment is not large in absolute terms. Moreover, foreign investment flows to developing countries, including the NICs, have fallen in the 1980s (see Table 16-1). In the western hemisphere, which used to be the major recipient of foreign direct investment, the flows to developing countries were more than halved from 1981 to 1984. Latin America, which accounted for 12 percent of worldwide flows of foreign direct investment only a little more than a decade ago and once accounted for 14 to 15 percent, is now down to about 7 percent. On the other hand, the countries of Asia and the Pacific, which a decade ago accounted for only 6 to 7 percent of the total flows of foreign direct

Table 16-1. World Flows of Foreign Direct Investment, 1970-84 (*percentage of total inflows*).

Host Region	1970-71	1977	1980	1981	1982	1983	1984
Developing market economies	77%	73%	78%	73%	65%	73%	78%
United States	9	16	36	49	35	29	46
Western Europe	45	46	36	24	27	32	25
Developing countries	23	27	22	27	35	27	22
Western Hemisphere	12	14	13	15	16	9	7
Asia and the Pacific	5	7	8	9	13	13	11

Note: Switzerland, Western Asia, including China, and the centrally planned economies of Europe are not included in the data.
Source: United Nations Centre on Transnational Corporations (1986: 6).

investment, increased to 13 percent in 1983 but are now down to 11 percent.

The decrease in investment flows to the NICs implies that the rest of the developing countries receive practically nothing in terms of foreign direct investment. If we talk about Africa, we can basically forget about foreign direct investment, except for natural resource development. But with decreasing prices for minerals, commodities, and even oil, resource development is accounting for less and less in terms of foreign investment. For these countries there is little encouragement in the general picture.

There are a number of reasons for the low levels of foreign investment into the developing world. One is that the debt-service difficulties of the early 1980s have required wideranging austerity policies. Economic policy in the debtor countries reduced aggregate demand and weakened market prospects, thereby discouraging investment. This is the case for the newly industrializing countries in Latin America, and it is also the case for some Asian countries, such as the Philippines.

Protectionism also has an impact on foreign investment. Protectionism in developed countries decreases interest in export-platform investment, something that the NICs in South East Asia have been especially successful in attracting. Insofar as protectionism limits a country's foreign exchange earnings from exports, it is more difficult for debtor nations to service their external debts. As a result, protec-

tionism discourages foreign direct investment into the indebted countries. Unless one can deal with both the debt problem and the protectionism problem, there is very little likelihood that foreign direct
investment to the NICs will increase.

An additional factor is the uneven pattern of economic growth
that has characterized the world economy in recent years. Economic
recovery has been largely confined to the developed economies, with
only a few developing countries, such as Brazil and the Republic of
Korea, participating in the upswing. The lack of large and growing
internal markets in the developing world make it difficult to attract
foreign investment aimed at exploiting domestic markets. And in
many cases, developing countries have placed restrictions on foreign
investment in order to promote activity by their nationals in key industries such as computers and telecommunications. Moreover, with
some of the largest industrial countries running large current account
surpluses or, as is the case with the United States, seeking to reduce
a deficit, the prospects for continued export growth from NICs is
increasingly uncertain.

We need a number of coordinated measures, which are hopefully
on the horizon, in order to solve the debt crisis and stimulate the
growth of internal markets. The plan put forward in 1985 by United
States Treasury Secretary James Baker is an attempt to stimulate
new lending to debtor countries. This would allow these nations to
move away from their present reliance on austerity policies, aimed at
increasing their foreign exchange earnings to meet debt-related payments. The Baker plan, however, although an important step in the
right direction, is not enough. We need a decisive move to roll back
protectionism and a coordination of policies among OECD countries
to stimulate growth. Europeans, however, seem unwilling to take on
commitments for stronger growth, while Japan hesitates on the issue
of macroeconomic coordination.

In formulating policies regarding investment flows to developing
countries, it must be recognized that such flows are related to trade,
foreign aid, and flows of loan capital. Investment cannot replace a
decline in loan funds and official aid; more important, a fall-off in
these other forms of capital will likely cause a further decline in
direct investment flows because transnational corporations will not
look favorably on countries that are experiencing loan payment difficulties, are being bypassed by official development agencies, or have
instituted austerity policies. Thus, in advocating the important con-

tribution that foreign direct investment can make as part of a solution to problems of development, there must be recognition of the need for simultaneous progress on problems of indebtedness, trade, monetary issues, and political stability.

The United Nations, for a decade, has been sponsoring negotiations on a code of conduct for transnational corporations, in an effort to create an international investment climate that will help increase foreign direct investment and further economic development. The international political and economic climate has, of course, changed quite markedly since the mid-1970s. The code that is evolving is no longer based solely on establishing standards of behavior for transnational corporations. It is very much a code that includes obligations on the part of host countries as well as corporations.

There appears to exist a broad commonality of interests, on the part of both host developing countries and TNCs, in establishing mutually acceptable standards of behavior in the area of foreign direct investment. The existence of such a framework in international trade, with GATT, contributed to rapid worldwide economic growth after World War II. The inability to reconstitute such a framework in international finance over the last decade and a half has clearly been a negative factor in the world economy.

Final agreement on a code, however, continues to be elusive. Among the issues that remain outstanding, for example, are the establishment of procedures governing nationalization of property and the payment of compensation to foreign owners. Countries have yet to reach agreement on the applicability of international law and of national legislation to problems of international investment. Many developing countries have pointed out, for instance, that principles of international law were formulated before they had achieved independence and before international investment had attained its current importance in the world economy. Moreover, developing countries frequently use national legislation to protect their infant industries, a practice that many of today's developed countries practiced extensively in the past. All these issues are coming to the surface in the current debate over the treatment of services. Developed countries are seeking to apply the essentially free trade régime of GATT to services, while developing countries, arguing that foreign investment is much more important than trade in delivering the product across borders, are much more cautious in this regard.

Many of the specific unresolved points in the negotiations are more symbolic than real and could be resolved, if the main protagonists would make relatively minor concessions. Final agreement on a code would improve prospects for increased foreign investment to developing countries, and especially to the NICs. But although a widely accepted code is an important ingredient, it is not sufficient by itself. It must be accompanied by changes in policy on the part of the developed countries, such as those discussed above.

REFERENCES

United Nations Centre on Transnational Corporations. 1986. *Recent Developments Related to Transnational Corporations and International Economic Relations.* Report of the Secretary General E/C 10/1986/2.

17 TRADE AND FINANCE ISSUES FOR THE NICs
A Japanese Perspective

Toru Yanagihara

The future of the global economy will be shaped by the economic conditions and growth prospects of developing countries. Two sets of issues related to developing countries concern developed countries: (1) issues that arise from the success of development, most notably in the sphere of industrial development spearheaded by the newly industrialized countries (NICs) in East Asia and the need to adjust to the rising manufactured imports on the part of developed countries; and (2) issues that are related to the failure of development, of which the most dramatic and traumatic instance is the widespread famine in sub-Saharan Africa. The traditional approach to the North-South problem focuses on the disparity in the standard of living between the two groups of countries and remains highly relevant in this connection. Most developing countries fall between these two polar cases and exhibit varied combinations and degrees of success and failure. For example, Latin American countries are now suffering from a heavy burden of accumulated external debt that is the result of continued reliance on external borrowings over the 1970s, and their growth prospects are uncertain. On the other hand, new experiments in China and India aim at bringing management of the national economy more in tune with domestic and international market opportunities.

The diverse situations in the developing part of the world cannot be explained by reducing all economic problems to an all-purpose explanation like price distortions (as is fashionable at present). The developing world consists of countries in different stages and types of development, and the efficacy of market mechanisms cannot be assumed; it has to be examined. Supplementing as well as strengthening the working of the market mechanism constitutes an important aspect of creating development strategy, especially at an early stage of development. A market-oriented development strategy needs to address this question because eliminating price distortions alone might not generate positive responses. The goals and aspirations of developing countries must be understood on their own terms before they are evaluated and policy recommendations are prescribed. The advanced countries should endeavor to engage in a genuine dialogue to establish a collaborative framework and atmosphere for the resolution of global economic problems.

This chapter discusses industrial development and related issues in development strategy in the NICs and next-tier NICs. It reviews development experiences and presents situations of East Asian and Latin American NICs, identifies important explanatory factors for divergent performances, and draws implications for development strategy on the part of the NICs and next-tier NICs and for trade and assistance policies on the part of the developed countries. A brief discussion on the respective roles of the United States and Japan concludes the chapter.

NICs IN THE GLOBAL ECONOMY

One of the dynamic forces that reshaped the configuration in the global economy during the 1970s was the rapid growth of manufactured exports from a group of middle-income countries, which collectively came to be called newly industrialized countries (NICs), in increasingly diversified product categories. Because it occurred when the developed countries had to adjust to the OPEC-engineered oil price shocks and subsequent stagnation in economic activities, market penetration by NIC exports generated serious concern about the adverse effects on the level of industrial activities and employment in developed countries. The so-called gang-of-four East Asian NICs— Singapore, Hong Kong, Taiwan, South Korea—gradually upgraded the composition of their manufactured exports, thereby sustaining the momentum of export-led growth.

Over the second part of the 1970s the NICs and other developing countries also provided expanding markets for manufactured exports from the developed countries. Thus, the 1970s witnessed a mutually reinforcing expansion of trade flows between the developed and developing parts of the world. The process of trade expansion was partly fueled by the increased commercial lending to middle-income countries, which sustained continued current account deficits. It appeared that the world economy had recovered from the jolt of the oil price increase and was back on a growth trajectory again. In fact, some of the middle-income countries registered higher rates of growth after the oil price increase than had been previously the case, enhancing the optimism about the situation, although growth rates for most of the developed countries were diminished.

In retrospect, the late 1970s growth episode was the last phase of an inflationary expansion of the world economy—a boom just before a bust. The rupture came when the U.S. monetary authority shifted its policy stance decisively toward the control of inflation. This policy shift brought the U.S. locomotive to a complete halt for three years, induced other advanced countries to adopt similar monetary tightening, pushed up international interest rates to unprecedented levels, shrank the volume of world trade, caused primary product prices to plummet, and plunged the world economy into a prolonged recession.

The drastic change in the global economic environment in the early 1980s brought about by the anti-inflationary monetary control by the Federal Reserve Bank (the "Volcker shock") dramatically differentiated the East Asian and Latin American NICs in terms of the sustainability of the mechanism of economic growth. Here we will discuss some of the significant implications of the debt crisis for Latin American and East Asian NICs and for the global economy.

First, for Latin America the debt crisis meant not only the loss of one decade's progress in standard of living but also the loss of developmental prospects for decades to come. The sense of crisis was particularly acute because no new development model was readily available to restore the economy to a sustainable growth path. Second, the soundness of the economies of the East Asian NICs and the economic vitality of the Pacific Basin region were recognized, generating a positive evaluation of the region's growth prospects. Third, the debt crisis threatened major commercial banks and the stability of the global financial system. The extent of bank exposure to major debtor countries highlighted a new aspect of economic interdependence between the North and South. Fourth, in connection with the above, linkages and interactions in the global economy between countries and across issues (that is, trade and finance) were identified. Finally, based on these understandings, it now is recognized that a coordinated, cooperative approach to the management and resolution of the debt problem is needed.

Two salient issues of international concern are related to the growth prospects of the NICs and next-tier NICs. One is related to trade, and the other to external debt.

Prospects for the Growth of Manufactured Exports

The success of the NICs and other developing countries in rapidly expanding manufactured exports has generated protectionist sentiments in North America and Western Europe that favor managed trade in an increasing number of manufacturing subsectors. The most notable and notorious among all are import restrictions on textiles and clothing within the framework of the Multifiber Arrangement (MFA), an umbrella agreement under GATT auspices covering bilateral quotas negotiated between exporting and importing countries. Since the first arrangement, the short-term arrangement on cotton textiles, was concluded in 1961, international trade in textiles has been under an internationally negotiated managed trade scheme. During this period the scope of the restrictions—in terms of duration, product coverage, and the number of countries involved—expanded and eventually led to the MFA. It is clear that trade restrictions have become the rule, rather than an exception, in textiles and clothing. Managed trade is firmly established in this important branch of manufacturing.

Protection of the steel industry dates back to 1967 when the Japanese and European steel export associations submitted letters of voluntary export restraint agreement to the U.S. Department of State. In the mid-1970s, following a sharp rise in imports from Japan, the United States negotiated a marketing agreement with Japan setting a limit on the growth of steel imports. The trigger price system in the United States and a similar system in the European Economic Community introduced in 1977 were ostensibly designed to forestall unfair competition caused by dumping. The intent of those systems was to curb imports from lower-cost producers, as subsequently became evident as the United States and the EC moved to more openly protective measures based on quantitative control. As a result, virtually all inflow of steel products into the United States and the EC is managed now.

Japan has avoided resorting to explicit import restrictions under MFA and has not applied import controls on steel products, despite rising concerns among textile and steel industries about the rapid increase of imports from developing countries, notably East Asian NICs. It is unlikely that Japan will change its present policy in these industries. Japanese manufacturers in textiles and steel tend to be more efficient and adaptive to changing market conditions than their counterparts in the United States and the EC. The Japanese government is committed to the promotion of free trade and is strongly opposed to introducing new protective measures. There are, however, several problem areas related to market access for manufactured exports from developing countries. First, import quotas are applied to silk and leather products, which mostly affects Korea, Taiwan, and China. Second, tariffs on processed products tend to be higher than those on raw materials, which poses disincentives to manufacturing activities by raw material producing countries. Third, in some cases tariffs on processed products from developing countries are higher than those imposed on similar products from developed countries. Differential tariff rates on plywood from Indonesia and the United States are a case in point. Finally, there remain less formal, but no less important, obstacles to the access to Japanese markets, such as administrative guidances and business practices, although their significance is difficult to assess.

Many other product categories have been subjected to restrictive trade measures by developed countries and there are signs that protectionist sentiments are on the rise. This concerns the developing countries because they need to expand exports to maintain the momentum of growth (in the case of the East Asian NICs), to regain that momentum (Latin American NICs), or to be initiated into that growth (next-tier NICs). It is not evident how harmful those protectionist practices are. After all, Japan and the East Asian NICs have faced restrictions on a wide range of exports but have managed to keep high growth rates. It may be argued that restrictions have spurred exporting firms to upgrade their products and public policies that support continuous change in industrial structure, thereby contributing to the dynamic efficiency of the growth process. It also may be possible to argue that ceilings placed on exports from relatively advanced countries help less well-established countries get a foothold in export markets. This certainly was the case with the export to the United States of color television sets from Korea and Taiwan when Japanese exports were restrained. On the other hand, some import quotas are set based on past performance, and thus relative positions of exporters tend to be frozen. Quotas on steel imports imposed by the United States after 1983 are a particularly damaging instance of this approach because the full brunt of import reductions (in terms of percentage share of U.S. consumption) fell on small suppliers, mostly developing countries. As is suggested in this example, the manner of implementation may matter more than the goal of protectionist policy.

It is sometimes argued that an important adverse effect of protectionism is to discourage prospective exporters from adopting an outward-looking development strategy. Two conceptually distinct, although practically overlapping, issues are involved.

The first relates to an export pessimism based on a perception of widespread protectionist practices. In this connection it is important to remember that the growth of manufactured exports since the mid-1970s has been substantial despite the proliferation of protectionist restrictions. Protectionism has risen accordingly as import penetration has but has not halted or reversed the rising trend of imports in most cases. Furthermore, even if total exports are restrained, it is still possible for latecomers to achieve export growth by raising their share of the market. The U.S. scheme of quotas on textiles incorporates favorable treatment of small exporters. (Steel quotas treat them unfavorably, as is discussed above. The Jenkins bill would have had similar but much more disastrous effects on latecomer textile exporters.)

Market forces operate to raise the relative contribution of low-cost producers at the expense of high-cost ones. For example, the share of East Asian NICs in the U.S. imports of clothing and plywood rose steadily throughout the 1970s. There are signs that the ASEAN four (Malaysia, Thailand, the Philippines, and Indonesia) have begun to encroach the market position enjoyed by the NICs in labor-intensive subsectors within the manufacturing sector. Sometimes protective measures can work in favor of lesser exporters, either by design or as an unintended side effect.

One important factor in the growth of manufactured exports from developing countries is the practice of outsourcing by multinational enterprises (MNEs) either in the form of offshore production or overseas procurement. Outsourcing by MNEs has accelerated and been spurred by an increased international flow of manufactured products from lower-cost producers. MNEs tend to favor free trade, and the more that an industry is dominated by MNEs engaged in outsourcing the stronger will be the industry's support for free trade. Tariff provisions 806 and 807 for offshore assembly and a recent elimination of tariffs on semiconductors in the United States are cases in point here.

The advisability of an outward-looking development strategy comes under question in circumstances of widespread protectionism. Other things being equal, reduced access to the world market due to protectionism tends to diminish the return, in terms of export growth, of an outward-looking development strategy. Nonetheless, diminished effectiveness of the outward-looking strategy does not necessarily make it less effective than alternative ones. As far as foreign exchange availability remains a binding constraint to economic growth, export-oriented strategies promise better growth performance even under less favorable external trade environments than do other approaches. What is required is to strengthen export orientation to make the most of a less than favorable situation. Some economists argue that inward-looking strategies are appropriate under the expectation of worsening trade environments. The argument seems to be logically flawed, however, insofar as foreign exchange availability constitutes an effective constraint on the financing of economic development. Inward-looking strategies, with built-in antiexport biases, would prove more costly in a worsened trade environment than in a buoyant one in which incentives and efficiency are not critical for export expansion.

The preceding argument applies most directly to the group of primary commodity-exporting countries trying to expand manufactured exports. Diminished prospects for export earnings from primary commodities, along with reduced availability of external finance, make it imperative for those countries to pursue export-oriented industrialization in order to sustain economic growth over the long term. Losses in terms of trade suffered in the early 1980s after the commodity boom of the 1970s are a serious blow to economies that depend heavily on primary products. They should be viewed as a mixed curse, however, insofar as the commodity boom was regarded as mixed blessing. It was a mixed blessing because of its adverse impacts on the manufacturing sector through intersectoral resource reallocation effects (the so-called Dutch-disease effect) and also on economic policymaking in terms of widespread inefficiency, waste, and corruption.

Low export prices for primary products increase the relative profitability of manufacturing activities in general, and reduced export earnings, with the consequential depreciation of exchange rates and fiscal austerity, make export-oriented manufacturing particularly appealing for both private business and the government. Moreover, the bad habits of politicians and bureaucrats are less affordable in bad times. For these economic and political reasons, development strategies emphasizing manufactured exports today enjoy better domestic conditions for success than they did in the 1970s.

The Debt Problem

Most Latin American countries are now afflicted with high levels of external debts incurred in the 1970s. The debt problem affects long-term growth because interest payments increase and new loans become difficult to obtain.

Whether debt accumulation becomes a problem or not, however, depends on the sort of assets that are being created as counterparts to external debts. If productive investment is financed by external borrowing and the capacity to earn or save foreign exchange has been improved beyond the growth of debt-servicing burden, debt accumulation will not create a problem.

The tasks of the debt-ridden developing countries are (1) to enhance foreign exchange earning capacity so that interest payments on existing debts can be made and (2) to aim for the maximum growth rate sustainable under the severe restrictions imposed by the worsened balance of payments. Now that foreign exchange is scarce, development policy and macroeconomic management will have to reflect that change. Structural adjustment to cope with the debt problem must enhance the ratio of output (earning) per input (use) of foreign exchange for the national economy as a whole. In order to accomplish this goal, price and incentive systems must be restructured so that private cost and benefit in the use or earning of foreign exchange reflects its scarcity.

The purpose of structural adjustment, in short, is to improve production efficiency and export performance by using the market mechanism in development policy and macroeconomic management. Policy measures for structural adjustment fall into two groups: (1) measures for eliminating distortions in the incentive system biased toward domestic market-oriented activities and for strengthening of export incentives and (2) measures to support technical, managerial, and institutional changes instrumental to improve production efficiency.

Correcting the distortions in price structure is expected to realign industries according to comparative advantage, while the reducing domestic demand compels enterprises to make efforts to rationalize technology and management and to step up export drive. In this context short-term stabilization policies can prove effective in promoting the goals of medium-term structural adjustment policy to improve production efficiency and strengthen export orientation.

Whether improved production efficiency and strengthened export orientation, prompted by stabilization policies, will make possible a shift to long-term economic development depends on the adaptability of the production sector and the availability of financing for new investments. Changes in the policy environment will encourage new economic activities. However, reactions to incentives in production and investment activities will vary greatly depending on whether adequate guidance and support policies are implemented.

What is recommended here is that an industrial policy be based on a long-range vision of changes in industrial structure such as the one employed in postwar Japan. The task of formulating and implementing a Japanese-style industrial policy requires use of investment criteria and sectoral preferences based on in-depth studies of actual situations and industrial sectors. For the industrial policy to produce satisfactory results, guidance and support measures should be taken on the supply side to supplement, and not hamper, the functioning of market mechanisms.

The resolution of the present debt problem of developing countries calls for effective coordination between debtor countries' policy reforms and the assistance and cooperation extended by advanced countries and multilateral institutions. That is true not only for the management of foreign exchange crises—for which there has developed a pattern of international cooperation involving the debtor country government, creditor country governments, the BIS, the IMF, and private banks—but also for the strengthening of the debt-servicing capacity of debtor countries through structural adjustment.

An effectively designed and implemented economic cooperation program must address the differing directions and central tasks of structural adjustment according to the type of developing countries, based on the level of development, factor endowment, and export composition. Cooperation should emphasize the key issues of structural adjustment thus identified.

For middle-income countries, the central task of structural adjustment is to shift from an inward-looking development strategy to an outward-looking one. Priority in economic cooperation therefore should be accorded to projects with high foreign exchange earning potential and to implementing reform programs designed to improve the policy environment.

For many low-income countries, structural adjustment applies mainly to the expansion of agricultural production. Financial and technical support that improves managerial and technical capabilities in the agricultural sector will be instrumental in increasing efficiency in resource use in response to changes in prices and incentives.

In extending assistance and support to structural adjustment programs, the progress of the programs should be monitored so that loans are used to improve productive efficiency and strengthen the foreign exchange earning capacity of the recipient country. Continuing policy dialogues with recipient countries will be instrumental in bringing about an improved policy environment through reforms in development policy and macroeconomic management.

Effective implementation of the monitoring and policy dialogue concerning structural adjustment programs is difficult and practically impossible on a bilateral basis. It therefore calls for an internationally coordinated scheme, perhaps centered around the structural adjustment leading (SAL) practiced by the World Bank.

The World Bank requests the recipient country of the structural adjustment loans to submit a proposal for a structural adjustment program and makes the phased disbursements of loans conditional on the achievement of main targets for policy reform. In this way, the World Bank is expected to play the role of the monitoring agency and thus provides the seal of approval in the realm of medium-term structural adjustment policy, much as the IMF has done in its domain of short-term macroeconomic management.

The World Bank's structural adjustment approach emphasizes the correction of distortions in the price and incentive structure with a view to giving freer play to market mechanisms. Such policy reforms will certainly constitute necessary conditions for the improvement of productive efficiency. However, they may not be sufficient, in themselves, to generate private responses to a changed policy environment. Guidance and support policies for strengthening organizational and institutional capabilities as well as financial assistance will increase productive efficiency both at the microeconomic (enterprise) level and at the macroeconomic (national economy) level. Such support and assurance from the government will be particularly valuable in the uncertain economic environments currently experienced in debt-ridden developing countries.

CONCLUDING REMARKS

The Baker initiative represents a recognition that orthodox stabilization and demand management alone is not sufficient to restore the creditworthiness of debtor countries. It is explicitly growth-oriented and emphasizes the need for structural reforms on the supply side. The new approach, focusing on productive structure and incentive schemes, addresses a broad range of development policies. The main thrust of the approach is a belief in the efficacy of the market mechanism and private enterprise system.

There are two potential problems that the new U.S. approach could encounter. First, the U.S. push for economic liberalization, especially in the realm of trade and foreign direct investment, could be taken as a scheme for economic domination by the advanced countries and could therefore generate opposition from debtor countries on both economic and ideological grounds. It is true that under the new realism in Latin America, market mechanism and private enterprises are viewed more favorably than before. It is also true that the explicit growth orientation of the new approach, in contrast to the austerity-oriented initial one, is better in tune with the developmental aspirations of developing countries. Nevertheless, it is possible that a single-minded imposition of Reaganomics could prove abrasive. Second, and closely connected with the above concern, the new U.S.

policy of using the World Bank and the Inter-American Development Bank as implementing organizations of the Baker initiative could turn their relationships with member countries from cooperative to adversarial. Policy-based lending based on restrictive conditions tends to become a source of conflict between multilateral lending agencies and recipient countries.

In this connection, it is worth noting the contrasting approaches to economic development of U.S. and Japanese policymakers. The dominant U.S. approach is functional in the sense that emphasis is placed on the working of market mechanisms and the private enterprise system. It is principle-oriented rather than result-oriented. The Japanese, in contrast, think mostly in terms of tangible production and investment activities and therefore are very much result-oriented.

Past Japanese experiences in the design and implementation of industrial policy are useful in preparing and implementing structural adjustment programs, in view of the emphasis given to long-term export growth and necessary organizational reform in successive programs for industrial upgrading in postwar Japan. In this sense, Japan seems to be in a position to be able to make a unique contribution to an internationally coordinated scheme to assist the structural adjustment efforts of debt-ridden countries.

Japan will not openly challenge U.S. leadership because its own approach is not clearcut and is difficult to articulate. In practice, however, there is ample room for Japan to pursue its own approach in the design and implementation of its economic cooperation policy. In Japan, economic cooperation is conceived almost exclusively in terms of project assistance with virtually no concern for policy issues. Japan tends to be receptive to the wishes of recipient developing countries because the basic purpose of its economic assistance is to win the goodwill of the recipient country, especially with regard to the secure supply of energy and other natural resources. This aspect of Japan's economic cooperation is reflected in the so-called national projects—projects that secure access to natural resources that are significant for national economic security.

Japan has recently become aware of its responsibility as a global economic power and the economic situation of developing countries from a broader perspective. This new awareness on Japan's part still needs to be translated into specific programs of economic cooperation with various groups of developing countries. There is a widely shared belief among Japanese policymakers involved in economic cooperation issues that the design and implementation of economic cooperation needs to be tailored to the specific conditions of developing countries. Particularly challenging is the design of development assistance to the debt-ridden countries because there the resumption of growth entails adopting a new development model.

Growth-oriented strategy needs to be accompanied by a vision of economic development in order to be convincing. The goal of enhanced efficiency needs to be backed up by the expansion of productive capacity to be compatible with sustained economic growth. The U.S. and Japanese approaches are, in principle, not mutually exclusive or contradictory but complementary because economic development requires the right framework and the right ingredients. It is not clear, however, how the U.S. and Japanese approaches can be effectively combined. Different approaches followed by the United States and Japan may well be integrated into a comprehensive program for helping restore and sustain an efficient growth path for the debt-ridden countries.

18 INTERNATIONAL PRESSURES AND POLICY CHOICES

Daniel F. Burton, Jr.

The newly industrializing countries (NICs) are not as much a distinct group of nations as an international event. It is difficult to define exactly what constitutes a NIC. No longer less developed countries but not yet industrialized nations, they range from small city-states, such as Hong Kong and Singapore, to potential economic giants like Brazil. But there is no question about the impact these nations are having on the U.S. and the international economy. The NICs are at the center of policy discussions about trade, debt, technology, foreign investment, and structural adjustment, and their part in these discussions will increase over the coming decade.

The current debate about U.S. policy toward the NICs is complicated by the fact that the costs and benefits of the NICs' international economic emergence have been distributed very unevenly across the U.S. economy. Some groups, such as U.S. consumers, have benefitted from the lower-priced goods offered by the NICs. Other groups, such as workers in U.S. manufacturing industries, have suffered disproportionately from the NICs' rising exports of manufactured goods to the United States.

The views expressed in this chapter are solely those of the author and not the Economic Policy Council of the UNA-USA. The findings and recommendations of the council's panel on the newly industrializing countries were published as a separate report.

Although the NICs are emerging as tough international competitors in many sectors, they also continue to face deepseated economic problems of their own. As Thornton Bradshaw (1986) put it,

> We have to think of policy not only in terms of emerging competitors that threaten to rapidly take over our markets, but also in terms of how to keep the NICs from bringing us down with them if they go into a downward spiral of slow growth, increasing unemployment, growing inability to pay debts and a general unraveling of their social structure. How to reconcile these diametrically opposed problems? We still face the first problem—that these countries will emerge one day. But the way in which they emerge and the timing of their emergence will depend on how we handle the old problems with possibly some new policies.

In assessing the policy implications of the NICs' economic emergence, it also must be recognized that their growing impact on the U.S. economy is closely related to the web of economic linkages that has grown up among nations. This new setting has fundamentally altered global economic relationships. In recent years, U.S. macroeconomic policy has had a series of unintended international repercussions that have been fed back into the U.S. economy and created new sets of problems. It would be a mistake to point to the NICs or other nations as exclusive agents of the problems that the United States is experiencing as a result of its macroeconomic policy and increased international economic linkages (Economic Policy Council 1984).

The purpose of this chapter will be to examine the economic impact of the NICs in three different areas: (1) trade, (2) finance and investment, and (3) structural adjustment. It will conclude with some overall findings and policy recommendations. The countries examined here are representative of the wide range of nations classified as NICs. Included are two small entrepot economies (Hong Kong and Singapore), two intermediate-size countries (South Korea and Taiwan), two large, resourve-rich, but highly indebted nations (Brazil and Mexico), and two less developed but potential global economic powers (China and India). This group is not meant to represent a definitive list of NICs[1] but to be indicative of the emerging group of countries that are changing the face of the international economy.

TRADE

Trade is central to U.S. economic relations with the NICs. Anxious to generate rapid economic growth and employment, to meet severe debt-service requirements, and in some cases to emerge as industrial powers in their own right, the NICs have emerged as active trading nations. In 1973 only one NIC—Brazil—ranked among the top twenty exporters. By 1984 seven of the eight NICs considered in this study ranked among the top twenty exporters (see Table 18-1).

The NICs' emergence as active international traders, together with the overall international economic climate of recent years, has resulted in rising NIC trade surpluses with the United States. In 1986 the eight NICs considered in this study accounted for one-fourth of the U.S. trade deficit (see Table 18-2).

Much of the increase in the overall U.S. trade deficit since 1981 has been attributed to the rise in the foreign exchange value of the dollar. Although the decline of the dollar since 1985 will help reduce the U.S. trade deficit with many industrial nations, it is, however, unlikely to have a major impact on the U.S. trade deficit with the NICs.

Table 18-1. Leading NIC Exporters and Importers in World Merchandise Trade in 1984 and Compared to 1973 (*percentage of world total*).

| | EXPORTS World Rank | | | IMPORTS World Rank | |
	1984	1973		1984	1973
Taiwan	12 (1.6%)	27 (.8%)	South Korea	12 (1.5%)	29 (.7%)
South Korea	14 (1.5%)	35 (.6%)	Singapore	15 (1.4%)	24 (.9%)
Hong Kong	15 (1.5%)	24 (.9%)	Hong Kong	16 (1.4%)	22 (1.0%)
Brazil	16 (1.4%)	19 (1.1%)	China	19 (1.3%)	23 (.9%)
China	18 (1.3%)	21 (1.0%)	Taiwan	20 (1.1%)	31 (.6%)
Mexico	19 (1.3%)	41 (.4%)			
Singapore	20 (1.3%)	23 (.6%)			

Source: GATT, *Prospects for International Trade*, Press Release 1374, Sept. 26, 1985 (reprinted in Aho and Aronson (1985: 107).

Table 18-2. U.S. Trade Balance with the NICs (*billions of dollars*).

	1977	1981	1985	1986
Brazil	$+ .09	$-1.1	$- 5.0	$- 3.5
China	- .05	+1.5	- .4	- 2.1
Hong Kong	-1.9	-3.1	- 6.2	- 6.4
India	- .09	+ .4	- .8	- .9
Mexico	+ .05	+3.8	- 5.8	- 5.2
Singapore	+ .3	+ .8	- .9	- 1.5
South Korea	- .8	- .4	- 4.8	- 7.1
Taiwan	-2.3	-4.3	-13.0	-15.7
NIC Total	-4.7	-2.4	-36.9	-42.4
Total U.S. *Trade Balance*	-39.2	-39.7	-139.7	-166.3

Sources: U.S. Bureau of Census (various years).
Note: Export, F.A.S.; import, C.I.F.

The currencies of the four Asian Tigers (South Korea, Taiwan, Hong Kong, and Singapore) are more or less tied to the dollar so that any decline in the dollar's foreign exchange rate is mirrored to some extent in the value of their currencies. As a result, the dollar's drop will improve their price competitiveness against such countries as Japan and West Germany (whose currencies have appreciated sharply against the dollar since 1985) and allow them to displace the exports of these countries to the United States. Furthermore, despite the dollar's slide, the currencies of Mexico, Brazil, and China have not appreciated against the dollar, so that the dollar's drop will not serve to improve U.S. trade with these countries. In addition, debt service requirements create overwhelming pressure for highly indebted NICs to run trade surpluses. And finally, companies that have closed plants in the United States and established foreign sourcing supply lines in the NICs will not readily abandon these arrangements in response to a lower dollar.

The NICs have become increasingly reliant on exports to U.S. markets in recent years. In 1984 and 1985 the United States took well over one-third of the total exports of the four Asian tigers, Brazil, and Mexico combined. By contrast, the proportion of the NICs exports to the EEC has actually declined in recent years (see Table 18–3 below), no doubt due in part to slow European economic growth.

Not only is the volume of NIC exports increasing, the composition of their exports is shifting. The NICs have focused on the export of manufactured goods. During 1980–82 manufactured goods amounted to 34 percent of total exports in Brazil, 9 percent in Mexico, 91 percent in Hong Kong, 81 percent in Korea, 42 percent in Singapore, and 92 percent in Taiwan (Morgan Guaranty 1985: 7). Increasingly, however, these manufactured exports are not limited to low value-added products but include more sophisticated goods. For example, from 1981 to 1985 South Korea's exports of electronics and tele-communications equipment to the United States doubled to $2.7 billion, almost as much as the $2.8 billion worth of textile and apparel exports it sent to the United States that year (Stokes 1986: 814).

The asymmetry of NIC exports to the United States compared to Japan and the EEC is even more pronounced when it comes to manufactured products. Japan's imports of NIC manufactures increased only marginally from 1981 to 1985, whereas the EEC's actually declined. By contrast, U.S.-manufactured imports from the NICs rose substantially over the past four years (see Table 18–4).

These trends fuel protectionist pressures in the United States and put the NICs in a position of extreme vulnerability. As Bill Eberle (1986: 814) stated,

> We are in an unsustainable situation with the third world today. In 1984 and 1985 the U.S. took something in excess of 60% of all the manufacturing exports from the third world, and it isn't just because of the dollar since the currencies of most these countries are tied to the dollar. We have a terrible reliance of the third world on the United States, which is creating problems for them and creating real pressure for us in the form of protectionist pressures.

U.S. protectionist pressures have focused on the NICs because of the large absolute size of their trade surpluses with the United States, the relatively closed markets of some of them, and the perceived propensity of some NICs to violate intellectual property rights, international labor standards, and human rights. There is also growing U.S. concern that the establishment of export production facilities by

Table 18–3. NIC Exports *(billions of U.S. dollars)*.[a]

	1976	1981	1985	1986
Hong Kong				
Total	8.5	21.8	30.2	35.4
To U.S.	2.5 (29%)	6.1 (28%)	9.3 (31%)	11.1 (31%)
To Japan	.6 (7%)	1.0 (5%)	1.3 (4%)	1.7 (5%)
To EEC	2.0 (24%)	4.1 (19%)	3.7 (12%)	5.1 (14%)
South Korea				
Total	7.7	21.3	28.9	35.6
To U.S.	2.5 (32%)	5.7 (27%)	10.5 (36%)	13.7 (38%)
To Japan	1.8 (23%)	3.5 (16%)	4.5 (16%)	5.4 (15%)
To EEC	1.2 (16%)	2.8 (13%)	3.0 (10%)	4.4 (12%)
Taiwan				
Total	8.2	22.6	30.7	39.7
To U.S.	3.0 (37%)	8.2 (36%)	14.8 (48%)	19.0 (48%)
To Japan	1.1 (13%)	2.5 (11%)	3.5 (11%)	4.5 (11%)
To EEC[b]	1.1 (13%)	2.9 (13%)	3.0 (10%)	4.7 (12%)
Singapore				
Total	6.6	21	22.8	22.5
To U.S.	1.0 (15%)	2.8 (13%)	4.8 (21%)	5.3 (24%)
To Japan	.7 (10%)	2.1 (10%)	2.1 (9%)	1.9 (8%)
To EEC	1.0 (15%)	2.3 (11%)	2.4 (11%)	2.5 (11%)
Brazil				
Total	10.1	23.3	25.6	24.6
To U.S.	1.8 (18%)	4.1 (18%)	6.8 (27%)	6.5 (26%)
To Japan	.6 (6%)	1.2 (5%)	1.4 (5%)	1.6 (7%)
To EEC	3.1 (31%)	6.4 (27%)	6.8 (27%)	6.1 (25%)

Mexico				
Total	3.5	19.4	24.0	16.6
To U.S.	2.1 (60%)	10.7 (55%)	15.0 (63%)	11.2 (67%)
To Japan	.2 (5%)	1.2 (6%)	1.6 (7%)	1.0 (6%)
To EEC	.3 (9%)	3.6 (19%)	3.9 (16%)	2.0 (12%)
China				
Total	6.1	21.5	27.3	31.4
To U.S.	.2 (3%)	1.5 (7%)	2.3 (8%)	2.6 (8%)
To Japan	1.2 (20%)	4.7 (22%)	6.0 (22%)	4.7 (15%)
To EEC	.9 (14%)	2.5 (12%)	2.3 (8%)	4.0 (13%)
India				
Total	5.0	6.8	9.8	10.3
To U.S.	.6 (12%)	.8 (11%)	2.3 (23%)	2.2 (21%)
To Japan	.6 (12%)	.6 (8%)	1.1 (11%)	1.2 (12%)
To EEC	1.2 (24%)	1.3 (19%)	2.1 (21%)	2.1 (20%)
All Eight Countries				
Total	55.7	157.7	199.3	216.1
To U.S.	13.7 (25%)	39.9 (25%)	65.8 (33%)	71.6 (33%)
To Japan	6.8 (12%)	16.8 (11%)	21.6 (11%)	22.0 (10%)
To EEC	10.8 (19%)	25.9 (16%)	27.2 (14%)	30.9 (14%)

a. Exports on F.O.B. basis.
b. All of Europe except the countries in East Europe.
Sources: IMF, *Direction of Trade Statistics* (1982, 1987); Taiwan Board of Foreign Trade (1986).

Table 18-4. U.S.,ᵃ Japanese,ᵇ and EECᶜ Imports of Manufactured Goods from the NICs (*billions of U.S. dollars*).

	1981			1983			1985		
	U.S.	Japan	EEC	U.S.	Japan	EEC	U.S.	Japan	EEC
China	1.2	1.3	1.6	1.6	1.1	1.3	2.6	1.8	1.6
Hong Kong	5.3	0.5	4.7	6.3	0.5	3.6	8.3	0.6	4.5
India	0.9	0.2	0.5	1.1	0.2	1.2	1.4	0.3	0.4
Korea	5.1	2.5	2.9	7.0	2.2	2.4	9.8	2.6	4.5
Singapore	1.9	0.4	1.4	2.6	0.3	1.2	3.7	0.5	0.4
Taiwan	7.8	1.4	3.0	10.9	1.5	2.5	16.0	2.0	2.8
Brazil	1.8	0.3	1.3	2.5	0.5	1.3	4.3	0.5	1.8
Mexico	5.1	0.2	.5	6.3	0.2	0.4	9.0	0.2	0.3
Total	29.1	6.8	15.9	38.3	6.6	13.9	55.1	8.4	11.4

a. U.S. and EEC's definition of manufactured goods in SITC numbers starting with 5, 6, 7, and 8.
b. Japan's definition of manufactured goods is "chemical machinery and equipments and others."
c. 1981, 1 ECU = U.S. $1.12; 1983, 1 ECU = U.S. $.89; 1985, 1 ECU = U.S. $.76.
Note: U.S. statistics on customs value basis; Japan and EEC on C.I.F. basis.
Sources: U.S. Trade Representative; Ministry of Finance of Japan; European Community Information Office, Euro Statistics.

U.S. corporations in the NICs is driving down U.S. wages and eroding the U.S. manufacturing base.

The NICs, however, see themselves as unfairly singled out by the United States. The Asian NICs argue that their export success is due to their ability to combine modern technology with high productivity and low wages. They point out that they have already responded positively to U.S. calls for reduced import barriers, removal of subsidies, and greater protection of intellectual property rights. Furthermore, they have independently embarked on "privatization" programs to reduce the role of the state and increase the role of the private sector and market forces in their economies. The Asian NICs further stress that many of their exports to the United States are generated by U.S. corporations and that Japan and the EEC contribute much more to the U.S. global trade deficit. Latin American NICs, on the other hand, claim that the United States encourages them to increase their trade surpluses in order to generate the foreign exchange necessary to service their foreign debt and then criticizes them when this results in more exports and fewer imports.

The NICs also complain about industrial countries' restrictions on their exports. Successive rounds of trade negotiations have served to reduce tariff barriers among industrial nations. These tariff reductions were extended to developing countries (LDCs) under the most-favored-national clause, even though LDCs did not generally offer equivalent concessions. In part because of the lack of such concessions, however, tariffs were reduced less on LDC exports than on the exports of industrial countries. And because the current tariff structure escalates from raw materials to finished goods, it discriminates against processing activities in developing countries. Nontariff barriers also reflect this discrimination against exports from developing countries. In 1985, 12.9 percent of U.S. imports of agricultural and manufactured goods from developing countries faced nontariff barriers, as opposed to only 3.9 percent of U.S. imports of these goods from industrial countries. The comparable figures for the European Community are 21.8 percent and 10.5 percent and for Japan, 9.5 percent and 10.5 percent (Balassa et al. 1986: 158).

Many of the NICs have embraced specific economic programs to increase exports and accelerate the shift toward manufactures. These programs differ from country to country but are widely viewed in the United States as a source of unfair competition. Of all the NICs only Hong Kong has pursued predominately neutral, market-oriented trade and domestic economic policies. In South Korea the government decided in the mid-1970s to emphasize capital-intensive heavy industry, such as shipbuilding, steel, and automobiles. The country borrowed heavily in international markets and made large credits available to private business groups, and the government itself even stepped into take over some projects. The emphasis was later broadened to include high-technology industries, especially electronics. These programs have not been universally successful (Korean shipbuilding and semiconductors face severe overcapacity), but they have resulted in export surges to the United States in such industries as steel and electronics.

Taiwan, by contrast, has not concentrated industrial projects in the hands of a few large business groups. Instead, it has financed economic growth through domestic savings and relied on small and medium-size entrepreneurs. Because of a lack of large business conglomerates, the government undertook most of the heavy industry projects and encouraged the private sector to enter into joint ventures and high-technology projects requiring lower capital inputs. Much of Taiwan's high-technology drive is centered around the science park at Hsinchu.

Mexico and Brazil have followed different strategies. Mexico introduced the National Industrial Development Plan (NIDP) in 1979 and the Global Development Plan (GDP) in 1980 to promote balanced agricultural and industrial development. International loans and large-scale government spending of oil revenues were to provide the engine for growth, whereas the long-term goal was the evolution of an industrial economy that would supersede reliance on loans and oil. Strict control over foreign investment and local content laws designed to spur the shift toward manufacturing were key elements in the overall plans. The debt crisis of 1982 and the precipitous drop in oil prices that began in 1985, however, have severely undermined this strategy (Economic Policy Council 1983).

Brazil has promoted industrial production by actively encouraging manufactured exports and placing strict limits on imports and foreign investment. Brazilian import restrictions cut across all sectors. Automobiles, computers, and all products relating to national security must be produced in Brazil. Brazil's 1984 Informatica law, which prevents foreign manufacturers from owning more than 30 percent of a company that makes computer equipment, is especially controversial ("Industry Brief" 1986: 70).

As these examples illustrate, the NICs' success has been associated with a wide variety of economic circumstances and policies. Perhaps the major distinguishing factor of the NICs is their emphasis on manufactured exports. The conviction that foreign investment should be tightly controlled and a lack of respect for intellectual property are also characteristic of many of the NICs. Their basic strategy has been to use their low labor costs to gain a comparative advantage in low valued-added manufactured goods that require standardized, easily replicated technologies and relatively minor inputs of skilled labor. Once they have established themselves in these sectors, the NICs have rapidly shifted to the manufacture of more sophisticated goods by importing technologies and factories and upgrading the skills of their workforces. The NICs' challenge remains most intense in basic industries—textiles, apparel, steel, consumer appliances, and so forth—but it is also beginning to spread to high-tech and related areas.

The export success of the NICs in East Asia and the debt problems of the NICs in Latin America have led to a stylized, but inaccurate, contrast of the two regions' economic strategies. According to the stylized view, the East Asian model is outward oriented and driven by the free market with an emphasis on export-led growth and internal liberalization. As a result, it generates low inflation, little price distortion, high growth, increasing exports, and a low incidence of debt rescheduling. By contrast, the Latin American model is inward oriented and characterized by government intervention with emphasis on import substitution and debt-led development. Consequently it generates high inflation, great price distortion, low growth, stagnant exports, and a high incidence of debt rescheduling.

In reality both models are characterized by extensive government intervention. What appears to distinguish East Asia's economic performance is not the dominance of free enterprise but the highly effective collaboration between the private and public sectors. Shared goals and commitments together with a high degree of professionalism in the service of national economic development have characterized the region's economic strategy. Market forces and government intervention are not at odds with each other but carefully coordinated for national economic gain.

The NIC's market reserve policies and manufactured export push have had a tremendous impact on their trade with the United States and prompted growing U.S. concern that the NICs are preying on

U.S. markets. From 1981 to 1985, U.S. manufactured exports to Latin America declined by one-third, whereas U.S. manufactured imports from Latin America increased by 77 percent. In 1985 U.S. manufactured imports from Far Eastern developing countries and NICs were over three times the volume of U.S. manufactured exports to those countries (U.S. Bureau of the Census 1981, 1985).

These shifts are reflected in a widening U.S. trade deficit in manufactured goods that in 1986 amounted to over $140 billion. The unprecedented U.S. trade deficit, in turn, has raised questions about the strength of the U.S. industrial base and about the adequacy of the international trade system embodied by GATT. Not only does GATT cover a limited share of world trade, it is not handling well those areas that it does cover. Governments no longer adhere to many of GATT's rules, and significant new actions and issues have emerged that lay outside GATT's jurisdiction.

The U.S. push for a new trade round is an attempt to strengthen GATT and extend its coverage into new areas. Calls for the new trade round, however, are motivated more by fear of a breakdown than by hopes of a breakthrough. Supporters see the negotiations as a way to block rising international protectionism, whereas detractors see the new round as a necessary but insufficient response to unfair trade practices.

The issues that will be discussed in the new trade round include the unfinished business of previous rounds, such as subsidies, nontariff barriers, and emergency import protection. Strengthening the trading system by bringing sectors such as agriculture back under the auspices of GATT and extending GATT discipline into new areas, such as services, technology, trade-related investment, and intellectual property, are also on the agenda (Aho and Aronson 1986).

Led by Brazil and India, a group of ten developing countries resisted the inclusion of services on the agenda and instead demanded discussions aimed at improving world commodity markets. These countries claimed that as long as the industrial world protects its agricultural and textile industries, developing countries should not open their markets to U.S. services. A second group of developing countries that includes the Asian NICs, however, supported the U.S. call for liberalization in services because they see the new round as a means of keeping international markets open.

The Ministerial Declaration on the Uruguay Round hammered out at Punta del Este in September 1986 reflected the U.S. position that agriculture, services, trade-related investment, and intellectual property be included on the agenda. At the same time, however, it highlighted explicit exceptions for developing countries. It noted that the differential and more favorable treatment for less-developed countries that is embodied in Part IV of the GATT applies to these negotiations and that the developing countries are not expected to make reciprocal concessions that are inconsistent with their individual development, financial, and trade needs. The declaration also stressed that special attention be given to the problems of the least developed countries. But it also recognized that as the NICs' economic stature grows, they will be expected to be fuller participants in the world trade system and to accept new responsibilities for helping to manage the system.

FINANCE AND INVESTMENT

Just as Mexico's 1982 announcement that it was unable to service its foreign debt signaled the onset of the international debt crisis, Mexico's financial troubles of 1986 marked a new phase of the debt problem (Economic Policy Council 1984). By the beginning of 1986 the total indebtedness of developing countries had grown to well over $800 billion, more than double the 1979 level. Brazil was at the top of this list with a total foreign debt of $106 billion, followed by Mexico with $97 billion; South Korea had $43 billion.

The initial response to the debt crisis was a series of case-by-case reschedulings managed by the IMF and involving debtor countries, commercial bank creditors, central banks, and the Bank for International Settlements. These efforts were based on economic austerity programs as a prerequisite for new credits. As part of these programs, debtor nations reduced their fiscal budget deficits and ran up large trade surpluses.

Although these efforts contained the problem, the cost to debtor nations was high. The 1982 and 1983 recessions in Latin America that were triggered by the drying up of foreign capital flows wiped out much of the economic progress that had been made in the region since 1975. From 1981 to 1984 Latin America as a whole suffered a cumulative decline of 8.9 percent in gross domestic product per capita.

According to some estimates, unlike the 1970s when Latin America managed to borrow more money each year than it paid out in interest payments, the region has paid more to service its debt than it has received in new loans since 1982. In 1982 its net payments to its creditors were $18.4 billion; in 1983, $30.1 billion; and in 1984, $26.7 billion (Glynn 1985: 17). Some observers have pointed to this reversal in the flow of international capital away from developing countries to advanced industrial nations as "the central aberration of the debt crisis" (see Lever and Huhne 1986: 27).

These outlays on the part of debtor nations were financed in large part by surging trade surpluses. In 1984 Brazil's trade surplus was $13.1 billion and Mexico's $12.8 billion; in 1985 their trade surpluses were $12.4 billion and $9.5 billion, respectively. These trade surpluses have to a great extent been engineered by increasing exports to the United States and reducing imports.

Latin American debtors claim that they are subject to contradictory demands from the United States. On the one hand, the U.S. encourages them to run up trade surpluses large enough to service their foreign debt. At the same time, however, it criticizes them for the aggressive export tactics and import controls necessary to generate these surpluses. This contradiction underlies the highly skewed nature of the adjustment process, which so far has fallen mostly on the goods economies of the debtor and creditor countries.

Despite successive years of austerity and record trade surpluses by debtor countries, economic growth and renewed international bank lending remain elusive. Commercial bank lending to non-OPEC developing countries dropped from a high of just under $50 billion in 1981 to about $10 billion in 1984, as banks reduced their exposure to many highly indebted NICs (Overseas Development Council 1985: 175). Foreign direct investment flows to highly indebted NICs in Latin America have also declined, although they have increased in Asian NICs (see Table 18-5).

Capital flight is also a serious problem for highly indebted NICs. Not only does it deprive them of much needed resources for economic development, it aggravates their debt problems and makes foreign creditors unwilling to provide them with new loans. The problem is particularly acute for Latin America. In the absence of capital flight, Brazil and Mexico would have had much more manageable debt burdens. Although there is wide agreement that extensive capital flight has occurred in many highly indebted NICs, estimates of

Table 18-5. Total Foreign Direct Investment Flows *(millions of U.S. dollars).*

	1980	*1981*	*1982*	*1983*	*1984*
Mexico	$2,184	$2,541	$1,644	$ 454	$ 392
Brazil	1,913	2,526	2,922	1,556	1,598
India[a]	79	92	72	6	-37
China	57	265	429	636	125
Hong Hong	374	88	652	603	681
Taiwan	162	119	57	120	208
Korea	8	101	68	69	112
Singapore	1,669	1,916	1,803	1,445	1,458

a. Overseas Development Council.
Sources: IMF (1986); U.S. Bureau of Labor Statistics (1986).

Table 18-6. Estimated Net Capital Flight, 1976-85 *(billions of U.S. dollars).*

Brazil	$-30
Mexico	-60
India	-10
South Korea	-12

a. Based on year-end 1985 estimates.
Source: Morgan Guaranty Trust Company of New York (1986: March, p. 13; September, p. 6).

the size of these flows vary widely. Table 18-6 lists one of the most frequently cited estimates.

Debtors complain that they have followed the programs outlined by the IMF and now need a significant infusion of new capital. But commercial banks and investors fear that continuing economic mismanagement, corruption, and capital flight in debtor nations mean that new loans will be squandered without contributing to the infrastructure and solid economic progress necessary to service their debt.

In order to resolve this impasse, U.S. Secretary of the Treasury James Baker proposed a new approach in October 1985. In it Secretary Baker outlined three goals: (1) the adoption by "debtor countries of comprehensive macroeconomic and structural policies, supported by the international financial institutions, to promote growth and balance of payments adjustment, and to reduce inflation"; (2) a continued central role for the IMF, in conjunction with an enhanced role for the World Bank and other multilateral development banks, reflected in increased and more effective structural adjustment lending; and (3) "increased lending by the private banks in support of comprehensive economic adjustment program." The goal of the Baker plan is to funnel $29 billion ($20 billion from commercial lenders and $9 billion from the World Bank and other multilateral agencies) to fifteen major debtors over the next three years (*IMF Survey* 1985).

Although this approach has been endorsed by both debtors and creditors, there is some question about how effective it has been and whether it will be sufficient to balance the need for fundamental long-term structural adjustment in debtor nations with the need of substantial new capital infusions.

Senator Bill Bradley has also proposed a new debt strategy, which differs from the Baker initiative in that it calls for more funds, a cut in the annual interest rates commercial banks charge to developing countries, and a write-off of loan capital. Like Baker, however, Bradley emphasizes the important role of the IMF and the World Bank and the need for debtor countries to institute policies that will spur economic growth and stem capital flight as a condition for new loans.

STRUCTURAL ADJUSTMENT

With the rise of multinational corporations and with managerial talent, technology, and production systems easily transferrable among nations, industrial production is quickly moving around the world. The NICs have been quick to exploit this trend and establish themselves as manufacturing centers. Production of manufactured goods in the NICs has been accompanied by major export drives because domestic demand is not usually great enough to justify the necessary investments and the bulk of these exports have been to the United States. Although NIC exports have benefitted U.S. consumers, they have also contributed to dislocation in the U.S. foreign trade sector.

In 1981 the United States enjoyed a $5 billion surplus in its manufacturing trade; by 1985 this surplus had swung to a $113 billion deficit and in 1986 increased to over $140 billion. The United States already takes approximately two-thirds of the total manufactured exports of the LDCs. With the decline of the dollar relative to the currencies of Japan and Western Europe, the NICs are likely to displace the industrialized countries' as suppliers of manufactured goods to the United States and claim a growing share of the U.S. market.

The U.S. Commerce Department estimates that over 70 percent of U.S. manufacturing is subject to import competition, and the NICs aggressive export of manufactured goods has contributed to restructuring of industry and jobs in the United States. Many American workers have had to leave manufacturing jobs. The shift from jobs in the manufacturing sector to jobs in other sectors is made more difficult by wage disparities. In 1985 the average weekly earnings for manufacturing workers was $386, whereas workers in the financial sector earned $289, workers in retail trade $177, and workers in other service industries $261 (U.S. Bureau of Labor Statistics 1986: 219).

From 1973 to 1985, U.S. manufacturing production (measured in constant dollars) increased by almost 40 percent, yet manufacturing employment went down steadily. During that period total U.S. employment jumped from 82 to 110 million, but blue-collar jobs in the U.S. manufacturing sector declined by 5 million (Drucker 1986: 776). U.S. manufacturing is thus following the same trend that U.S. agriculture did a century earlier—increased output with fewer workers.

Although industrial dislocation due to imports creates adjustment problems that are often concentrated in a few sectors, protecting manufacturing jobs in the foreign trade sector can also be costly. Many corporations reject the notion of a choice between shifting production and jobs overseas or keeping them in the United States. The real choice, they maintain, is between shifting some U.S. production overseas or closing down the production facilities altogether.

Table 18-7. 1985 Hourly Manufacturing Compensation in the United
States and the NICs (*in U.S. dollars*).

United States	$12.82
Brazil	1.22
Korea	1.44
Hong Kong	1.75
Taiwan	1.46

Source: U.S. Bureau of Labor Statistics (1987).

Table 18-7 demonstrates just how great the wage gap is between
the United States and the NICs, and why U.S. firms find it so profitable to manufacture overseas and export their products back to the
United States, provided the low wages are combined with sufficiently
high productivity. The NICs themselves are beginning to face wage
competition from less developed countries. As a result, like the
United States and other advanced industrial nations, they are trying
to maintain their competitive advantage by increasing worker productivity, upgrading the skill level of their workforce, and creating a
cadre of highly trained managers. Consequently, they are beginning
to take over more complex aspects of production and to manufacture an increasingly wide range of advanced industrial goods.

Taiwan is indicative of the NICs' attempt to move up the manufacturing ladder. Taiwan initially depended on low wage rates to
attract foreign investors. This strategy proved to be very successful
in the short term but unsustainable in the long run because of lower
wage rate competition from other developing countries, such as Mexico and China. As a result, Taiwan has begun to develop a highly
skilled workforce as a lure for foreign investors. For example, the
largest employer in Taiwan is General Electric, but few of their employees are American. Taiwan's wage levels may be slightly higher
than in most other NICs and LDCs, but productivity is also higher
and workers are better trained. Skilled workers and technically
trained management are especially important to firms in the high-
technology sector. Taiwan's Hsinchu science park, which emphasizes
R&D and high-technology production, is indicative of its plans for
the future.

The NICs move up the manufacturing ladder will contribute to
heightened competition and adjustment pressures for an increasing

range of U.S. workers and industries over the next decade. Workers in the textile and apparel industry were among the first to experience the job dislocation stemming, in part, from imports. Steelworkers, autoworkers, and electronic assembly workers have all since experienced this same dislocation, and other workers in manufacturing are likely to feel the pressure in the future. As long as U.S. domestic economic dislocation remains widespread, adjustment will be difficult and resistance to manufactured imports will grow.

FINDINGS

In examining U.S. economic relations with the NICs, several observations merit attention. Some of the more salient findings are outlined below.

First, the *NICs have a pronounced reliance on U.S. markets.* The increase of the NICs' exports to the United States has far outstripped any increase to Japan and the EEC in recent years. The U.S. share of the total exports of the eight NICs studied here rose from 23 percent in 1975 to 33 percent in 1985, whereas Japan's share fell from 13 percent to 11 percent and the EEC's share dropped from 19 percent to 14 percent. In 1985 the United States took three times as many exports from these NICs as Japan and more than twice as much as the EEC. The NICs' dependency on the United States has added to the dislocation in the U.S. foreign trade sector, made the NICs vulnerable to any disruption in U.S. markets, and raised questions about whether the NICs have become excessively dependent on U.S. macroeconomic conditions.

Second, *exports of manufactured goods* have been a key to the NICs' economic growth in the past and will continue to be a major factor over the next decade. For the top ranking Asian NICs and India, manufactured exports account for the bulk of total exports (over 90 percent in the case of Taiwan and Hong Kong); for Latin America and second-tier Asian NICs, they account for a smaller but nonetheless significant portion of total exports. The NICs will be increasing, not decreasing, their manufactured exports, and if past experience is any guide many of them will be headed for the U.S. market. In 1985 the United States imported $55.1 billion of manufactured goods from the eight NICs examined here, whereas Japan imported only $8.5 billion and the EEC only $11.4 billion.

Third, the *NICs' reliance on exports contributes to the domestic adjustment problems already facing U.S. management and labor.* Because rapidly rising NIC exports accelerate the need for adjustment in the U.S. foreign trade sector, trade policy will be a central concern of the United States and the NICs over the next decade. Trade policy cannot be viewed in isolation, however, because such issues as macroeconomic policy, exchange rate swings, and foreign debt service requirements can swamp trade policy decisions.

Fourth, the *NICs have a lot to lose if the international trade system unravels.* Like Japan, many of the NICs have pursued a policy of export-led development. Such a strategy, however, depends to a large degree on access to international markets, especially in a slowly growing world economy. Failure to get a multilateral program to promote more open international trade will result in reciprocal bilateral and regional agreements that will work to the disadvantage of the NICs.

Fifth, as long as *U.S. macroeconomic policy leads to extensive domestic dislocation, U.S. trade policy will be under pressure* to deal with the disruptive employment effects of imports. During the early 1980s tight U.S. monetary policy and expansionary U.S. fiscal policy drove up the exchange value of the dollar and caused U.S. consumers and investors to purchase more foreign goods. As a result of this "leaky bucket" effect, the stimulative impact of U.S. macroeconomic policies on the domestic U.S. economy was limited, and U.S. unemployment rates remained high. Just as low unemployment buffers the job dislocations caused by trade, high unemployment makes the job dislocations caused by trade more visible and increases the pressure on U.S. trade policy to protect U.S. jobs. Consequently, when U.S. macroeconomic policy results in widespread domestic U.S. economic dislocation, trading nations like the NICs with large volumes of exports to the United States are the focus of increasing U.S. criticism.

Sixth, the *NICs' currencies will play an increasingly important international role* as they emerge as significant players in the global economy. As this process occurs, it will be crucial for the NICs to avoid competitive devaluations and to keep their currencies market oriented. Exchange rate adjustments can help reduce international trade imbalances and lessen protectionist pressure.

Seventh, many of the NICs are characterized by *extensive government intervention* in the domestic economy. The NICs are often divided into those countries that rely on free enterprise and encourage export led development and those that rely on government interventions and promote import substitution. In reality, widespread government intervention is common to virtually all of the NICs, and aggressive export programs do not exclude a high degree of import substitution. What seems to distinguish most of the successful NICs is the effective collaboration between the public and private sectors. Government interventions are closely coordinated with market-oriented solutions; development strategies have clearly defined objectives and priorities; and management is characterized by professionalism in the service of national economic development.

Eighth, the *financial burdens of highly indebted NICs put pressure on the goods sector of the U.S. economy.* In order to generate the foreign exchange necessary to service their foreign debt, highly indebted NICs have reduced imports and pushed exports. This move has hurt industries and workers in the U.S. foreign trade sector. Highly indebted NICs, especially in Latin America, have justifiable concerns about the need to earn the foreign exchange necessary to service their debt, but they should not be allowed to use debt as an excuse to keep their markets closed. Further measures to ease the debt crisis, whatever form they take, should be tied to dismantling trade barriers and promoting more open markets in the NICs.

Ninth, *foreign investment in the NICs* can make some contribution to easing the debt and trade difficulties confronting the NICs, but it is unlikely to play a major role in solving these problems in the near future. Growth of domestic demand in the NICs benefits all nations over the long term, and foreign investment can aid this process. Foreign investment is not an independent variable, however, but highly sensitive to such issues as indebtedness, trade policy, foreign exchange rates, macroeconomic management, and political stability. The NICs receive the majority of foreign direct investment in the developing world, but these flows have decreased in recent years. The trend of decreasing investment, particularly in Latin America, is likely to continue in view of the investment disincentives for multinational corporations in the form of price and remittance controls, import restrictions, failure to provide adequate protection of intellectual property, and so forth. There is much talk of replacing commercial lending to highly indebted NICs with equity in the form of foreign investment, but as long as impediments and disincentives

to foreign investment persist in these countries, there is little likelihood that it can be generated in amounts sufficient to substitute for
commercial bank lending.

Tenth, the changes taking place in the international economy have
created *a new premium on flexible adjustment.* With the rise of
multinational corporations and with managerial talent, technology,
and production systems easily transferrable, industrial production
is quickly moving around the world. Low wages may initially be
enough for a country to attract industry, but they are not enough to
keep it. Other developing countries are already undercutting the
NICs wage levels. Consequently, the NICs are beginning to compete
in terms of managerial know-how, workers' education and training,
and technology—all traditional preserves of the advanced industrial
nations. The ease of transferring productive assets among countries
and the ability of governments to create a national competitive advantage through industrial policies have raised fundamental questions
about the U.S. position in the international economy. Given the new
international environment and prevailing wage levels in the United
States, many Americans are beginning to question which U.S. industries and workers, other than those in some high tech and service
sectors, will benefit from freer trade.

Eleventh, *serious issues of the distribution of economic rewards
in the NICs* still exist despite the huge investments in technology and
education that have paid off in terms of dramatic aggregate economic
growth. Too often, dictatorships and internal political oligarchies
prevent the mass of the population—workers and potential workers—
from benefitting from expanded production and trade. Those countries whose growth and economic development continue to occur
under conditions in which workers do not have the minimal safety
and health protection, where child labor is a common practice, where
unions are forbidden, and where human rights are violated cannot
be expected to be treated as equal partners in trade and economic
affairs. It is neither inconsistent with the tradition of the United
States nor its present foreign economic policy aims to encourage a
fairer and more equitable sharing of the fruits of economic growth.

Twelfth, there are *no short-term solutions* to the trade and debt
problems facing the United States and the NICs. The foreign exchange rate realignments currently underway among the United
States and other industrial nations will not significantly ease U.S.
trade tensions with the NICs in the short term; measures stemming

from the new GATT round of trade talks are likely to take five years or more to implement; and most debt strategies now focus on the need for long-term adjustment. The best that can be hoped for in the short run is sufficient economic growth in the United States, other industrial countries, and the NICs to ease dislocation in the U.S. foreign trade sector and to further the growth of internal markets in the NICs.

The United States has no policy framework to deal with the findings outlined above. It continues to press for trade liberalization, but there is growing concern about U.S. competitiveness and adjustment in a world of open trade and rapid innovation. This confusion on the policy front underlies a fundamental problem. The NICs' transition to advanced industrial states is being played out in the broader global economy and is forcing major international adjustments. Because the NICs are neither less developed countries nor fully fledged industrial nations, they are confounding traditional policy responses. They play too large an economic role to be left outside of existing policy channels but insist that they are not yet mature enough to accept responsibility for their growing impact on the global economic system. Their in-between status has prompted a rethinking of long-standing economic relationships and the role of international institutions. New policy solutions must be found that help the United States make necessary adjustments and help the NICs accept the increased international responsibilities that go with their economic emergence.

POLICY RECOMMENDATIONS

1. *The U.S. Executive and Congress should make a high-level government commitment to trade with the NICs a key aspect of U.S. trade policy.* The U.S. Trade Representative's office is overextended and needs to be strengthened, but a stronger USTR will not necessarily mean better and more farsighted attention to the NICs in the absence of a unified, clearly defined U.S. policy commitment. The United States should vigorously enforce antidumping and countervailing duty laws, strongly protect U.S. intellectual property, self-initiate investigation of foreign unfair trading practices, and defend U.S. exporters against subsidy programs of other nations. If efforts to eliminate unfair foreign trade practices and open foreign markets through consultations fail, the United States should take tactical

measures—such as denying or limiting access to U.S. markets—to resolve these issues.

2. *The Ministerial Declaration on the Uruguay Round provides a good framework to address new trade issues, but governments and heads of state must lend their full support to these trade talks if this declaration is to lead to genuine reform.* The Uruguay Ministerial Statement outlines the importance of bringing agriculture, services, trade-related investment, and intellectual property into the multilateral trade system. Further progress in these areas is critical to the continued viability of the multilateral trade system, but they are not a substitute for an effective national trade policy, exchange rate adjustments that better reflect current economic realities, or a fiscal policy that promotes lower budget deficits and more U.S. savings and investment.

3. *The United States and the NICs should join forces in the coming trade round to open the markets of Japan and the EEC to more imports.* Exchange-rate realignments should result in increased U.S. and NIC exports to other industrial nations, but action is also needed on the trade policy front. The lack of access to the Japanese market and slow growth in the EEC have contributed to the NICs' increasing reliance on the U.S. market. This asymmetry in trade flows exacerbates U.S. economic dislocation and pushes the NICs toward a situation of extreme dependency on one market.

4. *To the extent that the upper-tier NICs decline to participate fully in the process of trade liberalization, they should not receive the full benefits of liberalized trade under the new trade round.* Although the Uruguay Declaration reaffirmed the principle of differential and more favorable treatment for less developed nations as embodied in Part IV of the GATT, upper-tier NICs should not be allowed to hide behind this provision. Their growing economic role carries with it the responsibility to be full participants in the trade system.

5. *The General Agreement on Tariffs and Trade (GATT) should be strengthened so that it can do more to guard against trade abuses.* The GATT Secretariat should have and use the power to initiate the exploration and study of protectionist trade policies, instead of having to wait for member governments to initiate trade complaints. Furthermore, the GATT surveillance system should be strengthened, and measures should be introduced to speed dispute settlements. These actions would strengthen the GATT. They could be negotiated

without penalizing individual GATT members and could serve as a bridge to the longer-term negotiations of the trade round.

6. *The new trade round should not distract U.S. attention from the domestic competitive handicaps that hamper U.S. trade performance*, such as insufficient incentives for civilian R&D by industry, an educational system in need of reform, and a failure to devise a system to ease the dislocation of U.S. workers and communities hurt by imports.

7. *The criteria for graduation from the Generalized System of Preferences (GSP) should be reviewed and the criteria for eligibility tightened.* GSP exempts developing countries from certain U.S. import duties. As a result of a two-year U.S. review of the competitive need limits on GSP products, advanced developing countries will receive a smaller share of GSP benefits, and some countries will lose their benefits entirely because of their practices in the area of workers rights. Present law states that GSP will be withdrawn for countries with per capita GNP above $8,500. This ceiling is too generous and should be lowered. The United States should not, however, look to graduation from GSP as the solution to our trade problems with the NICs. The sums in question are relatively small, and even if some NICs are graduated, GSP would still be available to other developing countries.

8. *U.S. government, business, and labor should give high priority to adjustment assistance and to the implementation of a comprehensive displaced-worker program for those permanently separated from their jobs as a result of trade.*[2] Much of the U.S. concern over trade with the NICs has to do with the tragic impact of widespread import penetration on many workers and industries and the need for more active labor market policy measures. Workers displaced by imports often face difficulties making job transitions because manufacturing industries are not growing fast enough to absorb them and because many of those sectors that are growing rapidly often offer low-skilled, largely part-time jobs that pay low wages and offer little in the way of insurance and other fringe benefits. Failure to facilitate the transition of workers displaced by imports to new jobs will lead to increasing calls for protectionism.

9. *Efforts should be made through the International Labor Organization (ILO) and other multilateral institutions to promote internationally recognized labor standards and a more equitable distribution of income in the NICs that would support an expanded domestic*

market. The United States cannot and should not try to compete with the NICs exclusively on the basis of lower wage rates. Among the fruits of industrialization and international trade are higher wages and an improved standard of living. The 1984 U.S. trade bill tied continued GSP privileges to observance of international labor rights, protection of intellectual property rights, and market access for U.S. goods, services, and investment; and the United States should continue to push for these conditions.

10. *The World Bank should do more to help defuse the global debt crisis but at the same time cannot forsake its commitment to project financing.* Its efforts in these two areas, however, will soon be constrained by limited funds, unless a capital increase is agreed and commited next year. In 1980 the bank began supplementing its project financing with policy-based loans meant to help improve the borrowing country's overall economic climate.[3] The conditionality that is an explicit paft of these policy-based loans helps promote sound economic management in debtor nations, and the World Bank should structure these loans so that they promote trade liberalization and a broadening of domestic markets.

11. *The IMF should encourage the NICs to keep their currencies market oriented and in some cases allow their foreign exchange values to strengthen.* The IMF has a key role to play in the supervision of foreign exchange rates. It has already worked with some highly indebted NICs with overvalued currencies to bring down their exchange values and should continue to exercise this vigilence in the future.

12. *Capital flight has been a major contributing factor to the debt problems now confronting some NICs, and they should take action to reduce the export of capital.* Capital flight reflects a lack of confidence of citizens in their governments' policies, and reversing it will require improvements in these policies.[4] In the short run, the NICs should maintain credible exchange rates for their currencies, keep real interest rates positive, and push for lower budget deficits to reduce monetary creation. Over the longer term, the NICs should focus on improving investor confidence by improving the overall economic environment, maintaining market determined interest rates, creating a stable monetary environment, and introducing more private sector oriented policies. Rather than simply try forcibly to repatriate flight capital, highly indebted NICs should try to tap international capital

markets and encourage not only their own citizens but also foreign investors to invest in their economies.

13. *As the NICs become more technically advanced and emerge as important players in the international economy, it will be necessary to promote an intense exchange of information and bring them into a cooperative framework of extensive consultation.* This exchange already takes place among the industrialized countries, both on an informal basis and through institutions such as the Organization for Economic Cooperation and Development (OECD). Admitting new members to the OECD is a lengthy process, and the United States should begin to discuss the possibility of expanding the OECD to include upper-tier NICs.

NOTES

1. Many other countries—such as some Southern European and Middle Eastern nations (Greece, Portugal, Spain, Yugoslavia, Turkey), other Latin American countries (Argentina, Venezuela), and other Asian countries (Malaysia, Thailand)—are also often classified as NICs.
2. For a thorough discussion of policy recommendations concerning the jobs problems facing U.S. workers, see Economic Policy Council (1985).
3. These loans can be used for balance of payments financing, provided that disciplined, long-term economic policies are followed (such as measures to stem capital flight, cut back government budget deficits, encourage the private sector, reduce corruption, and so forth).
4. According to some estimates, a sum equal to as much as one-half of the money borrowed by large Latin American debtor nations during the last decade has been exported. Moreover, capital flight from many highly indebted NICs continues, causing lenders seriously to reconsider new loans.

REFERENCES

Aho, C. Michael, and Jonathan David Aronson. 1986. *Trade Talks.* New York: Council on Foreign Relations.

Balassa, Bela, Gerardo M. Bueno, Pedro-Pablo Kuczynski, and Mario Henrique Simonsen. 1986. *Toward Renewed Economic Growth in Latin America.* Washingron, D.C.: Institute for International Economics.

Bradshaw, Thornton. 1986. "Comments before the EPC Panel on the Newly Industrializing Countries." New York, January 17.

Drucker, Peter. 1986. "The Changed World Economy." *Foreign Affairs* 64 (4) (Spring): 768-91.

Eberle, William. 1986. "Comments before the EPC Panel on the Newly Industrializing Countries." New York, May 19.

Economic Policy Council. 1983. *U.S. Trade and Economic Relations with Japan and Mexico.* New York: UNA-USA.

_____. 1984. *The Global Repercussions of U.S. Monetary and Fiscal Policy.* Cambridge, Mass.: Ballinger.

_____. 1985. *The Jobs Challenge: Pressures and Possibilities.* Cambridge, Mass.: Ballinger.

Flainn, Paul O., and Ellen Sehgal. 1985. "Displaced Workers of 1979-83: How Well Have They Faired?" *Monthly Labor Review* 108 (6) (June): 3-16.

Glynn, Lenny. 1985. "Is the Latin Debt Crisis Over? Don't Kid Yourself." *The Institutional Investor* (May): 87.

"Industry Brief." 1986. *The Economist,* March 29, p. 70.

International Monetary Fund. Various years. *IMF Direction of Trade Statistics.* Washington, D.C.: IMF.

_____. 1985. *IMF Survey.* Washington, D.C.: IMF.

Lever, Harold, and Christopher Huhne. 1986. *Debt and Danger.* Boston: Atlantic Monthly Press.

Ministerial Declaration of the Uruguay Round. 1986.

Morgan Guaranty Company of New York. 1986. *World Financial Markets.* New York: Morgan Guaranty.

Overseas Development Council. 1985. *U.S. Foreign Policy and the Third World: Agenda 1985-86.* New Brunswick, N.J.: Transaction Books.

Stokes, Bruce. 1986. "Korea: Relations Worsen." *National Journal,* April 5, p. 814.

Taiwan Board of Foreign Trade. 1986. *1986 Foreign Trade Development of the Republic of China.* Taiwan.

United States Bureau of Labor Statistics. 1986, 1987. *Statistical Abstract.* Washington, D.C.: U.S. Government Printing Office.

United States Bureau of the Census. 1981. *Highlights of U.S. Export and Import Trade.* Washington, D.C.: U.S. Government Printing Office.

_____. 1985. *Highlights of U.S. Export and Import Trade.* Washington, D.C.: U.S. Government Printing Office.

United States Department of Commerce. 1986. *U.S. Industrial Outlook.* Washington, D.C.: U.S. Government Printing Office.

INDEX

The acronym NICs stands for newly industrializing countries.

267

PROJECT PANEL AND PARTICIPANTS

Economic Policy Council Chairmen:

Robert O. Anderson
Former Chairman of the Board
Atlantic Richfield Company

Douglas A. Fraser
President Emeritus
International Union-United Auto
   Workers

Panel Cochairmen:

Thornton F. Bradshaw
Former Chairman of the Board
RCA

Robert D. Hormats
Vice President for International
   Corporate Finance
Goldman, Sachs & Company

Project Advisor:

Richard N. Cooper
Maurits Boas Professor of
   International Economics
Harvard University

Members:

Michael Alexander
Director
Gordon Capital

George J. Clark
Executive Vice President
Citibank, N.A.

Charles F. Barber
Former Chairman
ASARCO Incorporated

H. David Crowther
Vice President-Corporate
   Communications
Lockheed Corporation

281

Abe H. Raskin
Visiting Scholar
Woodrow Wilson International
    Center for Scholars

Robert V. Roosa
Partner
Brown Brothers Harriman & Co.

Richard J. Schmeelk
Senior Executive Director and
    Member of the Executive Committee
Salomon Brothers Inc

Jack Sheinkman
President
Amalgamated Clothing & Textile
    Workers Union, AFL-CIO

Joan Spero
Senior Vice President,
    International Corporate Affairs
American Express Company

Richard S. Weinert
Director
Leslie Weinert & Company

Lynn R. Williams
President
United Steelworkers of America,
    AFL-CIO, CLC

Additional Participants:

Michael Aho
Senior Fellow on Economics
Council on Foreign Relations

Thomas Bayard
Program Officer
The Ford Foundation

William Broderick
Director, International
    Governmental Affairs
Ford Motor Company

Jack Guenther
Senior Vice President
Citibank, N.A.

Catherine Gwin
Consultant
The Rockefeller Foundation

Iqbal Haji
Senior Economist
Office of Director General for
    Development and International
    Economic Cooperation
United Nations

Peter Hansen
Executive Director
U.N. Centre on Transnational
    Corporations
United Nations

James Merrill
Chief Economist, International
Marine Midland Banks, Inc.

Carol O'Cleireacain
Assistant to the Executive Officers
District Council 37
American Federation of State,
    County & Municipal Employees

James Parrott
Economist
International Ladies Garment
    Workers Union, AFL-CIO, CLC

Albert Rees
President
Alfred P. Sloan Foundation

John Sewell
President
Overseas Development Council

Bruce Stokes
Staff Correspondent
National Journal

Economic Policy Council Staff:

Daniel F. Burton, Jr.
Executive Director

Judy Farrell
Project Coordinator

Rose Carcaterra
Program Director

Maria D. Rivera
Secretary

ABOUT THE CONTRIBUTORS

Pedro Aspe Armella is Mexico's deputy secretary of planning and the budget. From 1983 to 1985 he headed the Instituto Nacional de Estadística, Geografía e Informática (Mexico's statistical agency). In 1980-82 Dr. Aspe was chief economic advisor to the minister of finance and in 1978-82 he was the head of the Economics Department at the Instituto Tecnológico Autónomo de México. Dr. Aspe received his Ph.D. in economics from M.I.T. in 1978.

Edmar Lisboa Bacha is professor of economics at Catholic University of Rio de Janeiro, Brazil. Previously he was president of the Brazilian Institute of Geography and Statistics; served on the faculties of various U.S. universities; and was a visiting professor at Yale, Columbia, and Harvard. Professor Bacha was also a member of the Research Advisory Panel for Industrial Development and Trade at the World Bank and of the Presidential Committee for Reform of the Brazilian University System. He is currently on the Executive Committee of the International Economic Association, Paris, and the Committee for Development Planning of the United Nations, New York.

John T. Bennett is an economist and president of the Korea Economic Institute of America, which he founded in 1982 in Washington, D.C. Previously, he spent twenty-six years in the Foreign Service in Asia, Africa, and Latin America.

Rose Carcaterra is program director of the Economic Policy Council. She received her B.A. degree from St. Johns University in psychology and sociology and has done graduate work in the field of computer science.

Robert F. Dernberger has been a professor of economics at the University of Michigan for the last twenty years, serving as director of the Center for Chinese Studies from 1983 to 1985. He received his formal training in Chinese studies and economics at the University of Michigan and Harvard, earning a doctorate at Harvard in 1965. Having made several visits to China, Professor Dernberger has written more than twenty-five articles and books on the problems of economic development and on comparative economic systems, with special reference to China's contemporary economy. His publications include an edited volume, *China's Development Experience in Comparative Perspective* and *China's Future*, coauthored with Allen Whiting.

Richard S. Eckaus is Ford International Professor of Economics and head of the Department of Economics at the Massachusetts Institute of Technology, where he also earned his Ph.D. He has an undergraduate degree in electrical engineering from Iowa State University and an M.A. in economics from Washington University in St. Louis. His expertise is in problems of developing countries, and he has done research and consulted in a number of such countries including Chile, Costa Rica, Mexico, Sri Lanka, India, Egypt, Jamaica, Portugal, and a number of other countries. He has focused on problems of overall policy, including investment allocations, balance of payments policies, and labor force planning.

Judy Farrell is project coordinator of the Economic Policy Council. Prior to joining the EPC staff in 1981, she was assistant to the Alateen Coordinator at Al-Anon Family Group Headquarters, an organization that serves the families and children of alcoholics throughout the world.

Peter Hansen is professor of International Relations at Odense University in Denmark. Since 1978 he has been on leave to serve with the United Nations, currently as executive director of the Centre on Transnational Corporations and prior to that as assistant secretary-general for Programme Planning and Coordination.

Tommy Koh is currently Singapore's ambassador in Washington, after having served for thirteen years as its ambassador to the United Nations. He is also a professor of law at the National University of Singapore, where he was dean of law from 1971 through 1974. He was educated at Harvard and Cambridge.

Ching-ing Hou Liang is professor of economics in the Department of Banking at the National Chengchi University. From 1981 to 1984 he was commissioner of the Taiwan Provincial Government. Professor Liang received his B.A. from the National Taiwan University and his M.A. from Vanderbilt University.

Kuo-shu Liang is professor of economics in the Department of Economics at National Taiwan University and chairman of the Chang Hwa Commercial Bank, Ltd. Professor Liang received his B.A. from National Taiwan University and his Ph.D. from Vanderbilt University.

Jay Mazur is president of the International Ladies' Garment Workers' Union. He is also a vice president and member of the Executive Council of the AFL-CIO.

John W. Sewell has been president of the Overseas Development Council since January 1980. His research has focused on U.S. economic, political, and security interests in development and on U.S. attitudes toward development questions. He has also written on development ethics and development in the Sahel region of Africa. He is the author of *The United States and World Development: Agenda 1980*, and a coauthor of *U.S. Foreign Policy and the Third World: Agenda 1985-86*, the seventh and tenth editions respectively in the council's annual assessment of U.S. relations with the developing world.

Bruce Smart is chief officer for international trade at the Department of Commerce. He was formerly chairman and chief executive officer of the Continental Group, Inc. He holds a degree from Harvard and a master's degree in civil engineering from the Massachusetts Institute of Technology. He served in World War II and Korea.

Michael Brackett Smith is deputy U.S. trade representative in Washington, D.C., with the rank of ambassador. He has held a number of government posts, including U.S. representative to GATT; chief negotiator for textile matters; chief textile negotiator of the United States; chief of Fibers and Textiles Division, Department of State; White House chief of presidential correspondence; principle officer, Lyon, France; deputy principle officer, Strasburg, France; and staff assistant to the undersecretary for economic affairs. Ambassador Smith graduated from Harvard College in 1958.

Stuart K. Tucker is a fellow at the Overseas Development Council. Prior to joining ODC, he was a research consultant for the Inter-American Development Bank, the Urban Institute, and the Roosevelt Center for American Policy Studies. He has written on many subjects, including U.S. international trade policy, the debt crisis and trade, the U.S. costs of the Third World recession, the Caribbean Basin Initiative, the Generalized System of Preferences, and Non-Tariff Barriers. At the council, Mr. Tucker is working in the areas of international trade policy and Latin American development. He holds degrees from the University of Virginia and the Johns Hopkins School of Advanced International Studies.

Toru Yanagihara is research coordinator for economic studies at the Institute of Developing Economies in Tokyo. He has served as a consultant to the World Bank and was a visiting scholar at both the University of California at Berkeley and Columbia University. He holds an international relations degree from the University of Tokyo and an economics degree from Yale University.

ABOUT THE EDITORS

Thornton F. Bradshaw is chairman of the MacArthur Foundation. He was formerly president of Atlantic Richfield Company and chairman and chief executive officer of RCA Corporation. He has also served as a naval officer, an assistant professor at Harvard Business School, and a partner in a management consulting firm.

Daniel F. Burton, Jr., is vice president of the Council on Competitiveness. He served as executive director of the Economic Policy Council of the UNA-USA from 1984 through 1986. He was a fellow in the U.S.-Japan Leadership Program in 1984 and has worked in the area of rural development in the Ivory Coast. Mr. Burton is the author of numerous articles on industrial policy and trade. He received his B.A. degree from The University of Pennsylvania and his M.A. from Columbia University's School of International Affairs, and did postgraduate work at the Sorbonne.

Richard N. Cooper is Maurits C. Boas Professor of International Economics at Harvard University. Previously, he served as under secretary for economic affairs, Department of State (1977–81); consultant to the National Security Council (1969–70); deputy assistant secretary of state for International Monetary Affairs (1965–66); and senior staff economist with President Kennedy's Council of Economic Advisers (1961–63). He was provost of Yale University from

1972 to 1974 and held the position of Frank Altschul Professor of International Economics there from 1966 to 1977. Professor Cooper received his Ph.D. degree from Harvard University and is a graduate of the London School of Economics. His numerous publications include *Economics of Interdependence.* He is a director of the Center for European Policy Studies in Brussels. In addition, he chairs the executive panel of the chief of Naval Operations, U.S. Navy, and is a member of the Trilateral Commission.

Robert D. Hormats is vice president for investment banking of Goldman, Sachs & Co. and director of Goldman Sachs International Corp. He joined Goldman Sachs in 1982, after serving as U.S. assistant secretary of state for economic and business affairs from May 1981 until August 1982. He also held the positions of deputy U.S. trade representative (1979–81) and deputy assistant secretary of state for economic and business affairs (1977–79). From 1974 to 1977, he was a senior staff member for international economic affairs on the National Security Council. Mr. Hormats received his Ph.D. degree from the Fletcher School of International Law and Diplomacy. In the spring of 1983, he was a visiting lecturer at the Woodrow Wilson School of International and Public Affairs at Princeton University. He has had numerous articles published in *The New York Times, The Washington Post, American Banker*, and the *Financial Times* of London.